CRIMES
THAT SHOCKED
BRITAIN

CRIMES
THAT SHOCKED
BRITAIN

NEW
HOLLAND

Laura Fulton

For Dennis Jarrett,
who believed in me

CONTENTS

FOREWORD

Murdered prostitutes, vicious gangsters, abducted children, mutilated corpses – what, exactly, is the point of revisiting some of the worst crimes Britain has ever seen? It's an important question and one worth asking.

Though the stories in this book are often the stuff of nightmares, there is the hope that much good will come from retelling these stories once again.

One reason to return to these famous crimes is for the sake of future generations. Many of these crimes happened at a time when the dissemination of information was much less prevalent than it is today.

It's likely that children were abducted just as frequently in the 1960s, but the limits of technology meant that fewer people heard those stories back then than they do today. Women have always been the victims of violence. Now those stories make the headlines a lot more frequently.

In repeating those chilling stories of abduction and murder, it is the hope that potential victims of those crimes will be able to learn from what has happened in the past.

Now conscious of the dangers of abduction, most modern parents are much more vigilant than their parents or grandparents ever were. Though it is vastly unfair and much work is being done to change the social climate, women are now highly aware of the dangers that are constantly present and take measures to protect themselves.

If even one life is saved – if even one woman knows how to protect herself because she knew what happened to another victim, if even one child makes it home safely because his parents heard the story of a child who was lost – then the lives of those victims will not have been lost in vain.

Not only have these stories encouraged people in the public to change their behaviour. In some cases, these crimes have also resulted in changes to police procedures and in legislation that have made it more difficult for criminals to obtain the means or the opportunity to commit the same offense.

Often this legislation comes up for debate. When it does, it is important for members of the public to remember the circumstances that inspired those regulations to be made law in the first place. It is the hope that, if that time ever comes, these stories will serve as a reminder to help keep those laws in place or assist in making those laws better.

Another reason to continue telling these stories centres on those criminals who are still alive. More than once, vicious killers who have committed truly vile acts of cruelty have been sentenced to life in prison – only to have a change in law or a government nearly set them free.

These criminals would love nothing more than to have the public forget the details of the heinous crimes they committed as they quietly do their best to convince a court to set them free. While rehabilitation sometimes happens and second chances are sometimes warranted, books like this one are meant to serve as a reminder of what those people once really were.

And while we remember those who sometimes haunt our dreams, it is also just as important to remember the brave men and women of the police force who put their lives on the line every single day to apprehend these criminals.

Often under extraordinarily difficult circumstances and many times bearing the brunt of harsh criticism, most of the officers in this book have demonstrated compassion, dedication and courage far above and beyond the call of duty. It is worth remembering the sacrifices that these men and women have made to keep the rest of us safe.

The same is often true of the members of the press core who, in many instances, put in an incredible amount of time, energy and concern seeking out the truth. More than once, it was through the cooperation of the media and the authorities that a criminal was apprehended and brought to justice.

More than anything, though, this book serves as a reminder that – whether the victim was an alcoholic prostitute or an innocent two-year-old boy – the value of human life is paramount, and murder is never justified. If for no other reason, this book has been written to say that these lives should never be forgotten.

Laura Fulton
April 2016

CHAPTER ONE

Jack the Ripper

(1888)

No book about sensational British crimes would be complete without a look back at Jack the Ripper, the serial killer who terrorized the Whitechapel area of London for several weeks in the autumn of 1888. Despite intense scrutiny by the media, both at the time of the murders and in the decades since, the iconic criminal has never been identified.

Though thousands of hours of research have been devoted to the case, many of the theories involving Jack the Ripper remain unresolved. Was the Ripper one man or part of a wider conspiracy? Were all of the murders connected or were they separate crimes perpetrated by unconnected killers? What could have motived a person (or persons) to take so many lives in such a brutal manner?

Experts even disagree on the number of victims that died at the hands of the Whitechapel killer. Most agree that five prostitutes were among those murdered, but other unsolved crimes occurred around the same time and place which may put the number as high as thirteen, if not more.It is important to note the environment in which the murders took place.

Called a 'rookery' in the colloquial terms of the day, the Whitechapel neighbourhood of London was by all definitions the worst sort of slum, notorious for its widespread crime, poverty and destitution.

Many 'Ripperologists' believe the story begins on 8 August 1888. It was a cool, clear Thursday night when Mary Ann Nichols stepped out for the evening. Life hadn't been easy for the 43-year-old mother of five. She'd separated from her husband eight years before, and he'd kept the children.

Though her ex-husband had agreed to pay her 5 shillings a week, within two years of the divorce, Mary Ann had fallen into prostitution (either to support herself or her rampant alcoholism or both) and the weekly allowance stopped. That August found Mary Ann sharing a room at a lodging house with five other women, including Emily Holland.

After spending some time at a public house called The Frying Pan, Mary Ann stumbled into the kitchen of her lodging house at 18 Thrawl Street shortly after midnight in the early morning of 31 August. She didn't have the 4 pence payment for her bed, though, and the deputy-lodging housekeeper threw her out.

About an hour later, Mary Ann ran into her friend and roommate Emily Holland at 2.30 in the morning. Emily found Mary Ann fantastically drunk and leaning against a wall. When Emily urged Mary Ann to return to the lodging house with her, Mary Ann reportedly replied, 'I've had my lodging money three times today and I've spent it. It won't be long before I'm back.'[1]

She never returned home that night.

A little over an hour after her last recorded conversation, at 3.40am a cart driver named Charles A Cross discovered the body of Mary Ann Nichols 'lying on her back lengthways across the footway'[2] at Buck's Row. Her skirts were raised almost to her stomach, and her legs were outstretched and slightly apart. Cross and another cart driver, Robert Paul, went to summon the police.

Within minutes, PC John Neil also came upon Mary Ann's body on his nightly patrol of the area. He could see right away that her throat had been slit from ear to ear.

Dr Rees Llewellyn was called to the scene where he gave his first quick examination:

Several injuries to the throat; her hands and wrists were cold, yet her body and legs were still warm; her chest and heart showed life to be extinct, estimating that she died no more than half an hour prior to the examination; very little blood around the neck; no marks of a struggle or of the body being dragged.

At the mortuary, Inspector John Spratling examined Mary Ann's body as she lay on the ambulance:

Throat cut from left to right with two distinct cuts being on the left side and with the windpipe, gullet and spinal cord being cut through; a bruise, possibly from a thumb, on the lower right jaw with another on the left cheek; the abdomen had been cut open from the centre of the bottom ribs along the right side; under the pelvis, left of the stomach, was another wound – jagged ... two small stabs on the privy parts; the knife used seemed to have been strong bladed; death almost instantaneous.[3]

It was an appalling crime, even for hardened Londoners who were used to the harsh realities of life and death. Just a few months before, on 3 April 1888, another prostitute named Emma Smith had been attacked by four men. Gangs of criminals often managed prostitutes at the time, and Emma may have been involved with the men – or trying to avoid them.

Whatever the reason, the men not only beat Smith. They also raped her with a blunt object so violently that they ruptured her peritoneum, a membrane that lines the internal organs. She died early the following day of her injuries, having never identified her attackers.[4] In other words, violence against women – especially poor women for whom prostitution was the only option – was nothing new in 19th century London.

But the work of Jack the Ripper shocked the public. (Some believed that Emma Smith was actually an early victim of the Ripper, but most agree her attackers were one of many criminal gangs operating in the area and not the work of the famed serial killer.)

Even more disturbing were the wounds that had been inflicted on the lower part of Mary Ann's body, most especially the deep, jagged wounds in Mary Ann's abdomen. Combined with several other cuts, both vertical and horizontal, these wounds left her intestines and other internal organs exposed.[5]

The inquest into Mary Ann's death began on 1 September, but before the inquest could reach its conclusion, the Ripper had struck again.

Like Mary Ann Nichols, Annie Chapman was living on her own, her husband and children all dead or institutionalised. By 1888, she was making her living day to day, staying in a lodging house. Fond of drinking, she was malnourished and fighting a disease of the lungs and membranes of the brain that was slowly killing her.

On 7 September, eight days after Mary Ann Nichols' last night, Annie wasn't feeling well but she pulled herself together enough to go out, hoping to earn the money she needed for her nightly lodging.

Just after midnight, the plump 47-year-old returned to her lodging house on Dorset Street, drunk by all accounts. A little over an hour later, the night watchman of the lodging house escorted her out when she didn't have the 4 pence for her bed that night. It was 1.35 in the morning, and it was to be the last time anyone was sure of having seen her alive.

It was nearly 6.00am when cart driver John Davis went outside his lodging house at 29 Hanbury Street and found the body of Annie Chapman lying between the steps and the fence. Her face was covered in blood, and her throat had been cut.

By the time police surgeon Dr George Phillips arrived at 6.30am, a crowd had already begun to gather. The deep, jagged incision on Annie's throat nearly encircled her neck. Nearby blood stains that corresponded with the position of the body combined with a lack of blood elsewhere to suggest that Annie had been killed on the spot at least two hours before.

It was a gruesome scene. Annie's abdomen had been cut open, and her intestines were found in a pile on the ground above her right shoulder. Part of her stomach was lying in a large pool of her blood above her left shoulder.

In light of the similarity in wounds and location, police investigators agreed that Annie Chapman had been killed by the same man who murdered Mary Ann Nichols.

Dr Phillips' post mortem examination revealed that the incision on Annie's neck was so deep that it reached through to her spine. Even worse, Annie's uterus, its appendages, the upper part of her vagina and most of her bladder had been completely removed. They were nowhere to be found.[6]

Annie's brutal wounds were chilling in their precision. Both her rectum and cervix had been left intact. Dr Phillips surmised that it would have taken the killer at least fifteen minutes to inflict the wounds and that he must have had some knowledge of the human anatomy. The doctor believed the killer had used a sharp, narrow blade 6 to 8 inches (15–20 cm) long, something like a slaughterman's knife or an amputating blade.

Upon hearing of the second murder, the public responded with great interest. In the days following Annie's death, onlookers flocked to 29 Hanbury Street. Some callous entrepreneurs took advantage of the spectacle, setting up food stands and selling refreshments to the crowds. Area residents began charging admission to allow people to see the murder scene from buildings on either side of the crime scene.

Though police hoped to apprehend the killer quickly, they soon discovered the enormity of their task. Statements from several witnesses were often contradictory or unreliable, and many were quick to point the finger at the much-hated immigrants in the area, especially the Jews.

Despite the public's overwhelming desire to help solve the case, the authorities had had little success when the killer struck for the third time.

Elizabeth Stride had been separated from her boyfriend for only three days when she took a lodging room at 32 Flower and Dean Street on 27 September. A prostitute whose husband and children had died, Elizabeth was also a heavy drinker. Between 1887 and 1888, she had incurred eight drunk and disorderly charges at Thames Magistrate Court.

Evidence suggests Elizabeth had had a date on Saturday night 29 September. Several witnesses recalled seeing her (or a woman who looked like her) in the company of a man throughout the evening. The two were seen hugging and kissing.

There is some discrepancy about an exchange that happened between a man (or perhaps two men) and a woman between 12.30 and 12.55am on the morning of 30 September outside the International Working Men's Educational Club at 40 Berner Street.

There may have been two men involved, or one man following the other, but the tone of the relationship between the man and woman – most likely Elizabeth – had turned ugly. A man looked to have been threatening her, and some witnesses reported hearing screams. It is unclear if this man was the same one who had been seen kissing Elizabeth earlier in the evening.

What we do know is that Elizabeth Stride was certainly dead or nearly dead when Jewish vendor Louis Diemschutz discovered her body at 1.00am outside the club on Berner Street. Her throat had been cut and recently. The blood was still pulsing.

Unlike the others, Elizabeth's clothing had not been disturbed and there was no sign of a struggle. When Dr Frederick William Blackwell arrived at the scene around 1.15am, he estimated that Elizabeth had only been dead for 20 or 30 minutes. Had Diemschutz arrived five minutes earlier, he might have witnessed the crime.

There has been much speculation about the difference in Elizabeth's death and those of the Ripper's other victims. The post mortem examination performed by Dr George Phillips indicated that she was most likely pushed to the ground and that the killer probably cut her throat as she fell or when she was on the ground.

The cut to Elizabeth's neck – a clean, 6 inch (15 cm) incision from left to right – was enough to sever her windpipe in two but did not go all the way to her spine.[7]

She also had not been disembowelled, a point for which the press named her 'Lucky Liz'. There is no concrete evidence to support why Elizabeth sustained fewer wounds than the other women. Some believed Louis Diemschutz interrupted the Ripper in his work. Others believed the man who killed Elizabeth was not the Ripper at all.

Either way, the night had not seen the last of murder. At the same time Louis Diemschutz was discovering Elizabeth's body, Catherine Eddowes was being escorted out of jail. The 46-year-old prostitute had been arrested at 8.30 the previous evening on a drunk and disorderly charge – she'd been making fire engine noises outside 29 Aldgate High Street.

She'd parted company with her partner, an Irish porter named John Kelly, at 2.00 that afternoon, hoping to get some money from her daughter for her night's lodging. She promised Kelly she would return by 4.00pm but it seems she must have been distracted at some point along the way.

Having had the chance to sober up in jail for a few hours, the mother of three grown children was taken from Bishopsgate Police Station and released into the night. Less than an hour later, PC Edward Watkins discovered Catherine's body in the southwest corner of Mitre Square – a spot well known for prostitutes to ply their trade – just 328 yards (300 m) from the police station and half a mile (800 m) from where Elizabeth Stride had been killed.

Lying on her back in a pool of her own blood, Catherine's throat had been cut. Her clothes were pushed up 'above her waist, her stomach was ripped up and her bowels were protruding'.[8]

The post mortem examination conducted by Dr Gordon Brown placed the time of death at around 1.30am, less than an hour after Elizabeth's.

Catherine had been decidedly less lucky than Elizabeth Stride. In addition to her throat being cut and her abdomen sliced open, Catherine's intestines had also been pulled out and placed over her right shoulder. A length of about 2 feet (60 cm) of her intestine had also been separated from the rest and placed on the ground between her body and her left arm.

Unlike the Ripper's previous victims, Catherine's face had also been horribly mutilated. Her eyelids had been cut through, her nose sliced to the bone from the bridge to the upper lip and the tip of her nose had been removed. Her cheeks had also been cut into triangular flaps and peeled back.

Many of Catherine's internal organs had been damaged by the killer's knife, including her liver, pancreas and vagina. Her left kidney and uterus had been completely removed, leading Dr Brown to believe that the killer had a clear understanding of the positions of these organs. He also surmised that the knife used was the same type that had been used to kill the others.[9]

It wasn't long before the press got wind of the double murder and the baffling investigation became even more difficult as well-meaning citizens drew the police in a number of wrong directions.

Efforts became even more muddled when someone calling himself 'Jack the Ripper' sent a letter to the Central News Agency on 27 September. Previously, the killer had been known as 'Leather Apron' or simply 'The Knife'. Now the brutal murderer had a nickname that would stick forever.

Though most experts discount the letter and a post card that followed on 1 October as a hoax, there is no way to be 100 per cent certain that the killer did not actually write the letter.

Rather than aiding the investigation, the correspondences sparked a slew of fake letters from writers calling themselves Jack the Ripper and wasted many valuable hours of police investigators' time.

While the police waded through misinformation, illegitimate letters and inaccurate eyewitness accounts, Mary Jane Kelly was debating whether or not she should leave London. The 25-year-old Irish blonde had recently returned to prostitution to repay a debt of 30 shillings she owed for rent on a tiny room in Dorset Street. She was terrified of Jack the Ripper and the realistic prospect of falling victim to him.

Just before midnight on 8 November, an upstairs neighbour saw Mary Jane return to her room with a man, presumably a customer. She was apparently drunk and a few witnesses reported hearing her singing until after midnight. By 1.00am, however, the singing had stopped.

There is some confusion around Mary Jane's movements for the rest of the night. A good friend of hers, a man named George Hutchinson who might have been an occasional customer, reported seeing Mary Jane and speaking with her at 2.00am near Flower and Dean Street. A short time later, he said he saw her returning in the direction of her room with a man, likely another customer.

Some neighbours in the vicinity of Mary Jane's room reported hearing cries of 'murder!' at different times during the night, but it was a common cry around the rookery and people often paid little attention to it. A few people were certain they'd seen Mary Jane as late as 10.00am on the morning of 9 November, but no one knows for sure.

What is certain is that, at 10.45am, Mary Jane's landlord sent his assistant Thomas Bowyer to collect some of the indebted prostitute's back rent. When she didn't answer the door, Bowyer looked through the window and made a grisly discovery – two lumps of flesh on the bedside table and the gruesome remains of Mary Jane's body lying on the bed.

It was after 2.00pm before Dr Thomas Bond joined Dr George Phillips on the scene to examine the body. The killer had taken advantage of the privacy of Mary Jane's bedroom to work at his leisure and the results were hideous in the extreme, as described in Dr Bond's post mortem report:

> *The face was gashed in all directions, the nose, cheeks, eyebrows and ears being partly removed. The lips were blanched and cut by several incisions running obliquely down to the chin. There were also numerous cuts extending irregularly across all the features.*
>
> *The neck was cut through the skin and other tissues right down to the vertebrae, the fifth and sixth being deeply notched ... Both breasts were removed by more or less circular incisions, the muscles down to the ribs being attached to the breasts ...*

The killer didn't stop there. Skin from Mary Jane's arms, hands and legs had been slashed and stripped to the bone. Part of her right lung was 'broken and torn away', part of her stomach was missing and her heart was 'absent'.[10]

Unlike Dr Phillips, Dr Bond did not believe the Ripper had any especial knowledge of the human anatomy, nor even 'the technical knowledge of a butcher or horse slaughterer'.[11]

Though rigor mortis prevented the doctors from making a more accurate assessment, Dr Bond believed the time of death was between 1.00 and 2.00am, contrary to statements from witnesses who claimed to have seen Mary Jane as recently as 10.00am.

It is here that the story of Jack the Ripper goes cold. Several other murders could have been the work of the Ripper, but many believe that these five (called the canonical murders) are the only ones that can be accurately attributed to the same person.

The biggest mystery, though, remains the identity of the killer. More than 100 books and countless articles have been written on the subject, including *They All Love Jack: Busting the Ripper* by writer and director Bruce Robinson, which was released in October 2015.

There is very little to go on. The only piece of physical evidence the Ripper ever left behind was a scrap of fabric ripped from an apron that Catherine Eddowes had been wearing the night she was murdered. The scrap was discovered a little over an hour after her body was found.

Several eyewitnesses have provided descriptions of men who were seen in the company of the victims shortly before their deaths, but prostitutes keep company with many men, any one of whom could have been the culprit.

Most accounts point towards a reasonably well dressed, middle aged man of average height, perhaps dark haired, possibly with a complexion slightly darker than that of the average English Caucasian of the time (though not necessarily). Literally hundreds of men could have fitted that description.

The killer's personality is somewhat more specific. Following the post mortem examination of Mary Jane Kelly, Dr Thomas Bond wrote a follow up report on all of the killings for Inspector Frederick Abberline, the lead investigator on the case. In it, Dr Bond said that the Ripper was 'a man of physical strength and of great coolness and daring'.

Bond believed the Ripper to be motivated at least in part by sexual deviance and that he was a solitary eccentric with a regular income, someone 'possibly living among respectable persons who have some knowledge of his character and habits and who have grounds for suspicion that he is not quite right in his mind at times'.[12]

The list of potential candidates is long and at times distinguished including a schoolmaster and barrister whose own family suspected him of being the Ripper, a Jewish misogynist who lived in Whitechapel and a Russian doctor who was also a convict. A few suspects are higher profile such as the Duke of Clarence and Avondale Prince Albert Victor, the physician to Queen Victoria, the father of Winston Churchill and children's author Lewis Carroll.

Whoever the Ripper was and whatever his motivation, these crimes left an indelible mark on the British psyche that has not dimmed in over 100 years. Though Jack may have been the first Ripper, he would not be the last. Several copycat killers have cropped up since the Whitechapel killer terrorized London, as we will see in chapters to come.

CHAPTER TWO

Dr Crippen

(1910)

For over a century, the name Dr Crippen has brought to the minds of Britain gruesome scenes of violence and death. What police found wrapped in a pyjama jacket at 39 Hilltop Crescent in Holloway has continued to horrify the nation, despite the discovery of recent evidence that casts doubt on the guilt of the mild mannered doctor about whom so many people once spoke so well.

The story of Dr Crippen begins on the other side of the Atlantic in the United States. By all accounts, Hawley Harvey Crippen was a small, unassuming man. Barely over 5 feet (152 cm) tall, the American homeopath wore glasses over his bulging blue eyes and tidy moustache. A disorder of his tear ducts caused him to blink constantly, which only contributed to his harmless appearance.

In 1884, Crippen graduated from the Cleveland Homeopathic Medical College, having previously studied at the University of Michigan Homeopathic Medical School.[1] Crippen married the seventeen-year-old girl he knew as Cora Turner in 1892 just three years after his first wife

Charlotte Bell died. When Charlotte died, Crippen's parents took over the care of his three-year-old son.

Cora would prove to be something of a handful. Born Kunigunde Mackamotzki, the New Yorker of Polish descent changed her name to Cora when she decided her birth name was too hard to pronounce and was keeping her from becoming a show biz star.[2]

Cora Turner was Crippen's polar opposite. She was the stereotypical 'ugly American'. Loud, bubbly, brash and not very ladylike, Cora was determined to become a famous opera singer.

Always looking for the next best thing, Cora had already been the mistress of a wealthy stove manufacturer when she met Crippen, a quiet widower thirteen years her senior. She thought the genteel doctor would be the perfect candidate to shower her with the lavish lifestyle she seemed to think she deserved.

Crippen did his best to appease his young wife, paying for numerous voice lessons and buying her the expensive clothes, furs and jewellery she wanted. After two years of lessons, however, she had yet to earn a single penny as a performer. In trying to keep up with his wife's expensive tastes, Crippen took positions first in Missouri and then in Toronto, Salt Lake City and Philadelphia, but his job as 'medical expert' was not enough to keep up with Cora's demands.

As Cora grew older, she became more and more irascible. Unable to have children and still unsuccessful as a performer, the once loving wife became more and more critical of her husband, finding fault in him at every turn.

When Cora finally did find a professional theatre engagement, she had gained so much weight that she earned the nickname 'the Brooklyn Matzos Ball', which was perhaps a cruel play on words of the stage name she had given herself, Macka Motzki.[3] She quickly changed her stage name to Belle Elmore. Despite Cora's lack of success and the expenses her ambition incurred, Crippen was reportedly still fond of her.[4]

Things changed for the couple in 1898 when Crippen took a position in London working for Munyon's Remedies, a patent medicine company. His American qualifications prevented him from practicing medicine, however, and he was little more than a glorified salesman.

Cora didn't seem to notice. She was convinced that she was much better suited to the classy music halls of England, which she considered much better than the vaudeville and burlesque shows in the United States. She did manage to get some regular work, but there was an artists' strike on at the time, which may have provided her with opportunities she might not have otherwise had.

According to Crippen, Cora's attitude seemed to change when she arrived in England. He said that 'she had cultivated a most ungovernable temper, and seemed to think [he] was not good enough for her.' She even boasted to Crippen of the many men who found her attractive and that she was seeing on the side. These men would boldly come to collect her at the Crippens' home to take her out for the evening.[5]

Her career as a performer was unremarkable at best, but Cora was still able to make many friends in London. One friend of the couple, Dr John Herbert Burroughs, described Cora as 'vivacious, bright and cheerful, a very pleasant woman generally, and enjoying the best of health; she was fond of dress and jewellery; she and [Crippen] always appeared to be on good terms.'[6]

What Burroughs and others probably didn't know was that Cora was no longer interested in having intimate relations with her husband. It wasn't a general lack of interest in sex, however. When Crippen went to Philadelphia for a six-month business trip in 1902, Cora reportedly had an affair with Bruce Miller, an American performer and prize fighter.[7]

Despite Cora's expensive tastes, in 1905 the Crippens were able to move from their one-bedroom flat on Store Street to 39 Hilldrop Crescent, a large semi-detached house in the North London suburb of Holloway. With the extra space, the couple was able to supplement their income by taking in lodgers including German students and various stage performers.

Cora used the additional income to pay for her expensive outfits and wigs, but she wasn't willing to pay for a maid to help run the house. Instead, she expected her husband to perform many of the household duties like lighting the morning fire and cooking breakfast for the lodgers – even polishing their boots – before he went into the office in the mornings.[8]

While Crippen was busy working a full time job and looking after the household, Cora found other pursuits. In 1908, she was appointed Honorary Treasurer of the Music Hall Ladies Guild, a position that allowed her to get to know several important figures in London's theatre world. Though unsuccessful as a performer, she was apparently well liked and respected by many of her peers.

In addition to entertaining her theatre friends, Cora also kept busy maintaining affairs with some of their lodgers. On at least one occasion, Crippen reportedly found her in bed with one of their paying guests, a situation that was nothing unusual.[9]

It was around this time that Dr Crippen began an affair of his own with his typist, a young woman named Ethel Le Neve whom he'd met several years before. Like Cora, Crippen didn't go to very much trouble to keep his affair a secret. His relationship with Ethel was common knowledge among the Crippens' circle of friends.

When Cora found out about her husband's affair, she did what she always did – she belittled and ridiculed him. The affair between Crippen and Ethel didn't seem to bother Cora until Ethel fell pregnant. Cora had had an ovariectomy shortly after getting married, but the thought that a woman eight years younger than she might be able to give her husband the child she couldn't was enough to infuriate Cora.

It looked like the marriage was over and that Cora was prepared to leave her husband penniless. On 15 December 1909, Cora gave twelve months' notice to the Crippens' bank that she would be withdrawing the entirety of the couple's savings, around £600.[10]

Shortly after giving notice to the bank, however, Ethel miscarried and Cora decided to stay with her husband. According to Cora's good friend and fellow performer Lil Hawthorne, Cora said at a dinner party in January 1910 that 'Harvey and I have decided to start life all over again' and then to Crippen, 'We've both done things we're sorry for, but that's all in the past, isn't it, dear?'[11]

It was around this time, on 17 January 1910, that Dr Crippen placed a suspicious order with a chemist in New Oxford Street, Lewis and Burrow's. His order for five grains of hyoscine hydrobromide was so unusually large that the chemists had to obtain a special shipment from their wholesalers, a shipment Crippen collected two days later.[10] According to the chemists' records, Crippen intended to use the drug – commonly found in nausea and vomiting medicines – for 'homeopathic preparation'.[11]

One discrepancy in this order was later revealed by Marin Kernow, manageress for Munyon's Remedies, for whom Crippen was still working at the time on a part time basis. When he placed the order with Lewis and Burrow's, he indicated that he was making the order on behalf of Munyon's. According to Ms Kernow, however, no one at Munyon's knew anything about the order.

'On January 19 last I was working with [Crippen],' Kernow later testified. 'I was keeping the books. I know nothing about the purchase of hyoscine on that date; no cash was paid out for such a purpose, nor is there any entry in any book.'[6]

Though she insisted Crippen was a very kind and pleasant man, Kernow indicated that Crippen must have ordered the drug for use on his own personal patients. The supposition is possible, as Crippen had been seeing private patients on the side for years.

It seems as though the last people to see Cora Crippen in London were Paul and Clara Martinetti, retired music hall performers who shared dinner with the Crippens on the night of 31 January 1910.

What happened after the Martinettis left remains a mystery. According to Harvey Crippen, the couple had a terrible fight during which Cora said she was leaving him (a threat she'd made often of which he took little notice). He also told the police that his wife had asked him to 'cover up the scandal with their mutual friends and the Guild the best way he could'.[12]

The following day, Ethel Le Neve delivered two letters to the Music Hall Ladies Guild. The letters – which had been dictated by Crippen to Ethel – indicated that Cora had been called suddenly to America due to a family illness and, as such, she was resigning her position with the Guild. In the letters, she said she was too busy preparing for the trip to write the letters herself. The letters were signed 'Belle Elmore'.

In the days following her sudden departure, Crippen began pawning his wife's jewellery, ending up with a sum of almost £200 (more than the salary he normally earned in a year). On the night of 2 February, Ethel Le Neve slept at 39 Hilldrop Crescent and thereafter began to stay on the premises frequently.

Despite Crippen's protests, Cora's friends at the Guild found her disappearance a little too convenient. When Lil Hawthorne asked about Cora, Crippen told his wife's friend that it was someone in his family, not Cora's, who had fallen ill in San Francisco.

Cora's friends grew even more suspicious on 26 February when Crippen showed up at the Music Hall Ladies Guild annual ball with Ethel Le Neve on his arm. It seemed odd to the ladies of the guild that Ethel should be wearing one of Cora's lavish gowns and a very expensive brooch that had been one of Cora's favourites.

It also seemed odd to the ladies that none of them had received so much as a postcard from the gregarious Cora. When one of the ladies asked Crippen for an address at which she could write to Cora, his only response was that she was 'right up in the wilds of the mountains of California' and that he would pass on an address for his wife as soon as he had one.[13] When Lil Hawthorne asked about Cora again, Crippen said that he'd heard she was ill but that he didn't think it was serious.

In March 1910, Ethel moved permanently into 39 Hilldrop Crescent, posing as a maid. She'd told her landlady that Crippen had promised to leave his wife and marry her. While Ethel openly wore Cora's gowns, furs and jewels, Crippen mentioned to Cora's friends that Cora was growing more and more ill.

Finally, on 24 March, Crippen sent a telegram to Lil Hawthorne saying that Cora had died. As soon as Crippen sent the telegram informing Lil Hawthorne of his wife's sudden death, he set sail for France with Ethel Le Neve for a short holiday.

Upon his return the following week, he was bombarded by Cora's friends, all of whom wanted to know more about his recently deceased wife. The only address he could provide where Lil and the ladies could send flowers was that of his son in San Francisco.

Crippen said that Cora wasn't being buried but cremated and that her remains were being returned to England. He told the ladies that they shouldn't bother sending any tokens of remembrance as anything they sent would arrive too late.[10] All of his neat explanations added to the sense of extreme and unlikely convenience for those who knew and loved Cora.

Crippen tried to carry on living his life has he had before, but his attempts at deflecting the ladies became less and less convincing, especially when they discovered that Cora had not contacted any of her friends or relatives in New York on her journey through to California. By July, Cora's ashes had still not arrived from America, and Lil Hawthorne took the matter to a friend she knew through the Guild, a detective at Scotland Yard.

In charge of the newly formed serious crime squad, Detective Superintendent Froest sent Detective Chief Inspector Walter Dew and Detective Sergeant Mitchell to investigate. On 8 July 1910, the two detectives went to 39 Hilldrop Crescent. Crippen was not home, but Ethel directed the policemen to the doctor's office.

It was during this interview that Dr Crippen confessed that Cora had not actually died. In his statement to the police, which took over five hours to complete, he explained that he had stopped sleeping with Cora four years previously, as she was quite taken with Bruce Miller, the prize fighter with whom Cora had been having an affair.

He said he'd hoped the story of her death would deter people from asking too many questions. He'd kept secret the fact of her many affairs to save himself from embarrassment.

'So far as I know, she did not die, but is still alive,' he told the police in his official statement. 'It is not true that she went away on legal business for me, or to see any relations in America. I did not receive any cables to say that she was ill, and it is not true that she was cremated at San Francisco, and that the ashes were sent to me, or that she sailed from Havre.'[5]

After taking this statement, the police searched Crippen's home on Hilldrop Crescent but, finding nothing, they left. It seemed the little doctor was telling the truth.

Had he carried on living in London with Ethel Le Neve by his side, Crippen might never have attracted any further attention. Instead, on 9 July, Crippen and Ethel left London for Belgium. They changed their names to Robinson and Ethel wore a disguise, travelling as Crippen's teenaged son.

On 11 July, Detective Chief Inspector Dew returned to the Crippen home to clarify some dates but discovered Crippen and Ethel were gone. The departure of the doctor and his lover seemed highly suspicious to the detective, who thought perhaps the police had better give the Hilldrop residence a closer look.

Four days later, the authorities made a gruesome discovery. Hidden in the floor of the cellar at 39 Hilldrop Crescent was the decaying tissue of a human body including heart, lungs, trachea, oesophagus, liver, kidneys, spleen, stomach, pancreas, small intestines and most of the large intestine along with some decaying skin.

There was no head, no limbs and no bones except for one that looked to be that of a human thigh. There were also no reproductive organs. In his notes, famed pathologist Sir Bernard Spilsbury described the remains:

> *Human remains found 13 July. Medical organs of chest and abdomen removed in one mass. Four large pieces of skin and muscle, one from lower abdomen with old operation scar 4 inches [10 cm] long – broader at lower end. Impossible to identify sex. Hyoscine found 2.7 grains. Hair in Hinde's curler – roots present. Hair 6 inches [15 cm] long. Man's pyjama jacket label reads Jones Bros, Holloway, and odd pair of pyjama trousers.*[10]

Two damning clues pointed to Dr Crippen as the perpetrator of a gruesome murder. One was a mark on the decaying skin that was similar to a scar Cora Crippen had carried as the result of her ovariectomy operation. The other was the result of a toxicological analysis carried out by Scotland Yard that uncovered lethal levels of hyoscine hydrobromide within the remains.

Word spread quickly and soon every port on the map was on the alert. Excited members of the press helped spread descriptions of Crippen and his mistress, whipping the public into a frenzy, and it wasn't long before people around the world were looking for the pair. The case became a global sensation as articles about Dr Crippen circulated far and wide.

By now, Crippen and his lover were in Belgium. On 20 July, Crippen and Ethel boarded the *Montrose*, an ocean liner bound from Antwerp for Canada, still travelling incognito.

We can only imagine what was going through the doctor's mind, perhaps that he was finally free of his unhappy marriage and escaping to a new life with his true love. Whatever he was thinking, he didn't seem to consider how he and Ethel must have appeared to their fellow passengers. The two were seen to be much more affectionate with each other than would be typical for a father and his teenaged son, so much so that the two aroused the suspicions of the crew.

On 22 July, Captain Henry Kendall of the *Montrose* sent a Marconi wireless message to Scotland Yard, informing the authorities that he felt certain the father and son calling themselves Robinson were actually the couple everyone had been looking for. It was the first time in history that wireless technology had been used to apprehend a fugitive on the run from the law, making Dr Crippen's a landmark case.

In a dramatic turn of events, Crippen found Inspector Dew waiting for him on 31 July at Father Point in the Gulf of St Laurence. Dew had taken a faster ship and beaten his suspect to Quebec. Boarding the *Montrose*, Dew arrested both Crippen and Ethel and returned the couple to England to stand trial separately for the murder of Cora Crippen.

It seemed to be an open and shut case. The remains of a human body had been discovered in the doctor's house. Forensic doctors determined that the remains had most likely been buried around the same time Mrs Crippen was last seen.

The remains, furthermore, contained lethal amounts of the same type of deadly drug Dr Crippen had ordered shortly before his wife went missing (most of which was never found) and the skin on the remains bore a mark prosecutors insisted was the same as Cora Crippen's abdominal scar.

The fabric of the pyjamas found in the cellar, furthermore, had not been in use until a few months before, so the remains could not have been buried before the Crippens moved in, the prosecution insisted. Even worse, Crippen himself had admitted to the police that he had lied about his wife's disappearance.

Crippen's demeanour during his trial didn't help either. At one point, as the prosecution attempted to establish that the mark on the flesh found in Crippen's basement was the same as Cora Crippen's scar, the doctor was handed a grisly piece of evidence:

> *The hideous moment in which the pieces of his dead wife's skin were handed round in a soup plate for inspection left him, alone of all the people in that crowded court, quite unmoved. He peered at them with an intelligent curiosity as though they had been mere museum specimens. Not by one word or tremor did this frail little man betray any sign of his terrible position.*[5]

Crippen argued that the remains could have been in the basement prior to his taking up residence in the house. He insisted he'd used the deadly drug to make medicine for his patients (which is why it could not be recovered). He further maintained that his wife had run away with another man and that he had no idea what had happened to her.

The jury was convinced by none of his explanations. The only point on which he was able to persuade them was that Ethel Le Neve had had nothing whatsoever to do with his wife's disappearance. On that point, they believed him and Ethel was acquitted.

Though Dr Crippen proclaimed his innocence to the end (and numerous people connected with the case claimed Dr Crippen was the kindest man they had ever known), it took the jury only 27 minutes to find him guilty. At 9.00am on Wednesday 23 November, he was hanged at Pentonville Prison and buried in the prison graveyard.

It would seem that the story that garnered so much attention worldwide ends here, but the discovery of recent evidence casts doubt on the outcome of the case. An article published in *The Journal of Forensic Sciences* in 2010 reports the findings of a study that compared that the DNA of the remains found in the Crippens' cellar in 1910 to that of Cora Crippen's living relatives.

'Based on the genealogical and genetic investigations presented here,' the article concludes, 'the remains found in Dr Crippen's coal cellar were not only not Cora Crippen's, they were not even female.'[14]

So what really happened at 39 Hilldrop Crescent? If the remains were not those of Cora Crippen, whose were they? Who left them there? And what actually happened to the doctor's wife? These questions will probably never be fully answered.

CHAPTER THREE

The Case of the Brides in the Bath

(1915)

Sometimes murder happens when love goes wrong, like (perhaps) in the case of Dr Crippen, but what happens when a dangerously criminal mind marries for the sake of opportunity? One famous answer is the notorious fortune hunter George Joseph Smith, who broke the hearts of numerous young women for his own personal gain.

While there is little denying Smith was a reprehensible man who preyed on lonely spinsters, there remains some question as to whether or not he was actually guilty of the crime for which he was convicted in the summer of 1915.

One reason Smith was able to operate as effectively as he did has to do with the climate of the day. Between 1815 and 1880, England saw huge numbers of eligible young men leaving the UK to search for their fortunes in the British colonies, especially during the gold rushes of Australia, New Zealand, South Africa and the United States.[1] The effects of this migration resonated for years and by 1910, women in England outnumbered men by half a million.[2]

Enter the dashing, dishonest George Smith. Born in 1872 in the East End suburb of Bethnal Green, the cockney was only nine years old when he was sent to Gravesend Reformatory for seven years on charges of theft. Shortly after his release in 1888, he spent another seven days in jail, again for theft. More charges for theft and then larceny followed in 1891 and 1896, both of which resulted in sentences of imprisonment and hard labour.[3]

After his stint in prison for larceny, Smith went to Leicester and opened a baker's shop at Russell Square. It was there he met Caroline Beatrice Thornhill, who was quickly enamoured with Smith. Theirs was a short engagement and in January 1898, George Smith (calling himself George Love) and Beatrice Thornhill were married. Beatrice's relatives strongly disapproved of Smith, so much so that they didn't attend the wedding.

It wasn't long before the baker's shop at Russell Square failed and Smith took his young wife with him to London, where he was to live off of her industry. Over and over, he found positions for Beatrice to work as a domestic servant. He also persuaded her to steal from her employers. When she was eventually caught, she went to prison, but as soon as she was released, she implicated her husband in her crimes.[4]

Smith was sentenced to two years in prison with hard labour for his role in Beatrice's offenses. When he was released in October 1902, he discovered Beatrice had left the UK. Fearing Smith might exact revenge upon her, she had emigrated to Canada.[3]

Beatrice never filed for divorce, but Smith's status as a legally married man didn't stop him from 'marrying' a second time. He'd already found a second 'wife' in 1899 while Beatrice was still in prison, this time a woman from London who ran boarding house. Smith spent a lot of time travelling, he told his new bride, so it was nothing unusual for him to disappear for months at a time. It was also nothing unusual for him to return and demand money from her.

At first glance, there was nothing remarkable about Smith, but it seems he often had an amazing effect on women, especially those who were slightly older than the standard marrying age of the time. His second 'wife', whose identity has remained a secret, described his irresistible charm:

He had an extraordinary power ... This power lay in his eyes ...
When he looked at you, you had the feeling that you were being
magnetised. They were little eyes that seemed to rob you of your will.[5]

It wasn't long before Smith had managed to talk his second 'wife' out of every penny she had. No longer useful, she saw less and less of George until eventually he stopped coming back to her altogether.

In June 1908, Smith set another trap when he met a widow named Florence Wilson. After a three-week engagement, Smith married Florence in London. Only days later, on 3 July, Smith convinced his newest 'wife' to withdraw all of her savings and give the money to him. Florence was not suspicious when her new husband snatched up the sum of £30 because, as she said in a later statement to the police, 'He knew I had no pocket.'[3]

She was also not suspicious when he took her away on a cheap holiday. She didn't become suspicious, in fact, until Smith went out for a newspaper and never came back.

When she returned to her flat where the two had set up house together, she discovered that he'd already been there. Smith took everything, sold it and made off with between £80 and £90. It was the last Florence ever saw of Smith or her money.

Over and over, George Smith worked his magic on women who believed he loved them. On 30 July 1908, less than a month after conning Florence Wilson and promptly disappearing from her life, he married a naïve girl named Edith Pegler.

Edith didn't seem to mind waiting at home while her 'husband' went out on the town in the evenings or disappeared for weeks, sometimes months, at a time on 'business'. Whenever she ran out of money, Edith would return to her mother, with whom she would live until her husband came to collect her again. Smith's relationship with Edith continued in this on-again, off-again manner for the next seven years.

Smith was still living with Edith when he met and quickly married another spinster named Sarah Freeman in October 1909. Like others before her, Sarah believed Smith's story that his money came from a wealthy aunt and that he was an antiques dealer. She also believed his name was George Rose, yet another pseudonym Smith used to stay one step ahead of his victims.

Smith convinced Sarah, who worked as a clerk, that he was just a little short of the funds he needed to set up an antiques business. His newest bride willingly obliged her husband, not only emptying her savings but also selling some government stock she'd prudently put away.

On 5 November, Smith took Sarah for a day out at the National Gallery. At the gallery, Sarah waited patiently while Smith excused himself to the restroom. She was still waiting when he returned to their flat, emptied the lot and disappeared with everything Sarah had, which he sold for around £400 – about four years' wages for the average working man.[5]

Smith next met Beatrice Mundy, the 31-year-old daughter of a bank manager who had died and left the spinster with a large trust fund overseen by her uncle. Though Beatrice (known as Bessie) received only £8 per week from the account, her £2500 trust fund continued to grow.

Smith quickly married Bessie on 26 August 1910. The same day, Smith wrote to Bessie's uncle, saying his bride was in 'perfect health' and asking the uncle to forward 'as much money as possible'.[6]

The trust had been set up in such a way that even Bessie was unable to access the entire amount in the account, but Smith managed to make arrangements with the solicitors to withdraw as much as he could and by December 1910, he had taken the accumulated interest on the trust, a sum of £135.

As soon as he had the money, Smith promptly left Bessie, saying that she had given him a disease called 'the bad disorder' which she had contracted from her failure to be 'morally clean'.[5] Smith returned to Edith Pegler and the two relocated to Bristol in early 1912.

Bessie hadn't seen Smith in over two years when, in a bizarre moment of coincidence, she happened to see him out in public. She had been staying with a friend in Weston-super-Mare when she went for a walk on the esplanade one day and bumped into the man she believed to be her husband.

Smith once again turned on the charm, telling Bessie that he had been looking for her. Remarkably, Bessie soon forgave him for everything.

Still eager to get his hands on Bessie's trust fund, Smith began making inquiries. On 2 July 1912, he learned that the only legal way he could access the money was if she were to leave it to him in a will. The very same day, the couple went to see a solicitor to draw up their wills, Bessie leaving her considerable fortune to Smith and Smith leaving his meagre assets to her.[6]

On 8 July, the wills were attested. The following day, Smith sent Bessie to haggle for a second hand bathtub. It was an unusual purchase for Smith. According to Edith Pegler, the 'wife' with whom he had spent the most amount of time, Smith rarely took a bath.

Edith later said that she had never seen Smith look for an apartment with a bath and that he had often told her that he 'did not believe in using baths in apartment houses which other people had access to'.[3]

On 10 July, just two days after the wills were finalised, Smith took Bessie to a local doctor. The two had recently taken up rooms in the holiday resort town of Herne Bay, which was beautiful, trendy and not easily accessible from London, where Bessie's family lived.[7]

Smith chose this moment to tell Bessie that she had been having fits. She had a form of epilepsy, he said, that featured violent seizures. When Bessie said she'd never had a seizure, only a headache, her husband claimed that it was a symptom of her disease that she wouldn't remember having had the fits or even recovering from them. Smith took Bessie to see a doctor, Frank French, who prescribed a sedative for her.[3]

It was just past midnight in the early morning of Friday 12 July when Dr French was called to Bessie's bedside. Smith claimed she'd had another fit, but the doctor could find nothing wrong with her beyond clammy hands, not surprising considering it was a warm summer night. He prescribed another sedative.

Later that day, on the afternoon of 12 July, when Dr French saw Bessie and Smith out walking, she looked the picture of health. At her husband's suggestion, however, she wrote a letter to her uncle, telling him about her fits.[6]

Around 7.00am on the early morning of Saturday 13 July 1912, Bessie began the arduous task of filling the second hand bathtub her husband had purchased just a few days before, bucket by bucket. Smith went out to buy fish, but returned a short time later.

At 8.00am, Dr French received a note from Smith: 'Can you come at once? I'm afraid my wife is dead!'[5]

When Dr French arrived, he found Bessie dead in the bathtub, naked and partly submerged, her legs resting out of the water on the end of the tub. In her right hand, she still clutched a bar of soap, a small detail that would later become very important.

Bessie's family tried to contest the hasty will Bessie had drawn up less than a week before her death. At the inquest, however, Dr French testified that he had previously treated Bessie for epilepsy and that he had found no signs of a struggle or any other evidence of foul play.

Bessie's death was deemed accidental and within six months, the whole of her trust fund totalling £2,579, 13 shillings and 7 pence had been forwarded to George Smith.[7]

Within a year, Smith was on the lookout for another wife. This time, the unlucky candidate was a 25-year-old private nurse named Alice Burnham. Smith met Alice in October 1913 at Southsea in Hampshire.

Alice's father took an instant disliking to his daughter's future husband. In his statement to the police, Mr Burnham described Smith as having a 'very evil appearance, so much so that he could not sleep whilst Smith was in the house …'[3]

Despite her father's misgivings, Alice and Smith's wedding went ahead on 4 November 1913, the day after Alice's life had been insured for £500.

Smith quickly appropriated nearly £30 from Alice's bank account plus another £104 that her father owed her. As soon as the life insurance policy premium was paid, Smith took Alice away for an unseasonal seaside holiday.

On Wednesday 10 December 1913, the couple arrived in Blackpool and took lodging with a couple named Mr and Mrs Crossley. It was Smith's second choice of accommodation. Smith had decided against their first choice when he discovered the apartment had no bath.

Almost immediately upon getting settled, Smith took his new bride to see a Dr Billing because she had a headache.

On the evening of Friday 12 December, Smith asked Mrs Crossley's daughter to draw a bath and then took his wife out for a walk. The couple returned just after 8.00pm. Fifteen minutes later, the Crossleys were having their tea in the kitchen one floor below the Smiths' bathroom. Moments later, they noticed a water stain growing across their kitchen ceiling and dripping down the wall.

Within minutes, an out of breath Smith appeared with two eggs he said were for breakfast and then went upstairs. Almost immediately, he yelled down to the Crossleys to fetch a doctor. They called for Dr Billing, who discovered Alice dead in the bath.[5]

The inquest into Alice's death was held the following day and Dr Billing ruled that she had 'accidentally drowned through heart failure when in the bath' and that there was no evidence of any criminal activity.[8]

Like with Bessie, Smith had Alice buried in a common grave only days after her death. Smith immediately returned to Edith Pegler in Bristol. Between the life insurance pay out and the sale of Alice's possessions, Smith walked away with around £600.

Between his two most recent wives, Smith had pulled in well over £3000, an enormous sum for the time, but he was not ready to give up on his lucrative scam. On 17 September 1914, after travelling around Britain for several months with Edith, Smith married a maidservant named Alice Reavil in Woolwich.

Four days after the wedding, after clearing out the maidservant's scant saving of £90 and stealing everything she owned, Smith took Ms Reavil for a tram ride and left her in a public garden, never to return. When he brought the girl's clothes home to Edith, he claimed he'd been able to get a good deal on them at a sale.[5]

Nearly three months after abandoning Alice Reavil, Smith reacquainted himself with Margaret Lofty (known as Peggy), a 38-year-old spinster he'd met in Bath earlier that year. Peggy had been engaged to be married but had broken off the plans when she discovered her fiancé was already married. When Smith returned to her, she was overjoyed that she would be able to marry after all.

Before plans could go ahead for the wedding, however, Peggy had to take out a life insurance policy in the amount of £700. The policy was finalised on 4 December. On 17 December, Smith married Peggy and the two went immediately to London where they took rooms at Highgate. As soon as they were checked in, Smith took his bride to see a doctor who gave her a prescription.[3]

On 18 December, Peggy visited her solicitor and drew up a will in which she left all of her assets to her husband. She then withdrew the entire amount of her savings account, only £19. That evening, Smith told the landlady he was going out to buy tomatoes for their dinner while his wife took a bath.[8]

At around 8.00pm, the landlady was ironing in the kitchen when she heard the sound of splashing in the couples' bath followed by a sigh. Soon after, she could hear the sound of someone in the front room playing a church hymn on the harmonium. Ten minutes later, Smith rang the doorbell, claiming to have forgotten his key.

Once again he was shocked to discover his wife dead in the bath upstairs. Once again, the inquest was held immediately and deemed an accidental death. Once again, Smith returned to Edith Pegler.

Unlike the others, however, Peggy died in London – not some sleepy seaside village – and in January 1915, *News of the World* ran the sensational headline BRIDE'S TRAGIC FATE ON DAY AFTER WEDDING.[5]

The publication ran nationally, and it wasn't long before Alice Burnham's father saw the story about Peggy. So did Mr Crossley, who had let rooms to Alice on her tragic honeymoon. Though the names of the husbands were different, both men thought the circumstances surrounding the deaths of the two brides were too alike to be coincidence.

On 3 January, Joseph Crossley wrote to Scotland Yard, pointing out the disturbing similarities between the recent death of Peggy Lofty and that of Alice Burnham a year before.[8] Alice's father sent a similar letter to the Aylesbury police.[3]

It was at this point that things began to come unravelled for George Smith. Police throughout the nation immediately began making quiet but extensive inquiries and soon learned of the death of Bessie Mundy.

Within the month, the authorities had gathered enough evidence to make a holding charge against Smith. On 1 February 1915, Smith was arrested just as he was leaving his solicitor's office. He had been sorting out the collection of his latest wife's life insurance policy.

The police told Smith he was being arrested for making a false entry in a marriage register, but on 23 March – after the authorities exhumed the bodies of the three women for further examination – Smith was charged with the murders of Bessie Mundy, Alice Burnham and Peggy Lofty.[9]

Smith's was a landmark case. The ten-day trial, which lasted from 22 June to 1 July, saw no fewer than 264 exhibits and the testimony of 112 witnesses from 40 different towns.[3]

Also, Smith was only on trial for the murder of Bessie Mundy because British law prohibited trying a prisoner for multiple murders at once. The prosecution, however, wanted to establish that Smith had a history of murdering his wives. To this end, they brought in evidence from the deaths of Alice Burnham and Peggy Lofty. The judge allowed it, setting a precedent that would apply to the court for decades to come.[4]

The defence hung on two key elements. First, Smith purchased 'endowment' life insurance policies for both Alice and Peggy, which returned about half as much money as 'all-life' policies. Smith's solicitors argued that if he had intended to kill the women, surely he would have purchased 'all-life' policies. The premiums on both types were about the same.[3]

The other, more telling argument was that none of the three women had had any marks on their bodies indicating a struggle. If Smith had held their heads under the water, the defence argued, the women would have fought back. As one solicitor asked, 'If you tried to drown a kitten, it would scratch you, and do you think a woman would not scratch?'[6]

The prosecution, however, claimed that Smith had only bought the endowment policies as a way to lessen suspicion. The all-life policies would have attracted too much attention, they argued.

They also pointed out that Bessie Mundy had never shown any signs of being epileptic and was unlikely to suddenly start having seizures at the age of 35.[3] Pathologist Bernard Spilsbury (who also testified in the case against Dr Crippen) noted that when Bessie Mundy's body was found dead, she was still clutching a bar of soap. He argued that if she had truly had a seizure or had fainted, her hand would have relaxed.[4]

The prosecution posited that Smith had surprised all three women, rendering them suddenly unconscious before they could take steps to defend themselves.

Spilsbury explained that sending a sudden rush of water up the nose and throat could stimulate the vagus nerve, which connects the brain to the heart, and cause an instant loss of consciousness.

To demonstrate his theory, the prosecution performed an experiment for the jury using the same bathtub in which Peggy Lofty had died. A female volunteer dressed in a bathing costume lay down in the water. Then, with a quick jerk, a male volunteer quickly raised her legs and gently pushed down on her forehead.

The woman immediately lost consciousness and nearly died before she was resuscitated. Throughout the ordeal, however, she suffered no marks or bruises. The jury was convinced and within 22 minutes, they returned a guilty verdict.[6]

But was Smith guilty? Notorious self-styled lawyer Giovanni Di Stefano, who claims to have defended Slobodan Milosevic and Saddam Hussein, has reportedly uncovered evidence that 'clearly shows' how Home Secretary Sir John Simon 'persuaded' the judge to secure a guilty verdict against Smith to draw attention away from the war that was raging throughout England and France at the time.[9] This evidence, however, has not been forthcoming, and Di Stefano is currently serving a fourteen-year sentence for fraud.[10]

Whatever the truth of Di Stefano's claims, George Joseph Smith was convicted for murder on 23 June 1915, claiming to the end that he was innocent. Outside the court, Edith Pegler wept. All appeals denied, Smith was hanged less than a month later on 4 August 1915 at Maidstone Prison, having never shown one moment of remorse.[5]

CHAPTER FOUR

10 Rillington Place

(1953)

Though killers often proclaim their innocence – even in the face of overwhelming evidence to the contrary, as in the case of George Joseph Smith – sometimes justice is not served and the wrong man is executed. Such may or may not be true in the case of 10 Rillington Place.

There is little doubt that John Christie carried out a series of horrifying murders in his flat in Notting Hill, but there has been much speculation regarding the guilt or innocence of his neighbour Timothy Evans. Since the original events transpired in 1953, the case has taken the spotlight several times in the debate surrounding the death penalty and the disturbing possibility of the miscarriage of justice.

John Reginald Halliday Christie had what appears to have been a fairly uneventful childhood. He was one of seven children who grew up in a stable, financially comfortable home.[1]

Born in 1898 in Black Boy House, Halifax, Christie seemed normal by all accounts – exemplary, even. He was a model Boy Scout (rising to the level of assistant Scout Master), he sang in the choir and he was at the top of his class in maths. From a young age, he was interested in medicine and would help in the first aid room and read medical books.[2]

Most of what is known of Christie's young life was related by Christie himself in a number of interviews he gave after his arrest, and there is little to confirm or deny his assertions. According to Christie, his mother was 'a wonderful woman who lived for the happiness of others' while his father was stern, strict and proud though not unusually abusive. 'I always lived in dread of him,' Christie once said.[3]

If Christie is to be believed, he was always fascinated by death. He related one story about seeing his first dead body:

> *All my life, I never experienced fear or horror at the sight of a corpse. On the contrary, I have seen many and they hold an interest and fascination over me. The first one when I was about [twelve] years old and quite clearly I remember. I was not in any way worried or perturbed.*[4]

In fact, he later described 'the trembling sensation he felt as both fascination and pleasure'.[2]

Other than his fascination with death, the only other indicator that anything was amiss with Christie was his feeling of sexual inadequacy. As a teenager, Christie once found himself unable to perform with a girl. As a result, he was teased mercilessly by his friends. 'All my life since, I have had this fear of appearing ridiculous as a lover,' he later recounted, saying that he felt 'doubtful of [his] own sexual capabilities'.[4]

In 1914, the First World War began, and Christie was quick to enlist. He was only seventeen when he joined as a private in September 1916, but he wasn't mobilised until the following April. It was around this time that Christie began frequenting prostitutes, which he would continue to do throughout his time in the military.[5]

One important event in Christie's life happened in June 1918. While on active duty in France, he was injured by a blast of mustard gas. Though Christie later claimed that the gas left him blind, hysterical and unable to speak for over three years, there are no medical records to confirm these symptoms. He did, however, receive a disability pension for a short time, and the injury left him with a distinctive rasping, gravelly voice.[2]

Other than a couple of minor incidents, Christie did well during his time in the army, and his character was assessed as 'very good'.[6] After leaving the army, Christie returned to Halifax in the autumn of 1919 and in May 1920, he married Ethel Waddington, a placid girl from Sheffield. According to Christie, theirs was a happy marriage. He said that she 'made me an excellent wife and was devoted to me'.[7]

From his ordinary childhood and exemplary (if unremarkable) time in the military, Christie's life took a turn for the worse less than a year after his wedding. He'd taken a job as a temporary postman and was jailed for nine months when he was caught stealing money out of letters.[2]

Christie had a few other run-ins with the law before he split with Ethel in 1923 and left Halifax. According to Christie, she'd had an affair with her boss when she had been drinking. There is no evidence (other than Christie's word) to support his claim, but it might have been true. Ethel was an attractive woman and Christie himself admitted that the couple rarely had sexual relations as he continued to have performance issues.[8]

Following the separation, Christie began drifting, sometimes unemployed and often in trouble with the law. In 1929, he was arrested again, this time for a 'murderous attack' on a prostitute with whom he'd been living. Though he'd managed to get off with minor punishments previously, this time he was sentenced to six months of hard labour.

After another stint in prison for stealing from a priest who'd befriended him, Christie contacted Ethel and persuaded her to take him back. It was 1933 when she went to live with him in London.[2]

Despite the reunion with his wife, Christie continued seeing prostitutes. Supposedly his appetites became more violent and began to include some necrophilia. He was suspected of several assaults against women but never charged.[9]

In 1938, Christie and Ethel moved into 10 Rillington Place, and five years later, Christie got his first taste of murder.

A young Austrian woman named Ruth Fuerst arrived in London in 1939. She was a munitions worker and also rumoured to work as a prostitute on the side. In 1943, she fell in with Christie, who was working as a Special Constable at the time. Ruth soon began to regularly return with him to Rillington Place while Ethel was out.

It is believed that Christie killed Ruth by accident during what is now known as erotic asphyxiation – that is, strangulation during sex. It was August 1943 and Ethel was meant to be in Sheffield when Christie brought Ruth back to the flat as usual. This time, however, it all went wrong.

Shortly after discovering that he'd gone too far and had killed Ruth, Christie received word that Ethel was on her way home. He quickly stashed Ruth's body under the floorboards and then quietly moved her into the shared garden at Rillington Place. Ethel returned home, never suspecting a thing.[10]

It would be over a decade before anyone knew what had become of Ruth.

Having seen how easily he could get away with murder, Christie put more thought into his next victim's death. Christie met the respectable 32-year-old Muriel Eady at Ultra Radio Works where he was employed, having left the police force at the end of 1943.

The two were quite well acquainted by November 1944 when Christie invited Muriel back to his flat.[9] Muriel suffered from bronchitis and when Christie told her that he knew of a remedy, she believed him. Once at Rillington Place, Christie mixed a solution of Friar's Balsam with hot water in a jar and had Muriel breath the inhalant.

What Muriel didn't know was that Christie had attached a second hose to the jar, this one piping carbon monoxide gas from the kitchen stove. When the gas had rendered Muriel unconscious, Christie raped and strangled her then buried her dead body in the garden beside Ruth Fuerst.[10]

Four years later, a new couple named Timothy and Beryl Evans moved into the top floor flat at Rillington Place. The Evanses and Christies soon became friends.

With an IQ of only 65 or 70 (depending on the source), Timothy Evans might have been mentally disabled, much different than his neighbour John Christie, who had an IQ of 128. With a violent temper and a low level of intelligence, Evans, who worked as a lorry driver, had a hard time holding down a job.[9]

In October 1948, just over six months after the Evanses arrived, Beryl gave birth to a baby girl, Geraldine. The couple didn't manage their small income very well, and Timothy Evans seemed to take little interest in Geraldine.

When the nineteen-year-old Beryl discovered she was pregnant a second time in late 1949, she didn't think another baby would improve the family situation. Beryl told her husband she was going to have an abortion, and Evans reluctantly agreed.

What happened next is still up for debate. What we do know is that, in November 1949, Timothy Evans turned himself in at the police station in Merthyr Tydfil, saying he'd killed his wife.[11]

At first, Evans claimed that he had bought an oral solution that was meant to terminate his wife's pregnancy. When the solution accidentally killed her, he said, he hid her body in a drain outside the house. He then arranged for someone to look after Geraldine, he added, and left town.

The police searched the drain Evans described but found nothing. After being confronted by detectives, Evans changed his story, insisting that his neighbour John Christie had killed his wife by mistake in a botched attempt to perform the abortion.

Searching the house and grounds at Rillington Place, the police found little but a stolen briefcase. It was a small clue but enough to arrest Evans on a charge of theft. A second, more thorough search uncovered the bodies of Beryl Evans and her one-year-old baby Geraldine. They had both been strangled and there was evidence that Beryl had been sexually assaulted.[11]

This second search, though more thorough than the first, failed to uncover any further evidence. No one noticed that a woman's femur (that of Muriel Eady) was being used to prop up the fence. The police also didn't find it suspicious that children had discovered a woman's skull in the rubble left behind from the Blitz in the property just over the wall from where the Christies and the Evanses lived.[12]

On Friday, 2 December 1949, Timothy Evans gave two statements to officers at Notting Hill Police Station. In these statements, he explained in detail how he'd strangled his family, saying that Beryl had been running up debt.

Because the law prevented him from being tried for two murders at the same time, the Crown chose to prosecute Evans only for the murder of little Geraldine. There was no way, they believed, he could garner any sympathy for killing a baby.[2]

Evans' trial, which began 11 January 1950, seemed little more than a formality. He'd spent over an hour, after all, explaining to the police how he'd killed his wife and daughter.

Later, Evans retracted his confession, saying his neighbour John Christie had actually killed his wife and baby, but no one believed Evans' accusation. When Christie took the stand, the seemingly reputable former policeman and wounded war veteran testified for the prosecution. Christie's testimony helped see Evans convicted.

On 9 March 1950, after losing his appeal, Timothy Evans was hanged at Pentonville Prison, insisting to his last words that Christie had been the real killer.[9]

For all that is unconfirmed, it is certain that around 12 December 1952, John Christie's wife Ethel disappeared. He explained her absence to the neighbours with a flimsy story about how she was in Sheffield visiting relatives. At the same time, he told her Sheffield relatives that she was ill and unable to communicate with them.

After Ethel's disappearance, Christie became more and more irrational. He'd lost his job and was collecting benefits, but it wasn't enough to live on. He had to sell most of his furniture and Ethel's wedding ring to pay the rent. Without Ethel around to discover his dark side, however, Christie was free to murder at will.

In the months to come, Christie would kill at least three more women: Kathleen Maloney, a 26-year-old prostitute from Southampton, in January 1953; Rita Nelson, a 25-year-old pregnant prostitute from Belfast, later the same month; and Hectorina MacLennan, a 26-year-old Scottish girl, in March 1953. All were gassed, raped and strangled, the same as Muriel Eady, and stashed around the property at 10 Rillington Place.[10]

Whether from the growing odour, remorse, fear of being caught or some other reason, John Christie left 10 Rillington Place on 20 March 1953. Needing quick cash, he sublet his apartment to a young couple, demanding three months' rent up front. When the real landlord came by that evening, he discovered Christie gone and the new couple cheated out of their money. He told them they had to leave the following day.

With Christie's ground floor apartment now empty, the landlord said that new upstairs tenant, Beresford Brown, could use the vacant kitchen. Like the rest of the apartment, Christie's kitchen was unkempt and smelled foul, so on 24 March, Brown began the process of remodelling. He'd just removed a strip of wallpaper when he caught a glimpse of a woman's bare back through the rough boards and contacted the authorities.[11]

That day, the police discovered three bodies in the kitchen alcove, those of Kathleen Maloney, Rita Nelson and Hectorina MacLennan. Later that night, they uncovered the body of Ethel Christie from beneath the floorboards and the following day, they finally unearthed the bodies of Ruth Fuerst and Muriel Eady.

In addition to the bodies, the police also discovered Christie's horrifying collection – samples of four different types of pubic hair. According to Dr Lewis Nickolls, the director of the Metropolitan Police Forensic Science Laboratory, at least one of the samples could not have belonged to any of the corpses already uncovered. Nickolls drew the conclusion that at least one more person had fallen victim to Christie, possibly four.[13] The search for Christie began.

Less than a week after the first of the bodies was discovered at Rillington Place, Christie cracked. At 11.20pm on the night of 29 March, Norman Rae, chief crime reporter at *News of the World*, received a mysterious phone call.

When he heard the words 'You recognise my voice?' Rae immediately knew that the man on the other end of the phone was John Christie. Like everyone else who had been at the trial of Timothy Evans, Rae was very familiar with Christie's distinctive, raspy voice.

After five days of living on the street and dodging the police, Christie was ready to come forward. 'I can't stand any more,' he told Rae. 'They're hunting me like a dog and I'm tired out. I'm cold and wet and I've nothing to change into.' Christie told Rae that he would give an exclusive interview in exchange for a meal, a smoke and a warm place to sit.

Rae agreed (stipulating that he would have to contact the authorities immediately after the interview), but moments before the reporter was meant to meet with the elusive criminal, two policemen happened to come by the meeting place, unaware of Rae's appointment with Christie. Seeing the police, Christie got spooked and ran.

Two days later, a uniformed policeman named PC Thomas Ledger was walking his usual beat when he discovered a cold, wet, miserable Christie on Putney Bridge. At first Christie gave the officer false information, but Ledger recognised the little glasses and half-bald head and the jig was up. Christie was arrested and brought into custody.[2]

Over the course of the next several days, Christie admitted to killing all of the women. At first, he tried to maintain his innocence.

According to Christie, on 14 December 1952, Ethel had begun having convulsions in the night. He could do nothing to restore her breathing, he said, so he'd done her the kindness of ending her life by strangling her. (In reality, it's likely she'd begun to suspect her husband's true nature and that he'd taken measures to silence her.) The other murders, he said, were acts of self-defence or abortions gone wrong.

In the end, however, Christie confessed to raping and murdering the women. The only death he could not be held responsible for, he insisted, was that of baby Geraldine. With a plethora options, the Crown opted to prosecute Christie for the murder of his wife.

In the same courtroom in which Timothy Evans had been convicted, Christie's trial began on 22 June 1953. The judge immediately rejected Christie's initial insanity plea, stating that, 'The mere fact that a man acts like a monster cruelly and wickedly is not of itself evidence that he is insane.'

Three days later, the jury found Christie guilty after only 85 minutes of deliberation. On 15 July, he was hanged at Pentonville Prison on the same scaffold and by the same executioner Timothy Evans had been three years earlier. He was 54 years old.[10]

It wasn't long before questions began to arise regarding the true guilt or innocence of Timothy Evans. What were the odds of two men killing in exactly the same way coincidentally living in the same house? It seemed highly unlikely.

Much has been made of Timothy Evans' low IQ. His was reportedly between 65 and 70, but 95 per cent of people who are tested fall between 70 to 130,[14] which means Timothy was possibly 'normal' if on the low end of the scale. Was he incapable of understanding the consequences of his actions, or did the much more intelligent Christie (who was certainly a killer) manipulate him?

At the same time, Timothy went into detail when he confessed to murdering his wife and daughter. Would an innocent man confess, simply to protect his friend and neighbour, knowing the confession would most likely result in his own execution? Or did Timothy perhaps commit the murders under the tutelage of his sinister neighbour?

Also, no one knew Christie was a killer when Beryl and Geraldine died. Why would Timothy have thought to accuse Christie who, at the time, was not known to have ever killed anyone?

In light of all of the questions that arose about Timothy Evans following the conviction of John Christie, Home Secretary David Maxwell-Fyfe commissioned an immediate inquiry to ascertain if an innocent man had been wrongly executed.

QC John Scott-Henderson conducted interviews with over twenty witnesses to the two sets of crimes – including John Christie shortly before his execution – and came to the conclusion that Evans did murder both his wife and child.[11]

Questions still remained, however, so in 1965 a second independent inquiry was opened to question the validity of Evans' conviction and execution. Home Secretary Sir Frank Soskivce charged High Court Judge Sir Daniel Brabin with re-evaluating the evidence in question.

Unlike with the previous inquiries, Brabin did not believe that the same person must have killed both mother and child. 'They were separate killings,' he said, 'done I think for different reasons.'

There were several factors that made Brabin's job a difficult one. There was no question that the authorities had made many mistakes in handling Evans' case. Also, as Brabin pointed out, 'One fact which is not in dispute and which has hampered all efforts to find the truth is that both Evans and Christie were liars. They lied about each other, they lied about themselves.'

In the end, Brabin handed down an explosive verdict:

> *'I have come to the conclusion that it is more probable than not that Evans killed Beryl Evans. I have come to the conclusion that it is more probable than not that Evans did not kill Geraldine.'*

The year following Brabin's inquiry, Timothy Evans was posthumously pardoned and his body removed outside the walls of Pentonville Prison.[15]

Many were convinced of Evans' innocence. One famous example is *Ten Rillington Place*, a book published in 1961 by Ludovic Kennedy that in 1971 was made into a movie of the same name starring Richard Attenborough as Christie. Kennedy argued that Evans had not killed his wife and baby. Instead, Christie was responsible for both deaths and framed Evans. According to Kennedy, the police coerced Timothy's confession by questioning the mentally impaired man day and night.

A more recent book, *The Two Killers of Rillington Place* by John Eddowes, claims exactly the opposite. In the book published in 1994 by Little, Brown and Company, Eddows argues that Evans did indeed kill both his wife and child, and that Beryl's eventual death was not Timothy's first attempt to kill her. Eddowes also asserts that Beryl Evans was not even present at Rillington Place when John Christie supposedly killed her.[16]

Regardless of the truth of the circumstances, which will probably never come fully to light, the questions surrounding the execution of Timothy Evans was instrumental in the abolition of the death penalty in Britain. Labour MP Sydney Silverman wrote extensively about Evans' case, and in 1965 he succeeded in suspending the death penalty for five years. The abolition of punishment was made permanent in 1969.

Even so, the case remains controversial. While it is now (mostly) agreed that Timothy Evans was hanged for a murder he did not commit – that of killing his daughter Geraldine – there is still plenty of evidence to suggest that he was guilty of the murder of his wife Beryl.

The case came before the law once again almost forty years later. Unsatisfied with Evans' pardon, his family sought an appeal, but in March 2004, the Criminal Cases Review Commission (CCRC) refused to refer the case back to the Court of Appeal. The CCRC deemed the 1966 pardon was enough to establish the miscarriage of justice and restore the Evans family's reputation.

Evans' half-sister Mary Westlake carried on with the case and hired solicitor Bernard de Maid to challenge the CCRC's decision. In the end, a judicial review declared Timothy innocent of the murder of his daughter,[17] but it remains undecided whether justice was ever truly served or not.

CHAPTER FIVE

The Great Train Robbery

(1963)

Few crimes in British history have displayed the audacity of the one that has come to be known as simply the Great Train Robbery. On the morning of 8 August 1963, a gang of thieves led by Bruce Reynolds pulled off one of the most lucrative heists the world has ever seen, making off with £2.6 million without firing one shot.

These days, the 1960s often conjures up images of The Beatles and the conflict in Vietnam but at the time, the majority of the British population was recovering from the recent war and just trying to get by. For many, the idea that a small band of regular blokes could get away with such a fortune was enough to raise the bandits to the level of folk heroes.

Part of the reason the robbery became such a national phenomenon is because, in the words of Bruce Reynolds, no previous crime had received such wide coverage:

> *1963 was really the advent of media across the whole of the country. People had got television sets where they hadn't had them before.*

A lot of them looked on the Great Train Robbery as being the first media covered robbery that there'd ever been.[1]

Bruce Richard Reynolds was born into poverty in central London in 1931. His mother died when he was just a toddler and his father struggled to get by as the Great Depression continued to plague the world.

Eager to have the finer things in life, Reynolds became a thief at a young age, always preferring to rely on cunning rather than violence. 'The threat of violence was often needed, of course,' he said in a 2013 interview, 'but I saw using it as a failure.'[2]

It wasn't long before Reynolds became well known among his associates for his love of luxury. Called a 'gentleman thief', he cut quite the figure with his handmaid suits, extravagant sports cars and fine cigars. Reynolds was already a seasoned criminal when he helped plan and execute the theft of £62,000 in cash wages from the British Overseas Airways Corporation (BOAC) on 27 November 1962.

That chilly Tuesday, Reynolds joined Gordon Goody and Charlie Wilson along with driver Roy James and Ronald 'Buster' Edwards at the Hatton Cross branch of Barclays Bank. The five men calmly and carefully executed their well-planned attack, making off with the huge fortune and escaping in sleek Jaguars – in broad daylight and with hardly any bloodshed.[3] The five men would meet again in less than a year's time to accomplish the crime that would go down in history.

According to Reynolds, the famous heist on the Royal Mail train was planned as a 'war on authority'. So many British lives had been lost during the First and Second World Wars, and no one was eager to see more young men sent off to Vietnam. The robbery, Reynolds argued, was a way of sticking it to the establishment.[1] Whatever Reynolds' political reasoning, he certainly stood to profit personally from the robbery enormously.

On Thursday, 8 August 1963, the Travelling Post Office (TPO) was making its way from Glasgow to London as it had without incident every single night since 1838. On board was a load of mailbags full of packets of bank notes collected over the recent holiday weekend, some destined for banking head offices in London, others an allotment of £5 notes that were being withdrawn from circulation.

Along the way, the train made several stops, collecting a total of 128 mailbags. In these bags were over 600 packets containing £5, £1 and 10 shilling notes equalling £2,595,997.10. Even more tempting, there were no police or security guards on the Royal Mail train. It had never occurred to those in charge that the train and its highly lucrative cargo would be a target, so few precautions had been taken.[3]

As the train approached London, Bruce Reynolds waited at Leatherslade Farm in Buckinghamshire. With him were Gordon Goody, Charlie Wilson, Roy James, Jimmy White and a dozen others. Four would never be positively identified. They were known only as Mr One, Mr Two, Mr Three and an older man nicknamed Pop.

A rough Irishman born in 1930, Gordon Goody began his life of crime stealing cattle when he was just a boy.[4] The night of the hit on the train, Goody had nine previous criminal convictions, including robbery with violence.[3] Described as charismatic, articulate and witty, Goody later said, 'I had the worst record of all of them. [The judge] said I was the saddest case in front of him, and said my powers of leadership would have won me medals in a war.'[4]

Charlie Wilson, the treasurer of the gang, had grown up with Bruce Reynolds, and like Reynolds, his mother had died when Wilson was young. A big man with piercing blue eyes, he would go on to live an extraordinary life of crime.[5] The youngest of the gang was 27-year-old Roy James, an amateur race car driver who stood barely over 5 feet (152 cm) tall and had a reputation for being the best getaway car driver around.[3]

A former soldier, Jimmy White was famous for being precise and organized. A long time friend of Bruce Reynolds, he'd spent much of his life after leaving the army pursuing legitimate business interests, but when the army cut his pension, he turned to crime. The night of the train robbery, he'd been on the run for ten years.[6]

In the early hours of the morning that Thursday, a convoy of three vehicles left Leatherslade Farm to meet the train. Leading the way was

Bruce Reynolds, who sat beside Ronnie Biggs, John Daly and Roger Cordrey in a Series Two Land Rover driven by the man known as Mr Two.

Ronnie Biggs had known Reynolds for over ten years. Born in London in 1929, he found himself in trouble with the law several times as a teenager for theft. After two years in the Royal Air Force, Biggs was dishonourably discharged and again turned to crime.[7]

John Daly and Bruce Reynolds were brothers-in-law, having married sisters Barbara and Frances. A massive Irishman sometimes called Paddy, Daly weighed in at over 220 pounds (100 kg). Originally a florist in Brighton, Roger Cordrey found himself on the wrong side of the law when his gambling habits grew out of control. Cordrey was recruited by Reynolds for his expertise with railway signals.

Driving behind Reynolds, the second vehicle in the convoy was an Austin lorry with Mr One at the wheel. With him were Mr Three and Charlie Wilson alongside Buster Edwards, Tommy Wisbey, Bobby Welch and Big Jim Hussey.

Born in Lambeth in 1931, Buster Edwards had been a florist, barman, boxer and nightclub owner. He'd worked with Reynolds and Gordon Goody the previous year in the BOAC robbery.[3] Tommy Wisbey had been a bookie but was more useful to Reynolds as someone who could intimidate the train staff. 'I was one of the heavies,' Wisbey later said.[8] Two other heavies were Bobby Welch, a nightclub boss and gambler, and Jim Hussey, a painter and decorator with criminal leanings.

Roy James brought up the rear of the convoy driving a Series One Land Rover. With him were Jimmy White and Gordon Goody.

Shortly after 1.30am on 8 August, the convoy arrived at Bridego Bridge, a railway bridge running over a small country lane. The men parked the vehicles and got into position while Roy James and Roger Cordrey climbed the nearby telephone poles and cut the overhead wires.

The first step in the plan was to stop the train, which meant tampering with two sets of signals. The 'dwarf' signal with its amber bulb would slow the train and the 'home' signal 300 yards (274 m) south glowing red would stop it.

Reynolds, Cordrey and Daly went to work on the 'dwarf' signal. Cordrey knew exactly how to rig a switch with an external battery to the amber bulb. When the moment came, it was Daly's job to flip the switch and conceal the green bulb with a black leather glove. Though the green bulb would still be illuminated, the driver wouldn't be able see it. He would only see the amber bulb and slow down.

With Daly in place, Reynolds and Cordrey joined the rest of the gang at Sears Crossing further down the line from the dwarf signal. Here, Cordrey climbed the gantry over the tracks and again rigged a switch that would illuminate the red 'home' signal, telling the train's driver to stop the train.

Once the train was stopped at Sears Crossing, the plan was to uncouple the locomotive and the first two cars immediately behind it – including the High Value Packages (HVP) car – from the rest of the train. Then one member of the gang, the man called Pop, would drive the locomotive to Bridego Bridge where the gang would break into the HVP car and unload the cash into the vehicles waiting on the country lane below.

Despite careful planning, Reynolds and his accomplices misjudged a couple of details that could have undone their entire plan. They didn't anticipate, for example, that a nearby telephone exchange operator would alert technicians less than 90 minutes after the phone wires were cut. Also, John Daly inadvertently alerted a signalman when he unscrewed the green bulb rather than simply covering it with the black glove.

But luck was on the side of the thieves. The driver of the Royal Mail train, a 57-year-old man named Jack Mills, followed the unusual signals and put on the brakes.

At 3.03am, the train came to a stop at Sears Crossing, and Mills' fireman jumped down from the cab to investigate what the drivers believed to be a faulty signal. In an interview with the BBC three days later, Mills said, 'My mate went down to telephone, which is the usual custom. And he said these telephone wires have been cut – I didn't realise it was a trap, even then.'[3]

While Jimmy White and Roy James uncoupled the engine and the first two cars, other members of the gang swarmed the cab of the locomotive.

Unexpectedly, Jack Mills fought back. To subdue him, at least one of the men struck Mills a number of times with a 'cosh' or bludgeon.

All of the men who mounted the attack on the cab were wearing balaclavas, so it was hard to identify which of the gang resorted to violence. Several members of the gang later claimed to have been the one who bashed Mills, including Hussey, Biggs and Edwards, but the truth will likely never come out.

One incontrovertible fact is that seven years following the incident, Jack Mills died of cancer. His family, however, believe that Mills never fully recovered from the wounds he sustained during the robbery and that the injuries he suffered during the attack led to his death.[9]

Once the cars were uncoupled, it should have been a simple task to drive the engine and the two remaining cars the short distance to Bridego Bridge.

When the replacement train driver Pop climbed into the cab, however, he realised that the diesel engine was quite different to the local trains he was used to driving. As it turned out, he couldn't operate the locomotive at all. In the end, Ronnie Biggs had to revive a groggy Jack Mills to drive the locomotive to Bridego Bridge.

Once there, the gang unloaded the mailbags into the waiting vehicles. The men instructed the few postal workers remaining on the train to wait 30 minutes before contacting police, and then Reynolds' gang made their escape.

As the convoy made its way back to Leatherslade Farm, the postal workers left on the remaining ten cars at Sears Crossing thought something was suspicious. They managed to contact the authorities and at 4.20am, the alarm was raised and police began one of the biggest manhunts in history. Led by Detective Chief Superintendent Jack Slipper, the investigation was run by the Flying Squad at Scotland Yard and senior detectives from the Buckinghamshire Police.[10]

Back at the isolated farm, the gang was enjoying their spoils. In his later years, Gordon Goody would describe the haul, a massive pile of cash reaching from the floor to the ceiling. 'It was a sight to see,' Goody recalled.[11]

It was to be a short-lived celebration, however. The plan had been for the gang to lay low for a couple of weeks, but low flying RAF aircraft (completely unaware of the gang's location) had been going on training runs nearby.

The gang spooked, split the money – some of which was set aside for two informants who had passed along vital information but were not present – and went their separate ways.[10]

News of the heist spread across the country with dizzying speed and soon every newspaper and radio station was reporting the story. Then, on 13 August 1963, the gang's hideout was discovered. The farm was rife with evidence including empty mailbags, the getaway vehicles and, most importantly, fingerprints.

Even worse for the robbers, many of their criminal associates who were meant to help them hide tipped off the police and the thieves began to fall, one by one.

The first of the robbers to be caught was Roger Cordrey, the man who had rigged the signal lights. The former florist was arrested in Bournemouth on 14 August 1963 after he tried to pay three months' rent on a garage flat in 10 shilling notes and was sentenced to twenty years in prison. Released in 1971, he went back to quietly selling flowers. He retired to Swanage where he died in 2005 at the age of 84.[12]

The treasurer of the gang, Charlie Wilson, was caught on 22 August 1963 in London and earned the nickname 'the silent man' when he stayed quiet during police questioning. Four months into his 30-year prison sentence, he broke out of Winson Green Prison in Birmingham and seemed to disappear into thin air.

Four years later, he was arrested again on 24 January 1968 in Canada. The last of the gang to be released from prison in 1978, Wilson quickly returned to a life of crime. Eventually, he moved to Spain where he lived in luxury until he was murdered in 1990, allegedly over a drug deal gone wrong. He was 58 years old.[13]

Arrested on 4 September 1963, Ronnie Biggs' role in the robbery was fairly small – he was the one who had found the incompetent replacement train driver Pop. Biggs became one of the most well known members of the gang when he climbed the wall and escaped Wandsworth Prison, having served only fifteen months of his 30-year sentence. He managed to elude the authorities for years, getting plastic surgery to change his appearance and then hiding out in Australia and Brazil.

After decades of living a glamorous life on the run, Biggs finally returned to the UK in 2001, broke and needing medical attention. Making a deal with *The Sun*, he flew home where he was immediately arrested and returned to prison. There he suffered several strokes and when he could no longer eat, speak or walk, he was released from prison on compassionate grounds on 6 August 2009. He died four years later, not long after the release of his memoirs *Odd Man Out*.[14]

Gang heavies Big Jim Hussey and Tommy Wisbey were arrested within days of each other on 7 and 11 September 1963. Hussey served just eleven years of his 30-year sentence before his release in 1975, just over a year before Wisbey in 1976. Both later received convictions for drugs and assault, despite attempts to make it in small business. Hussey died on 12 November 2012, aged 79.[15] As of this writing, Tommy Wisbey lives in London. He self-published his memoirs, *The Wrong Side of the Tracks*, in January 2015.[8]

One key player who was not involved in the robbery itself was solicitor Brian Field, who organised the hideout at Leatherslade Farm. He was also meant to organise someone to clean the hideout after the gang left.

In the end, the cleaner Field hired took his money without ever doing the job, allowing police to uncover the evidence that would be the gang's undoing. Arrested 15 September 1963, Field was originally sentenced to 25 years but on appeal he saw the sentence reduced to only five years. He died at the age of 44 in a car accident in 1979.[16]

One of the main organisers who later claimed to have been the mastermind of the entire affair, Gordon Goody was arrested 3 October 1963 and was promptly sentenced to 30 years in prison. Goody believed the court was out to get him and that the prosecution used false evidence to secure his conviction. After his release in 1975, Goody relocated to Spain where he opened a bar. He became a much-loved figure in the community before his death on 26 January 2016.

His death came two years after he released his memoirs *How to Rob a Train* in 2014, around the same time he appeared in the documentary film *A Tale of Two Thieves*.

In the documentary, Goody revealed the identity of the famed Ulsterman, a postal worker who gave the gang sensitive information that made the robbery possible. Goody identified the man as Patrick McKenna, with whom Goody reported met on a number of occasions prior to the robbery. McKenna (whose family was astounded to hear of their father's involvement) died several years before the documentary was made and could neither confirm nor deny the allegation that he had been involved.[4]

Muscle man Bob Welch remains the oldest living member of the gang. Arrested 25 October 1963, Welch was sentenced to 30 years in prison. Released in 1976, the 87-year-old is now confined to a wheelchair.[17]

Though many of the gang enjoyed their notoriety in their later life, John Daly – the one who botched the simple job of covering the light bulb – was happy to return to anonymity. Arrested on 3 December 1963, Daly was acquitted when the prosecution failed to prove that Daly actually participated in the robbery. He returned to Launceston where he quietly worked as a respectable dustman and street cleaner until his death at the age of 82 in April 2013.[18]

Getaway driver Roy James was arrested on 10 December 1963 and was sentenced to 30 years in prison. After his release in 1976, he tried to return to car racing but he was never successful. He was 61 when he died from heart disease in August 1997.[19]

Though a dozen men were found guilty in early 1964 (two of whom were later found innocent), three of the known criminals managed to elude the police – for a while, anyway.

The nondescript Jimmy White, who helped uncoupled the train cars, managed to live in England for three years following the heist before anyone recognised him. In April 1966, he was finally arrested and sentenced to eighteen years in prison. Following his release in 1975, he moved to Sussex.[20] Little more seems to be known about White, including the date of his death.

Buster Edwards, the former boxer, dodged authorities until September 1966 when he turned himself in to the police. Supposedly he was avoiding his criminal associates, who all wanted a slice of the train robbery pie. Upon his released in 1975, he opened a flower stall outside Waterloo Station.

In 1988, the film *Buster* was released, a story about Edwards' life starring Phil Collins as the popular thief. Edwards reportedly suffered from depression and alcoholism, however, and when he was found hanged in a garage beside his flower stall in November 1994, the police deemed the death a suicide. He was 62 years old.[21]

Of the all the men identified as having been involved in the robbery, leader Bruce Reynolds evaded police the longest. For six years, Reynolds hid out in Mexico, Canada and France. When he returned to Britain in November 1968 – broke and alone – he was soon arrested and sentenced to 25 years, only ten of which he served.

After his release in 1978, he managed to make a modest living writing books and consulting on films about his most infamous crime, including *The Train Robbers* written by Piers Paul Reed in 1979. When he died 28 February 2013 following a lengthy illness, the list of celebrity gangsters in attendance at his funeral was long and infamous, including Ronnie Biggs, Bobby Welch and a number of other underworld figures.[22]

In the years since the famous heist, the robbers have often been seen as heroes – cultural icons on the level with Bonny and Clyde or Ned Kelly – but many fail to see the romance in the theft.

Most of the money was reportedly never recovered but rather lost or stolen by associates of the robbers who had been conscripted to keep the money safe, and few of the seemingly glamorous thieves enjoyed any lasting benefit from having been involved in the crime.

Justice Edmund Davies, the judge who handed down the famously long sentences, hoped to deter future thieves from trying to follow in the footsteps of Reynolds and his gang. At the first round of trials in 1964, Davies called the robbery 'a crime which in its impudence and enormity is the first of its kind in this country. I propose to do all in my power to ensure that it is the last of its kind ... Let us clear out of the way any romantic notions of daredevilry.'[23]

Whether the Great Train Robbery will be remembered as a gallant act of bravado or as a violent act of criminal greed, one thing is certain – it won't soon be forgotten.

CHAPTER SIX

Jack the Stripper

(1965)

There are a number of reasons young women might turn to prostitution, most of which are not pleasant. Once involved, women who resort to the profession often find themselves in precarious circumstances in which they become vulnerable to those who seek to do them harm.

One such criminal mind has been dubbed Jack the Stripper, a serial killer who haunted working girls in the West London suburb of Chiswick in 1964 and 1965, possibly longer. The murder of at least six prostitutes has been attributed to the Stripper, whose identity is uncertain – and is likely to remain so until police files on the case are opened on 1 January 2050.

Police first became aware of the killer on 2 February 1964. At 1.15pm, oarsmen from the London Corinthian Sailing Club came upon the body of a young woman in the water of the Thames River, bumping against a pontoon near Hammersmith Reach.

Upon investigation, pathologist Dr Donald Teare discovered bruising around the woman's jaw and was able to identify a piece of fabric caught in the woman's throat as matching that of her panties. Other than a pair of stockings, which had been rolled halfway down the woman's legs, the body was naked.

Authorities soon had a name to go with the face. Hannah Tailford was a 30-year-old waitress from Northumberland who had received four convictions for prostitution (and several others for theft) in previous years. She was a tiny brunette, standing only 5 feet 2 inches (157 cm) tall, the mother of three-year-old Linda and an 18-month-old son. At the time of her death, Hannah was pregnant.

When her body was found, Hannah had been missing for ten days from the flat she shared with her boyfriend in West Norwood, although one couple reported having seen Hannah at Charing Cross Station on 31 January. She'd said she was thinking of committing suicide, but the man had told her 'not to be daft'.

Forensic detectives studied the rise and fall of the river and determined that Hannah's body had been dumped in the water a mile and a half (1.6 km) upstream at Duke's Meadow, an area notorious as a spot for lovers and prostitutes at work.[1]

The exact cause of Hannah's death remains unknown. In his post mortem report, Dr Teare stated that he believed the cause of death was drowning, but head injuries suggested that she had been either knocked unconscious or drowned elsewhere and then moved to Duke's Meadow and into the river.[2] It was estimated that she had been in the water for between two and seven days.

Under the leadership of Detective Chief Inspector Benjamin Devonald, police with the Thames Valley CID interviewed over 700 people in connection with Hannah's death. In questioning members of London's underworld, the authorities learned little about Hannah's murder.

They did, however, learn that Hannah was more than simply a disadvantaged streetwalker. Hannah reportedly participated in kinky sex parties in the exclusive luxury neighbourhoods of Mayfair and Kensington, parties organised by a foreign diplomat who hired women through an agent.

Pornographic photographs of Hannah participating in group sex were also discovered, and it was believed she may have had copies she could have used for blackmail,[1] hinting at a possible motive for her murder. With so little to go on, however, authorities could determine neither the person who committed the crime nor the reason. Following the inquest, Hannah's case was left open.[4]

Hannah might have been dismissed as just another unfortunate prostitute who had met the wrong customer, but ten weeks later, a redheaded prostitute named Irene Lockwood met an eerily similar fate. On 8 April 1964, Irene's tattooed body was discovered at Duke's Meadow, tangled in the reeds along the water's edge. The 26-year-old had last been seen the previous day outside a pub in Chiswick.

A regular around Bayswater Road and Notting Hill, Irene was also involved in more than just soliciting on the streets. Like Hannah, she was known to work sex parties and appear in films. Also like Hannah, she was pregnant and small – only 5 feet (152 cm) tall. Irene too had been bashed in the head, apparently from behind, stripped naked and dumped on the banks of the Thames.[2]

It was hard for authorities to say what might have motivated a killer to take Irene's life. Was it a high profile client who feared she might reveal his identity? Was the killer a religious crusader, bent on cleansing the earth of immorality? Or, the most chilling possibility, was her death the work of a serial killer? DCI Devonald and Detective Superintendent Frank Davies had to consider all three theories.

Barely two weeks after Irene's death the killer struck again, this time 22-year-old prostitute Helen Barthelemy, who was often called Teddie. Though she didn't regularly work in the Chiswick area, her body was found in an alleyway just off Swyncombe Avenue in Brentford, only one mile (1.6 km) from where Hannah and Irene had been found.

Due to a lack of wounds on her throat, authorities determined that she had been seized (mostly likely from behind) and suffocated with a cloth or pillow. The post mortem examination concluded that, as with the others, Teddie had been stripped after her death and that she had been killed some time before being dumped in the alley.

Unlike the others, Teddie was missing three of her front teeth. A lack of other injuries suggested that these teeth had been removed after the girl's death.

Police learned that Teddie had been educated at a convent and had taken work as a housemaid before she became a stripper on Blackpool's Golden Mile. A year later, she was working as a prostitute in London, and she'd gained a reputation for catering to bizarre sexual appetites. She was also known to give away her services for free to black friends who were 'more sympathetic' and didn't 'go in all the time for kinky sex'.[1]

It was her affinity for black culture, in fact, that brought Teddie to the serial killer's hunting ground. She was a regular at the Jazz Club on Westbourne Park Road and Wraggs Café on All Saints Road. The last time she was seen, she'd been dancing and talking with African-Caribbean people at the Jazz Club. It was nearly dawn when she asked someone to hold her bag for her while she went outside. It was the last time anyone saw her alive.[5]

It was around this time that authorities began to link the deaths of Hannah, Irene and Teddie to that of another prostitute, Gwynneth Rees (also believed to have been called Tina Smart). Gwynneth had been found on 8 November 1963 at the Barnes Borough Council Refuse Disposal Plant although pathologist Dr Arthur Mant estimated that she had been dead for several weeks, possibly months, before her body was found.[6]

Authorities originally believed that Gwynneth had died as the result of a botched abortion, but now began to suspect that her death might have been at the hands of the same person who had killed the other three girls. Like the others, she was found naked except for one stocking and the police believed that she, too, had been killed elsewhere and dumped at the disposal plant.[1]

Further investigation revealed that Gwynneth was an East End prostitute who held twelve convictions for soliciting and one for theft. In light of the three more recent murders, authorities took another look at Gwynneth's death. One colleague of Dr Mant's determined that the cause of Gwynneth's death was strangulation.[7]

With three (possibly four) murders, it was becoming more and more possible – though by no means certain – that there was a serial killer on the loose, one who left his victims naked. Like another famous murderer who had terrorised London in 1888, this one also preyed on prostitutes and it wasn't long before the press had dubbed the elusive criminal Jack the Stripper.

Then came a break in the case. It seemed as though the search for the killer was over when Kenneth Archibald came forward. The 54-year-old bachelor was the resident caretaker of the Holland Park Lawn Tennis Club and co-owner of an after-hours drinking club that operated out of the tennis club from 11.00pm till 4.00am every night. The club attracted a number of underground figures and their associates, including Irene Lockwood. A few weeks after the club was discovered and closed, Irene's body was found.[8]

When police searched Irene's flat, they found a visiting card belonging to Archibald and questioned him. At first he claimed he'd never known the girl, but on 27 April 1964, Archibald went to the police and confessed to killing the girl. 'I killed her,' he told Detective Davies. 'I have got to tell somebody about it.'[1]

Despite the similarities in the cases, however, Archibald did not confess to killing anyone other than Irene, and a quick investigation determined that he could not have been responsible for the deaths.

On 19 June 1964, Archibald stood before the Acton Magistrates Court and pleaded not guilty. He recanted his confession, saying he'd been drunk when he'd made the statement. The magistrate committed him for trial, but on 23 June 1964, Archibald was found not guilty and acquitted.[8]

Archibald's bizarre sideshow had wasted many value hours of police time. The authorities were no closer to discovering the killer than before. They did, however, have some vital clues to lead them in the right direction.

Despite the similarities between Teddie and the other girls, there was one significant difference. Teddie's body had been dumped on dry land and, as such, had not suffered post mortem water damage.

Forensic scientists first noticed that her body was particularly dirty, suggesting she had been hidden before being dumped. More importantly, investigators found minuscule flecks of coloured paint still clinging to her skin – orange, yellow, green and black. Further examination revealed that the paint was the type used in automatic paint sprayers, most commonly used to paint cars, furniture and other types of metal.

The experts concluded that Teddie's body had most likely been stored in a closet or other small space near an industrial paint spraying facility. The nature of the high pressure spraying process meant that the paint was likely to find its way through even the smallest space around a door. They also determined that Teddie's body had lain on rough sacking, rubber matting and possibly a shelf.

There was no denying that all of the Stripper's victims came from the lowest echelons of society – poor prostitutes who held criminal convictions and engaged in activities deemed highly disreputable at best – but the social standing of the victims did nothing to deter the authorities. Police officers, detectives and forensic scientists all devoted hundreds of hours to finding the killer.

The authorities also got help from the most unlikely allies. Usually, those involved in the criminal underworld want little to do with the police, even in solving crimes perpetrated against their own. This case, however, was different.

The week following the discovery of Teddie's body, the head of Scotland Yard's CID unit, Commander George Hatherill, issued a statement asking prostitutes to come forward with any information they might have that would help with the investigation.

In his statement, Hatherill named the victims, including Gwynneth Rees, and promised that anyone who helped the authorities would do so in the strictest confidence. 'Police fear that if information is not forthcoming, yet another prostitute may be found dead,' he added. 'In particular, police wish to interview any prostitute who has been made to strip and has been assaulted.'

Hatherill later admitted to reporters that making the statement was something of a shock tactic but 'I want to get it home to these women that we want to protect them'.[1]

However shocking, Hatherill's tactic worked. Within hours, 23 prostitutes had contacted the authorities. Police also appealed to male customers to come forward with any information they might have had as well. By the end of April 1964, the authorities had spoken with 60 men and women who had come forward with information.[2]

In addition to waiting for volunteers to come forward, the police took the daring step of using decoys to lure the killer out of hiding. Six known prostitutes joined the police payroll, exchanging information for a small stipend. The girls were asked to report on customers with bizarre or unusual sexual appetites.

In addition to these working girls, a squad of undercover female police officers began posing as prostitutes. Shadowed by their male counterparts, these women put themselves at extraordinary risk, carrying tape recorders in an effort to obtain information.[2]

Despite the outpouring of assistance, the police were still searching when a near traffic accident brought them closer than they'd been throughout the investigation.

In the early morning of 14 July 1964, police received a phone call from an irate motorist who said he'd almost been hit by a dark coloured van speeding out of a cul-de-sac onto Acton Lane. Three minutes later, police arrived in a squad car and discovered the body of Mary Fleming sitting outside the garage of a house in Berrymeade Road, one street over. A neighbour had seen the body but had dismissed it, thinking it was a tailor's dummy.

There was little question that Mary had fallen victim to the Stripper. Only 5 feet (152 cm) tall, Mary had been attacked from behind and then stripped after her death. She had been dead for over three days when her body was found, leading police to believe that the killer had used the dark van to dump Mary's body before speeding away.[2]

Her lifestyle was similar to that of the other girls, as well. Mary had been working as a prostitute off and on since her arrival in London in 1954 and had convictions for soliciting and theft reaching as far back as 1956. The mother of two had last been seen around 5.00am on the morning of 10 July 1964 drinking at an unlicensed club. Four days later, she was dead.[9]

The police had little new to add to their investigation, other than that Mary's body also bore the same tiny flecks of paint that had been found on Teddie. Now the authorities were more certain that the same person was responsible for both murders.

After interviewing 8000 people and taking 4000 statements, the police were still no closer to finding the killer. It seemed as though the Stripper was becoming more brazen, though, and making fewer efforts to conceal his work. His dumping grounds were becoming more public, almost as though he was taunting the police.[1]

For the next four months, police continued to watch the areas where the victims had lived and worked – until the killer struck again. On 25 November 1964, the body of 21-year-old Margaret McGowan was found in a car park near Kensington High Street, where it had lain for at least a week. Experts determined she'd been dead much longer.

Stripped, strangled and flecked with paint, her body left little question as to who had killed her. As with Teddie, the killer also took one of Margaret's teeth.

One detail that set Margaret apart from the other victims was her involvement with the high profile Profumo scandal the previous year. Under the name Frances Brown, Margaret had testified in the defence of Dr Stephen Ward. The infamous osteopath had killed himself before a jury could convict him of pimping out prostitutes to high profile clients, including Secretary of State for War John Profumo.

Margaret's connection to the Profumo affair, however, did nothing to save her. The mother of three was last seen on 23 October 1964 by another prostitute and two men who hired the services of Margaret and her friend. This time, no one came forward with information about the murder.

With so many similarities between the victims, police psychologists began to draw a picture of their killer. They reasoned he was a small man, probably in a respectable position, possibly submissive and henpecked. They also believed he was a psychopath and a misogynist.

The killer had established a pattern of killing about every ten weeks, and in February 1965, he stuck to his schedule. In the early morning of 16 February 1965, the body of a prostitute named Bridie O'Hara was found behind a storage shed just off Westfield Road.[1] She had been suffocated and stripped, her naked body left only a short distance from the underground line.[10]

Once again, there could be no mistaking the killer. Standing only 5 feet 2 inches (157 cm) tall, the 28-year-old Bridie had eleven convictions for soliciting.[11] She was last seen the evening of 11 January 1965 at the

Shepherd's Bush Hotel where she spoke with several men she knew. That night, she climbed into the killer's car and was never seen alive again.

Police knew that the discovery of the killer's hiding place for the bodies near the paint shop would be a vital milestone in the case, and Bridie's body provided a few interesting clues. Bridie's body had been mummified – that is, dried out after she died – suggesting that she had been hidden near a source of heat. Traces of oil and fibres indicated that she had also been wrapped in a tarp as well.

The pattern was clear. The victims were always prostitutes who worked in West London, all between 5 feet and 5 feet 3 inches (152-160 cm) tall. Evidence suggested that they were all abducted between 11.00pm and 1.00am, suffocated or strangled, stored for a number of days and then dumped between 5.00am and 6.00am. Their bodies were all found within close proximity to each other and none of their clothes or personal effects was ever recovered.[1]

After the discovery of Bridie's body, Detective Chief Superintendent John Du Rose was appointed to investigate the case. He focused the efforts of hundreds of police personnel on finding the place where the killer stashed the bodies and any other clues as to his identity.[12]

Looking at another similarity among the victims, Du Rose developed a theory that drew an odd parallel between Jack the Stripper and John Christie – a taste for erotic asphyxiation, a view Du Rose later set forth in his memoirs:

> [The victims] had slight marks on the neck apparently made by fingernails, either by the murderer or by the victim in an attempt at self-defence ... Some had injuries and very slight bruising as though pressure had been directed in the region of the nose and mouth ... at the moment of orgasm, [the killer] became utterly frenzied ... [12]

In a bold move, Du Rose enlisted the help of the media to turn up the pressure on the killer. In regular press conferences, he told reporters that the investigation would soon end and that the list of suspects was growing shorter and shorter.

The hours during which the killer operated seemed to suggest someone who worked at night, such as a night watchman, but the police were not nearly as close to an arrest as Du Rose told the press. Somewhere, however, he hoped the killer was starting to feel the noose beginning to tighten.

Du Rose also increased the pressure on vehicles in the killer's known hunting ground. The police believed that the killer had abducted his victims by luring them into his car, so any car that crossed into the area three or more times was flagged for interview. Thousands of shamefaced men were discreetly interviewed, from clerks and factory workers to doctors and lawyers.

It had been weeks since Bridie's body had been found when the police finally discovered flecks of paint in the rear of a building on the Heron Factory Estate that matched those that had been found on the victims. Like they'd suspected, the building faced a paint spraying shop.

Hoping to prevent any further murders, Du Rose continued his ploy with the press, releasing a number of statements saying that the police were down to just a few possible suspects. The strategy worked. Ten weeks after Bridie's death, the police held their breath but no new bodies were discovered.

Around the same time the Stripper was due to strike again, in a seemingly unrelated incident, a quiet South London family man gassed himself to death with exhaust fumes. On 3 March 1965, the man left a note that read, 'I can't stick it any longer … To save you and the police looking for me, I'll be in the garage.'[13]

At first, the authorities thought nothing of the suicide, but further investigation revealed that the man worked the 10.00pm to 6.00am shift for a security firm. No physical evidence was ever found that connected the man with the Stripper murders, but there was enough circumstantial evidence that Du Rose felt reasonably certain they had found the killer.

The task force assigned to the case continued to investigate but the Stripper did not kill again and in July 1966, the investigation ended. With no confirmed suspect, the case remained opened. To this day, no one has been formally charged with the murders.[1]

In 1971, however, Du Rose published his memoirs, *Murder Was My Business*. In the book, Du Rose said that he was certain the security guard who committed suicide was the Stripper, but because the suspect was never arrested, charged or stood trial, his name was never released.

The following year, however, journalist Owen Summers wrote a series of articles that appeared in *The Sun*. Summers argued that the security guard in question could not have been the killer as he was in Scotland at the time of at least one of the murders. Summers went on to suggest that the real killer was a former police officer called Big John who had been dismissed for theft.[14]

A number of books have been written on the case, including *Found, Naked and Dead* by Brian McConnell (1975) and *Jack of Jumps* by David Seabrook (2007), but the truth of the matter remains a mystery.

At the moment, the National Archives will continue to keep the case files under lock and key until the year when the presumed killer will turn at least 85 years old.[15] Perhaps on 1 January 2050, when those files are released, Jack the Stripper will be positively identified at last.

CHAPTER SEVEN

The Moors Murders

(1966)

Chester Assizes was packed to the rafters that May afternoon in 1966 when a hush fell over the courtroom. Suddenly the screams of a little girl pierced the silence. Hardened police officers had to leave the room, unable to listen to the sounds of the child, gagging and begging for her life.

For sixteen long minutes, no one moved as the tape recorder rolled, playing the audio of ten-year-old Lesley Ann Downey's last moments alive. Behind a shield of bulletproof glass put in place for their protection sat the killers, both implacable and seemingly disinterested in the proceedings of the trial against them.

Ian Brady would go down in history because of the excessive cruelty of his crimes, but Myra Hindley, a woman in the prime of her childbearing years, would horrify the British public in a way the nation had not been shocked before.

In the 1940s, the Glasgow suburb of Gorbals – an impoverished slum on the south bank of the River Clyde – epitomized the worst of the inner city. Nearly 40,000 people lived in an area of only 252 acres, crammed eight or ten to a room in tiny flats crawling with rats.[1]

It was into this destitution that Ian Stewart was born on 2 January 1938. His mother Margaret was not married and would never reveal the name of her child's father. Unable to afford a babysitter, Margaret would often leave her infant alone while she went to work as a waitress. When he was only four months old, she gave the boy to another family to foster.[2]

The boy's foster parents had a difficult time managing their new ward. He had a terrible temper and would often bang his head into the wall.[3] Unable to socialize with his peers, he grew up spending much of his time alone, many times reading books about the Nazis.[2]

In 1951, he appeared before the Glasgow Sheriff Court for housebreaking and theft. It was the first of a further nine charges.[3] At the age of sixteen, he found himself facing a custodial sentence and was sent to live with his mother and her new husband Patrick Brady in Manchester. With the move, Ian Stewart became Ian Brady.[2]

It was around the same time that Brady began drinking heavily. In addition to books about the Third Reich, Brady collected a number of books on sadism, sexual perversion and the writings of the Marquis de Sade.[5] It wasn't long before he returned to his life of crime. In 1965, at the age of seventeen, he was charged with theft and sent to Strangeways Prison, where he would await his transition to borstal.

Borstal was meant to reform delinquent boys through hard labour and tough treatment, but more than once, borstals have made the news when stories of abuse, both physical and sexual, have been made public. One such case is Medomsley, where over 900 boys gave statements to police regarding ill handling in the 1970s and 80s.[4]

There is little information regarding what happened to Brady during his time at Strangeways, but on one occasion, he was quoted as saying that he felt the sentence that sent him to borstal was undeserved and that it was during his time there that he developed a 'bitter hatred of society'.[3]

It is difficult, however, to believe anything Brady ever said. In a 2012 letter to writer Jean Rafferty, Brady reportedly wrote, 'I began cultivating professional contacts in Strangeways at seventeen, mixing with adults while waiting three months for sentence to borstal and continued for the next two years of captivity, cross referencing exchange of information.'[6]

Whatever criminal contacts he may have made in prison and borstal had little apparent effect on his later life. There was only contact, in fact, that seems to have mattered – his girlfriend Myra.

Myra Hindley was born 23 July 1942 into the working class Manchester suburb of Gorton. Though she grew up in a small house crowded with family, Hindley had many fond memories of her childhood, including her uncle Bert who was a positive male influence in her life and her much-loved grandmother.

That serenity was largely shattered when her father returned from fighting in World War II. Now living in a separate flat, Myra and her mother became accustomed to regular beatings at the hands of Myra's father, especially after an aggravated war wound cost him his job at the local factory and his alcoholism took over.

Never the shrinking violet, Myra began fighting back at a very young age to protect herself and her mother, but as she neared the end of her teens, Myra's violence became less and less about self-protection. One of her uncles, Jim Burns, later said that her 'temper and childhood meanness' turned into 'major faults' as she grew older.[7]

It is tempting to look to the childhoods of Brady and Hindley for some sort of explanation, a way of understanding what motivated their later crimes. It's likely no authentic answer will ever be forthcoming. What is clear, however, is that when Brady and Hindley began dating in 1961, it was like throwing kerosene onto a fire.

Hindley was only eighteen years old when she went to work as a typist for Millwards Merchandising, a small chemical company on the outskirts of Manchester. She soon developed an attraction for 23-year-old Brady who was working as the store clerk.[8]

Hindley later made much of her girlish infatuation with Brady, claiming it was her love for him that made her so pliable to his influence:

> I'd always been a dreamer, falling in love with film stars. I was crazy about James Dean and Elvis, and had heard the phrase 'falling head over heels in love' – but never thought it would happen

to me. But as soon as Ian Brady looked at me and smiled shyly, that's exactly what happened.[9]

For several months, Brady paid little attention to Hindley but shortly before Christmas in 1961, Brady invited Hindley to go with him to see a movie about the Nazi trials at Nuremburg. It wasn't long before Hindley was following in Brady's footsteps, joining a gun club and buying a gun. She soon found out about Brady's criminal past, but it didn't seem to deter her.

In fact, the longer the relationship continued, the more twisted it became. Hindley willingly followed every instruction Brady gave her, dressing – and undressing – to please him, even posing for pornographic photos. At one stage, Brady planned a robbery, and Hindley never hesitated to play her part, taking all the necessary steps to see the crime carried out.[2]

With Hindley feeding the fire of Brady's criminal curiosity, the pair soon turned to more sinister crimes. On 12 July 1963, Brady reportedly told Hindley that he wanted to 'commit his perfect murder'. That evening, the two went trawling the neighbourhood for their victim, Hindley driving a van and Brady following behind on a motorbike.

Around 8.00pm, sixteen-year-old Pauline Reade was walking to a dance at the British Railways Club in Gorton. She knew Hindley, who was the older sister of Pauline's friend Maureen, so when Hindley asked if the girl would come help her look for an expensive glove she'd lost on Saddleworth Moor, Pauline agreed.[10]

That evening, Pauline's mother and brother spent hours searching for the girl – they would never find her.

Following the disappearance of Pauline Reade, several other children disappeared from Manchester. On 23 November 1963, just four months later, a twelve-year-old boy named John Kilbride went missing from the market in Ashton-under-Lyne. John's disappearance sparked a massive search operation with over 700 statements taken by police and 2000 volunteers turning out to help look for the boy. In the end, though, the efforts yielded nothing.[11]

Seven months later, on 16 June 1964, twelve-year-old Keith Bennett disappeared on his way to his grandmother's house. Later that year,

Lesley Ann Downey went to a local fairground on Boxing Day. She, too, went missing.[5]

Despite several hundred hours of searching and questioning, the police were no closer to uncovering what had happened to any of the missing children when they received a phone call that would change everything.

David Smith had met Brady and Hindley in August 1964, shortly after marrying Hindley's younger sister Maureen. The day following the wedding, Maureen and Smith took a day trip to the Lake District with Brady and Hindley. Smith was very impressed with the gracious Brady, who paid for everything throughout the day. It was to be the beginning of a tenuous friendship between Smith and Brady.[12]

In his memoirs, Smith later revealed that he grew to be afraid of Brady, especially after Brady confessed to Smith that he had killed before:

> I can't emphasize this enough – how Brady changed within the space
> of a year that we became friends. It was a colossal transformation
> from the Mr Nice Guy who invited me and Maureen round on our
> wedding night to his confession [that he had killed before].[13]

Smith would come to know Brady far better than he'd ever hoped on the night of 6 October 1965. That evening, Brady met his next victim, seventeen-year-old Edward Evans, at Manchester Central Railway Station and invited the apprentice engineer back to his house for a drink. In the waiting car, Brady introduced Edward to Hindley, saying she was his sister.

The couple returned with Edward to their house where the three shared a bottle of wine before Brady sent Hindley to fetch her brother David Smith, who was not prepared for what he would see as Smith later explained:

> When I first walked into the house, the door to the living room …
> was closed … Ian went into the living room and I waited in the
> kitchen. I waited about a minute or two then suddenly I heard a hell
> of a scream; it sounded like a woman, really high pitched. Then the
> screams carried on, one after another really loud. Then I heard Myra
> shout, 'Dave, help him,' very loud. When I ran in I just stood inside

the living room and I saw a young lad. He was lying with his head and shoulders on the couch and his legs were on the floor. He was facing upwards. Ian was standing over him, facing him, with his legs on either side of the young lad's legs. The lad was still screaming … Ian had a hatchet in his hand … he was holding it above his head and he hit the lad on the left side of his head with the hatchet. I heard the blow, it was a terrible hard blow, it sounded horrible.[14]

In total, Edward suffered fourteen blows from the axe before Brady strangled him with an electrical cord.[5] After witnessing the murder, the seventeen-year-old Smith later said, fearing for his life, he managed to disguise his horror long enough to help wrap up Edward's body. He then returned home and told his wife Maureen what her sister and Brady had done.

The following morning, a terrified Smith contacted the authorities and his statement led police to Hindley and Brady's address on Wardle Brook Avenue. There, the officers found the body of a young man locked in an upstairs bedroom.[15]

Police arrested Ian Brady for the murder of Edward Evans. Brady claimed that he and Edward had been in an argument in which Hindley was not involved. With no direct evidence to connect Hindley with the murder, police allowed Hindley to go free, but on 11 October, after the police uncovered several photos and documents, Hindley was arrested as an accessory to murder.[16]

The police had reason to believe that Hindley and Brady had killed before and that the pair had taken photos to record the locations of their buried victims.

Using photographs taken from Hindley and Brady's home, the police concentrated their search for more victims on Saddleworth Moor.

An eleven-year-old girl who lived near the couple was able to point the police in the right direction. She had been on several picnics with Hindley and Brady to Saddleworth Moor and was familiar with the couple's favourite spots.[17]

With these two vital guidelines, the police discovered the naked body of Lesley Ann Downey buried in a shallow grave on 10 October 1965. On 21 October, they also found the body of John Kilbride.[2]

A major break in the case came on 15 October when British Transport Police recovered a suitcase at Manchester Central Railway Station.[7] In it was the evidence that would help put Brady and Hindley behind bars – nine pornographic photos of Lesley Ann Downey, in which she was naked and gagged with a scarf, and a tape recording of the little girl pleading with her killers to let her go.[18]

Though the police suspected the pair was responsible for as many as eight murders,[5] the bodies of Lesley Ann, John and Edward were enough to bring charges against Brady and Hindley.

On 19 April 1966, the trial began at Chester Assizes. Both Hindley and Brady pleaded not guilty, but the evidence against them told a different story. Perhaps the most damning exhibit was the tape recording the couple had made of ten-year-old Lesley Ann Downey and the nine hidden photos of her that were discovered in the train station.

Daily Mirror crime reporter Brian Crowther was in the courtroom the day the tape was played:

> *There was utter silence as we listened to the little girl pleading. I had covered lots of big trials involving all sorts of killers but I had never seen grown men cry before as they did listening to Lesley. Policemen walked out of court because they could not bear it anymore. No one who heard that tape could ever escape from the memory. Lesley was in an awful mess, she was in absolute terror and you could hear it in her voice...*

> *The two least bothered people of all in the courtroom were Brady and Hindley. They were sat behind bulletproof glass that was put up around the dock because there were fears someone would try to kill them. But they were completely unconcerned with what was going on around them. They just exchanged looks with each other*

every day for the six weeks they were on trial. They did not care
about the evidence and did not appear to be listening to it.[19]

On 6 May 1966, both Brady and Hindley were found guilty of the murders of Edward Evans and Lesley Ann Downey. Brady was also found guilty of the murder of John Kilbride, Hindley accessory after the fact.[5]

The authorities felt certain Brady and Hindley were responsible for more murders, but continued searches of the vast moors yielded no further bodies. Both Brady and Hindley were sent to prison.

In 1985, Brady was declared criminally insane. At this point, he was moved to Ashworth Hospital, where he remained under close surveillance. Once at Ashworth, Brady began meeting with Fred Harrison, a journalist for the *Sunday People*, who was in the process of researching and writing a book about the murders.

It was during these meetings that Brady confessed to Harrison that, in addition to the three murders for which he was convicted in 1966, he had also killed Pauline Reade and Keith Bennett.[20]

With the confession, the authorities reopened the case. When asked about Pauline and Keith, Hindley agreed to help search for the bodies of the two children. On 10 February 1987, she made a formal confession to police, stating that she had indeed been involved in all five of the murders to which she had previously pleaded innocent.[21]

In a move that drew much criticism, the authorities took Hindley back to Saddleworth Moor on two occasions. Finally, on 1 July 1987, they uncovered the body of Pauline Reade, still dressed for the dance, her throat now cut.[22] Ian Brady also made a trip to the moors, but the body of Keith Bennett was never found.

Following her admission of guilt, Hindley began to tell her story, first in her original 1987 confession (a tape recording over seventeen hours long) and again in written form in 1998 when she began working with journalist Duncan Staff on a series of articles for *The Guardian* and a BBC documentary.

In both accounts, Hindley went into great detail describing how she would abduct each of the children by luring them into her car. She told of how she asked the children for their help – looking for a lost glove, helping to unload shopping or boxes – and the children would agree. She explained how she would then deliver the victims to Brady on the moors, where he would then take them away to rape and murder them.

Hindley's eagerness to distance herself from the worst of the crimes seemed a little too convenient for Detective Chief Superintendent Peter Topping who lead the investigation.

In his 1989 autobiography, Topping wrote of how he 'was struck by the fact that she was never there when the killings took place. She was in the car, over the brow of the hill, in the bathroom and even, in the case of the Evans murder, in the kitchen' and that he felt he 'had witnessed a great performance rather than a genuine confession'.[22]

Guardian journalist Duncan Staff also questioned Hindley's motives for cooperating with the authorities and with the media. Staff had 'no doubt' that she only helped the police in a bid to gain her own freedom:

> *Hindley often expressed distress at the fact that Keith Bennett was still missing. There was also little doubt that she believed it would be far more difficult for her to secure a release while one of her victims still lay on Saddleworth Moor.*[9]

After her confession in 1987, Hindley worked hard to be granted parole. She managed to gain the sympathy of a few high profile supporters, most controversially Lord Frank Longford and former editor for *The Observer* David Astor. She claimed that she had always been an unwilling victim, that Brady had coerced her into helping him and that she had since reformed.[8]

The authorities, along with the vast majority of the British public, however, disagreed and Hindley became known as the most hated woman in Britain. She was never released and on 15 November 2002, Myra Hindley died in prison at the age of 60.[5]

For all of Hindley's efforts to gain her freedom, Brady has made no such attempt. Instead, Brady has insisted on his right to die. In 1999, he went on a hunger strike in an effort to kill himself, but in March 2000 the High Court refused his demand. Ashworth staff members have been force-feeding him ever since.[2]

Forensic psychologist Dr Chris Cowley, who interviewed Brady extensively for his 2011 book *Face to Face with Evil: Conversations with Ian Brady*, agrees with the courts that Brady's claim is unfounded. 'If [Brady] went to prison I can't see him killing himself,' said Cowley in 2012. 'I'm not sure he's got the guts to do it or he'd have done it already.'[24]

In January 2015, Brady wrote a 750-word letter to Channel 5 News correspondent Julian Druker, complaining that he thinks he'll die soon. 'Had I divined the future of spending half a century in prison and the final fifteen years being force-fed by nasal tube in an unmonitored zoological cesspit of regression,' he wrote, 'I would've exited decades ago.'

Dr Cowley, however, believes the letter is just a bid for attention. 'Brady's a very egocentric person. He likes being in the limelight. I think probably at this point in time he's a little bit frightened that people aren't remembering him and people have maybe forgotten about him.'[25]

It will be interesting to see what Brady's death brings. Several sources report that Brady has written his autobiography, which is meant to be published upon his death.

In 2013, Sir Alan Keightley, a former head of religious studies at King Edward VI College, said that he had been meeting with Brady for the previous 25 years. Keightley revealed that, since their first interview in 1988, he had gathered thousands of hours of tape-recorded conversations.

According to Keightley, the 100,000-word manuscript based on these recordings is ready for release upon Brady's death. Keightley claims that the book includes Brady's confession to four additional murders, bringing his body count to nine, and gives details that implicate Myra Hindley more specifically in the crimes.

'The book has all the secrets,' said Keightley. 'It shows without a doubt that Myra Hindley was no bystander bullied into the killings by what she always claimed was Brady's Svengali-like hold over her.'

Though police are hesitant to put much stock into the claims of a convicted murderer and known liar, an unnamed publishing 'insider' says the book paints a black portrait of Brady's former lover:

Clearly [the book] is [Brady's] attempt to further blacken [Hindley's] name and undermine her previous accounts of her part in the Moors Murders, in which she portrayed herself as very much under Brady's control ... It contains graphic details about the individual killings and the sexual abuse of child victims in an extremely unsettling manner. Its aim is to directly implicate Myra Hindley in the sexual abuse of children. It describes in horrifying detail what Brady claims she did to the victims.[26]

With all of the accusations Brady and Hindley have thrown at each other since their original convictions in 1966, it is difficult to know which, if either, is telling the truth.

It is possible that Brady's graphic narrative is simply a fiction designed to remind the public of his name, distribute some of the blame away from himself and further taunt the families of his victims. Let us all remember just how much stock we can put in this man's word.

CHAPTER EIGHT

The Case of the Torso on the Train

(1968)

Jealousy, greed, hatred, insanity – there are endless motives for murder, but one of the most perplexing is the one that reportedly drove Suchnam Singh to kill his oldest daughter Sarabjit. Supposedly the Punjabi Sikh was only doing his duty by his firstborn and their family.

Following the partition of India in 1947, many Indians and Pakistanis emigrated from the subcontinent, hoping to leave behind the violence of the separation and the economic depression that had affected the region for decades.

One of the many places where these immigrants hoped to relocate was the UK. Seeing how the situation could be mutually beneficial, in 1964 the British government began a voucher scheme to recruit workers from throughout the Commonwealth, giving preference to teachers, doctors and nurses.

The Punjabi region, where most of the Sikhs had lived prior to India's independence, was one of the hardest hit by the separation and saw much of the worst violence. Little wonder, then, that the Sikhs of the Punjab were some of the first to take advantage of the 1964 voucher scheme.[1]

Suchnam Singh was one of thousands of immigrants to Britain who, like those of other nationalities, brought a unique diversity to the nation. The former schoolteacher from the small Punjabi village of Jullundor spoke excellent English, but he was willing to give up his profession when he arrived in England in September 1967 for the sake of his family.

Singh took a job as a factory worker, hoping the move to Britain would provide more opportunities for his children, especially his favourite oldest daughter Sarabjit. She had attended the School of Nursing in Delhi and once in England, she enrolled in the East Ham College of Technology.[2] Singh thought she might eventually train to become a doctor, but his hopes for his firstborn were not to last.

On 5 April 1968, the electric express had just pulled into Wolverhampton, having completed its journey from London Euston, when two off-duty drivers discovered an olive green suitcase in one of the passenger cars.[3]

Thinking the case belonged to a forgetful traveller, they took the piece of luggage to the lost and found department where Leslie Stevens, the clerk on duty, opened it and made a grisly discovery – the torso and arms of a woman.[2]

It was not the first time a murderer had tried to dispose of his victim's body in a suitcase. In April 1905, the bodies of a woman and her young twins were discovered in a trunk at Bannister of Kilburn, a furniture repository in the London suburb of Kensal Rise. They had been sealed in glue by Arthur Devereux, the husband and father of the victims.

Not long after, in 1907, Maria and Vere Goold murdered and robbed the wealthy Madame Emma Levin when they ran out of money gambling in Monte Carlo. They dismembered her body, packing her arms and torso in a trunk and her head and legs in a carpet bag, then called a porter to collect their luggage. They were apprehended in Versailles, having instructed the porter to send the trunk and carpetbag to London.

The summer of 1934 saw two trunk murders within a month of each other in Brighton. On 17 June, staff at the cloakroom of Brighton Station discovered the torso and arms of a woman inside a foul smelling trunk. The legs were later found at King's Cross Station, but the identity of neither the victim nor the killer was ever established.

Then on 15 July, the body of prostitute and dancer Violet Saunders was found in a box at a house near Brighton Railway Station. Her pimp Tony Mancini was never convicted for the murder, although he confessed to the crime in an interview 30 years later.[1]

The torso in the trunk discovered in the olive green trunk at Wolverhampton in 1968 was to prove no less perplexing for authorities.

While Dr Richard Marshall, pathologist at the Royal Hospital of Wolverhampton, began his examination of the torso, the authorities returned to the train and began their investigation. In a stroke of luck, the police learned that British Rail had taken a census of passengers at each stop the night before.

The train had not been very crowded and the officers were soon able to ascertain that the case had come onto the train at Euston. One witness at Euston reported seeing 'a black man' cross the barrier carrying a suitcase and that the same man had returned just moments later without the case.

Around noon the following day, a second case was found in the River Roding under the bridge in Ilford. Officers went to the scene where they opened the Indian-made suitcase and found a woman's legs.[3] Pathologist Robert Warwick of the Department of Anatomy at Guy's Hospital School of Medicine examined the legs and determined that they belonged to the torso that had been found on the train the previous day.

Professor Warwick's examination also concluded that the body parts belonged to an Asian woman between the ages of 18 and 30. She had not been a virgin at the time of her death, and she had recently undergone a gynaecological operation at the hands of someone who was not very skilled.

Warwick had found a lethal dose of barbiturates in the woman's system, but these drugs had not been the cause of death. He was also able to ascertain that the body had been dismembered by a saw with blue metal on one side and yellow on the other.[2]

Police began a massive, nationwide investigation to identify every passenger who had travelled on the train. After three weeks, the authorities were able to publish a drawing of the man they believed to be responsible for disposing of the suitcases, the most likely suspect for having killed the girl. The drawing was based on the description of the man who was believed to have been the first passenger to board the train at 10.40am on the morning the first suitcase was found.

Heading the investigation, Detective Superintendent Roy Yorke said, 'He was in possession of a suitcase and had a ticket to Wolverhampton. We believe he may have subsequently left the train and not travelled in it to Wolverhampton.' The *Birmingham Mail* printed the image of the suspect along with the police's request that the public look for a man with a 'long sad face'.

The newspaper also printed images of the clothing the girl had been wearing. Though the body had been wrapped in a green curtain, it had still been dressed in a pale blue embroidered tunic with a white pattern, a patterned blue hand-knitted sleeveless pullover and a pink cardigan.

The police had worked with garment experts, hoping the origins of the clothing might lead them to the killer, but the patterns of the clothing were unlike anything the experts had seen before.

Alongside the images, the authorities included an appeal written in the dialects of Urdu, Punjabi and Gujerati, hoping to reach as many people as possible, especially among the immigrant Indian communities. The strategy worked and nine people of subcontinental origin came forward.

These volunteers told police that the pattern of the blue jumper was one that could only be found in a small part of the Punjab, a region called Jullundor. They also revealed that the pattern was a type traditionally handed down from mother to daughter, so it would not have been included in any pattern books the authorities and experts had available to them. Knowing the specific origin of the victim gave the police a vital clue that would lead them in the right direction.[3]

A further examination of the girl's legs revealed two more clues. First, she had marks and calluses on her feet indicating that she had only been wearing European style shoes for a short time, which meant she had most likely only recently immigrated to Britain. Second, there was a scar on the girl's ankle, which was most likely the result of a surgical operation.

Agents began the tedious process of searching the records of hospitals and clinics for a Pakistani woman who had recently had a gynaecological operation that might have related to the scar on her leg.

At the same time, the hunt for the girl's head was on. Using helicopters, the police searched along the route of the railway between Euston and Wolverhampton while divers searched the Roding River, but the extensive search uncovered no further clues.

Then, on 8 May, a month following the discovery of the torso, Howard Perry was crossing Wanstead Flats on his bike. While stuck in a traffic jam, he happened to notice a canvas bag in the bushes alongside the road.

Thinking the sturdy bag looked to be in better shape than his own, Perry took it and shortly ended the mystery of what had become of the missing head. Now the authorities had a face to go with the torso and a cause of death – two blows to the skull with a blunt instrument.

Around the same time Perry found the head, the painstaking search through the hospital files turned up a Hindu girl who had been treated at the Barking Hospital. With a photo of the girl's face, Dr Gabriel Merriman was able to identify that the torso, arms, legs and head belonged to nineteen-year-old Sarabjit Kaur. Though he had not performed a surgery on the patient, he recalled that he had diagnosed the girl as pregnant the previous November.

Armed with her name, it was a relatively simple task to trace the girl back to her family's home on Fanshawe Avenue in Barking.[2]

When the police arrived on Saturday 11 May, less than a week after the discovery of Sarabjit's head, the man of the house was soft spoken and polite. At first, Suchnam Singh told the police that he only had two daughters, but after repeated questioning, he finally admitted that his third child, his oldest daughter, had left home in February three months before and that he didn't know where she was.

Singh insisted he had no photos of his oldest daughter, but when police searched the house, they found photos of the same girl whose corpse had been scattered throughout England. Singh also said he knew nothing of his daughter having ever been pregnant. Suspicious of the father's answers, however, the police took Singh in for questioning.

Once at the station, Singh's attitude towards the police changed. Now considerably less polite and cooperative, he refused to answer any questions but stuck to his story – his daughter had left home in February, he knew nothing about her ever having been pregnant and he could not identify any of the clothing that had been found in the suitcases.

He was detained overnight and the next day, lead investigator Detective Superintendent Yorke interviewed Singh, who was no more cooperative for his night in jail.

Rather than harassing the suspect, Yorke took a different approach. This was not the typical criminal with which he was used to dealing. This was a deeply religious man, sober and pious, who lived his faith in the clothes he wore and the food he ate. Yorke trusted Singh's faith would lead him in the right direction.

The following day, after being left alone in his cell overnight once again to think about what he'd done, Singh started talking.[3]

At first, he told the authorities that Sarabjit had taken an overdose of phenobarbitone meaning to kill herself and that she had sustained the blows to her head when a sewing machine fell on her. Singh said that when he discovered her body, he was in such a state of despair that he ran out of the house and was nearly hit by a car.

He said that eventually he went to his cousin, Hardyal Sandhu. Singh claimed that Hardyal discouraged him from going to the police, saying he would end up in trouble. He also claimed Hardyal helped him dispose of the body, but when the police questioned Hardyal, the cousin denied having any knowledge of or involvement in the affair. The officers believed him.

When traces of Sarabjit's blood were found in the family bathroom, the police returned to Singh. Finally, the truth came out.

On Tuesday 4 May 1968, Singh explained, his two younger daughters had gone to school as usual and his wife had gone out for the day, leaving Singh alone with his oldest daughter Sarabjit. He revealed that, before the family had left India less than a year before, his daughter had been in an intimate relationship with one of her cousins.

It was bad enough that the girl was no longer a virgin. Even worse, her lover was already married. Shortly after arriving in England, Singh learned that not only had his daughter been in the relationship but that she was still writing letters to her lover. Singh did not take the news well and started beating her.

His treatment of Sarabjit became so bad that in November 1967, she left the family home and moved into her own apartment in Ilford. A short time later, at a nearby clinic, Dr Gabriel Merriman told her she was pregnant. On 20 November, she went into hospital where the diagnosis was confirmed and Sarabjit learned she was twenty weeks along.[2]

For Sarabjit, this pregnancy was a big problem. The Sikh religion forbids premarital sex, especially for girls, and Sarabjit knew that her pregnancy would bring shame to her family in the eyes of other Sikhs. It would also make it more difficult for her parents to arrange a suitable marriage for her.[4]

The police knew Sarabjit had undergone a gynaecological operation. Though there were no records to confirm their suspicion, the authorities believed the operation was an abortion and that the scar on Sarabjit's leg was from the blood transfusion she would have received during the procedure. They also believed – but could never confirm – that the girl's parents had organised the abortion at the hands of a dubious practitioner.

What is known is that shortly following the diagnosis of pregnancy on 20 November 1967, Sarabjit returned to the family home and resumed living with her parents.[2]

Six months later, on 4 May 1968, Singh and Sarabjit had a heated argument. At one stage, he said, she came out of her room, screaming that she'd taken poison and that she'd also written a letter to her lover saying that she was committing suicide because her father would not allow her to marry the man she wanted.

According to Singh, she'd provoked him, saying that the police would accuse him of her death and hang him for murdering his own daughter.[1]

In his typical quiet manner, his hair neatly knotted beneath his traditional turban, Singh told the police how he'd flown into a rage, picked up the hammer the family used to break up coal and bashed his daughter twice in the head. When she fell to the floor, he believed she was dead.

Singh described how he changed out of his pyjamas and went to the hardware store in Ilford fifteen minutes away, where he bought a hacksaw. Upon his return home, he changed back into his pyjamas and put his daughter's limp body into a large plastic bag.

He had just begun to cut off the girl's head when she regained consciousness. She tried to defend herself and sustained a cut on her thumb in the process, but her father kept on cutting. Soon her head had been removed and Singh proceeded with the dismemberment.

The deed now done, Singh fastidiously drained the blood from the plastic bag into the bathtub. He then threw away his blood stained pyjamas, the hacksaw and the tainted hammer.[2]

Singh told the police how he'd packed his daughter's torso and arms into the olive green suitcase – the largest – her legs into the smaller case and her head inside the canvas bag. Now all he had left to do was get rid of the evidence, starting with the largest green case.

With his grisly luggage in tow, he took public transport to Euston Railway Station where he picked Wolverhampton at random off the indicator board. He bought a ticket, boarded the train, stowed the suitcase, left the train and returned home where he retrieved the second case.

It was at this point that he began to have second thoughts about what he'd done. Planning to go to the police, he got on a bus bound for Ilford.

En route, however, he changed his mind and threw the suitcase into the Roding River from a bridge on Romford Road. The following day, he strapped the canvas bag containing Sarabjit's head onto the back of his moped and threw it into some bushes on Wanstead Flats.[3]

Despite his confession, there were a few holes in Singh's story. One was that, prior to the Tuesday on which his daughter died, he'd asked his employer at the chemical company where he worked if he could have the day off, suggesting that Sarabjit's death was no momentary act of passion but that he'd premeditated the murder. It also seemed like no accident that there was no one else at home when the incident occurred.[2]

Finally, while the port mortem examination confirmed that Sarabjit had indeed ingested a lethal dose of phenobarbital, there was no way of knowing if she had actually taken the drug herself meaning to commit suicide (as Singh claimed) or if he had somehow coerced or tricked her into taking it.[3]

Authorities further discovered that large plastic bags were regularly used at the chemical company where Singh worked, and that the company also produced phenobarbital, a drug no doctor had ever prescribed for Sarabjit.

The evidence against Singh was overwhelming and in November 1968, his trial began at the Old Bailey. The case riveted the nation, with spectators queuing up daily to watch the proceedings.

Though Singh maintained that his daughter had meant to kill herself and that he'd merely lashed out in anger, another possible motive for the killing revealed itself. During the trial, references were made to an old Sikh custom whereby those who had disgraced themselves could atone for their sins if they were killed, dismembered and scattered, thereby bringing honour back to their families.[2]

It is a ritual still disturbingly common in Singh's native Punjab. On 4 January 2015, Sikhs Sandeep Kumar aged 24 and his bride Khusboo aged 22 were both hacked to death by family members because they had married without the consent of their parents.[5] In the Punjab's Gurdaspur region, a Sikh woman named Nargis met the same fate on 17 July 2015 for the crime of marrying a Christian.[6]

In Garnuthi, a village just south of Punjab, Dharmender Barak aged 23 and Nidhi Barak aged 20 were both killed on 18 September 2013 when their parents learned they'd planned to marry without the blessing of their families. The young woman Nidhi was beaten to death. Her fiancé Dharmender was dismembered alive.[7]

While these crimes may seem far removed from the Western philosophies of the United Kingdom, Singh's was not the first and certainly not the last honour killing to take place in Britain.

According to 2009 statistics from the Association of Police Officers, there are a dozen honour killings a year in the UK.[8] Seventeen-year-old Shafilea Ahme from Cheshire was killed by her parents in 2013 when she allegedly refused to marry the man they had chosen for her. In 2011, Gurmeet Singh Ubhi murdered his 24-year-old Sikh daughter Amrit when he discovered she was dating a white man. Surjit Athwal, a 27-year-old from Coventry, was killed in 1998 when she sought a divorce.[9]

Though honour killing is not specific to the Sikh religion, there are many cases that share a striking similarity with that of Sarabjit, such as the murder of Geeta Aulakh. In 2009, Geeta was found dying in the street in Greenford, West London. The mother of two had recently sought a divorce from her husband Harpreet Aulakh.

On her way to pick up her son from a child minder, Geeta was ambushed by two men. In the attack, she sustained serious head wounds but, more telling, her right hand had been cut off. One friend said that the dismemberment of the hand was particularly significant:

She was a Sikh and all Sikhs wear a metal bangle, the kara, on their right wrist. It is a permanent reminder to live a moral and good life and once it's on you can't get it off. So her murderer was both dishonouring her and perhaps trying to show she had been dishonourable – which is just barbaric. [10]

The authorities treated Geeta's murder as an honour killing, although some disagreed with this assessment. Whatever the reason, Geeta died within hours and her estranged husband was found guilty. [11]

Whether or not honour had anything to do with Sarabjit's killing, the court at the Old Bailey was not convinced by Singh's story of his daughter's attempted suicide. It took the jury only 90 minutes to find Singh guilty of his daughter's murder. He was sentenced to life in prison. [1]

CHAPTER NINE

The Kray Brothers

(1969)

From *The Godfather* to *Good Fellas*, filmmakers love to tell the story of glamorous gangsters who can get away with murder. It's no wonder, then, that several films have been made about Ronnie and Reggie Kray, the celebrity twins who will likely go down in history as Britain's most notorious mobsters, but many would argue that there is nothing glamorous about the infamous brothers.

London's East End has always had a reputation for attracting an eclectic community. The gritty neighbourhood that was once the hunting ground of Jack the Ripper sustained extensive damage during the Second World War and during the 1960s, 'under aged pregnancies, prostitution, illegal abortions, binge drinking and wife beating abounded in the crowded, TB-infested slums'.[1] It was this world that the Kray brothers would come to rule.

The twins became London celebrities, moving in exclusive circles with the likes of Diana Dors, Barbara Windsor and Frank Sinatra in addition to lords, MPs and famous sporting figures – but despite their high profile connections, the brothers couldn't evade the authorities forever.[2]

Born in 1927, Charlie Kray was the oldest of the three brothers. Twins Ronnie and Reggie were born within an hour of each other seven years after Charlie on 17 October 1934. They would soon begin to take after their grandfather, a famous local character around the East End known as Mad Jimmy Kray.

The boys grew up surrounded by the poverty of Bethnal Green. According to one 1932 government report, around 60 per cent of the children in Bethnal Green were malnourished and 85 per cent of the slum housing was unsatisfactory. But the twins were special. Nobody had twins and Reggie and Ronnie were gorgeous babies whom everyone spoiled, as their mother recalled:

> *Everyone who saw 'em seemed to love 'em ... Somehow with the twins you couldn't help it ... I always dressed the twins the same. They was such pretty babies. I made 'em both white angora woolly hats and coats and they was real lovely, the two of them. Just like two little bunny rabbits.*

Despite the poverty of the neighbourhood, the Kray family lived comfortably enough. The boys' father made a decent living selling secondhand clothes, gold and silver, and their mother treated them fairly and lavished them with love.[3]

When the Second World War came, the boys were evacuated and went to the country with their mother. They enjoyed their time in Suffolk, as evidenced by photos of them that appear in the 2013 collection *The Krays: From the Cradle to the Grave*,[4] but it wasn't long before the family was itching to get back to the city.

During the Blitz, the schools closed and the boys had the run of the neighbourhood, forming gangs and playing in the bombed out rubble with swarms of other children. Though the kids sometimes picked up lice and scabies from the debris, it was a generally happy time. 'Our mother saw that we never went hungry, though times was very hard,' Ronnie later said. 'But there'd always be potatoes and stew for dinner.'

From a young age, the boys earned a reputation for being polite to adults (especially ones who were acquainted with their mother) but vicious on the streets with the other children, as Ronnie recalled:

> We started gang wars. We had our own gang as early as I can remember. Reg an' me organised stone raids on the kids in the next street. Outside the house we always seemed to be fighting. Fought all the kids around. In the end we picked up such a name that if anyone was hurt or something broken, we'd be blamed. People called us the 'Terrible Twins'.

Like most of the other East Enders, they were also trained early not to trust the authorities. Their father had deserted from the army and spent nearly twenty years on the run. On several occasions, the boys lied to police officers to protect their father who would be hiding in the house or escaping over the back fence. It was just a way of life that no one in the neighbourhood violated.[3]

Already good with their fists, the boys began down a respectable road in their teen years that might have kept them away from crime and even led to legitimate success – championship boxing.

Both of their grandfathers had been fighters. On their father's side, Mad Jimmy Kray was well known in the local pubs for being aggressive and tough to beat.

Their mother's father, Jimmy 'Cannonball' Lee, was famous throughout the East End for his left hook – they called him the Eastern Southpaw. A world championship boxer in three separate weight divisions, it was Cannonball Lee who took the three Kray boys and taught them how to fight professionally.

Under the tutelage of Henry Berry, the twins and their big brother Charlie began working hard in the gym, and it wasn't long before local boxing managers began to take notice. Reggie especially showed promise, as one veteran trainer recalled:

Ronnie was a fighter, the hardest, toughest boy I've ever seen. To stop Ron you'd have had to kill him. Reg was different. Before he even started, it was as if he had all the experience of an old boxer in his fists. Once in a lifetime you find a boy with everything it takes to be a champion. Young Reggie was one of them.[5]

The boys did so well, in fact, that on 11 December 1951, they were selected to fight in an event at Albert Hall. Though Ronnie narrowly lost by the judges' decision and Charlie (who had once been the welterweight champion of the Royal Navy) took a serious beating, Reggie dazzled the crowd, winning his match in three rounds.[6]

After the bout at Albert Hall, Reggie was offered the chance to go professional, but his path to the British welterweight title ended abruptly a few weeks later when the twins were involved in a brutal fight outside a club in Walthamstow. The twins were taken in by police and their names appeared in the local papers.

According to the rules set forth by the boxing authorities, professional fighters were not permitted to engage in any sort of fighting outside the ring. When the boxing authorities heard of Reggie's involvement in the Walthamstow brawl, they immediately withdrew his license and with it any chance he might have had at making it as a professional boxer.

Shortly after the incident in Walthamstow, the twins were called for national service. Their older brother Charlie had cooperated when he'd been called up just two years before, going on to become a model sailor with the Royal Navy.

Only eighteen years old, the twins – called to serve with the Royal Fusiliers – were not so compliant. On their first day, they arrived at the Tower of London but before their commanding officer could finish his introduction, the boys were heading for the door. When the officer tried to stop them, Ronnie smashed the corporal in the chin and the twins kept walking.

They were soon returned to the Tower, but after a brief confinement, the boys were on the run again. Like their father before them, the twins would never really serve their country. Instead, they weathered any punishment set them and regularly lashed out against their superiors.

Every incarceration seemed to make the pair tougher and more resilient, as Reggie later explained in an interview: 'If you are weak and start worrying about others, they've got you where they want you. If you're tough and just don't care, you become invulnerable.'

Instead of letting captivity wear them down, the twins used their time in prison to their advantage, making connections with other convicts and learning the criminal trade. In the end, the twins were finally court marshalled in 1954 and given six months at the notorious Shepton Mallet Prison.

The sentence was by no means an accurate reflection of the infractions the twins had committed against the army, but it was enough for the military to give them dishonourable discharges and be shut of them. It was not the first time the authorities would have a hard time holding the Krays, and it wouldn't be the last.[5]

Now free of the military, the twins were able to devote all of their time to their illegal enterprises and lay the foundations of their criminal empire. They began with The Regal, a rundown billiards hall on Eric Street that attracted seedy clientele.

After several months of having the Krays hanging around the hall, playing billiards and socialising with friends, the manager was ready to sell. Since the twins' arrival, there had been a marked increase in the usual violence that had always plagued the place, and when someone threw fireworks at his guard dog, the manager gave up.

Once in charge of The Regal, the 21-year-old twins refurbished the hall into a classy hot spot. From the grand reopening, the Krays' place was an instant success. Not surprising, the violence dwindled away – the other gangs knew not to mess with the Krays.

Any attempt to intimidate the young brothers or cause trouble in their hall ended the night a Maltese gang came in at closing time and tried to bully the twins into paying for 'protection'. The gang, however, proved to be no match for the Krays, even when it was just the two of them against the entire Maltese crew.

Now a peaceful establishment, The Regal became the Kray brothers' headquarters. From the hall, they would meet with other criminals to plan robberies, store stolen goods and negotiate the sale of the merchandise. It wasn't long before the brothers began collecting and hiding weapons in the hall as well, everything from knives and swords to Ronnie's arsenal of firearms.[6]

Despite their criminal activities, The Regal thrived. Reggie was a natural businessman who was good at the financial side of the operation, and Ronnie was always the centre of attention, chatting and laughing with any and all who came into the hall. It was also Ronnie who gave the impression that his violent temper was always on a simmer, ready to boil over at any moment.

While violence may have been in their nature, Ronnie and Reggie Kray had another reason for always being on the defensive. Later in life, they both admitted to being gay but in the 1960s, they were eager to keep their sexuality confidential.[5]

They weren't alone in their secrecy. Until the Sexual Offenses Act of 1967, homosexuality between men aged 21 and above was a crime – it remained so in Scotland until 1980 and in Northern Ireland until 1982. Though the Krays had no trouble with breaking the law, they were concerned about public perception.

Antony Grey, who later became Secretary of the Homosexual Law Reform Society (HLRS), said that as a teenager growing up in the Krays era, he barely understood what it meant to be gay. He only knew that it was bad:

> *There was a hideous aura of criminality and degeneracy and abnormality surrounding the matter … We knew from experience that if you called the police and they suspected you were homosexual, they would ignore the original crime and concentrate on the homosexuality.*[7]

Even now, huge numbers of gay, lesbian, bisexual and transgender teenagers and adults report being stigmatised for their sexuality. In the

1950s and 1960s, that stigma was even greater. For the Krays, it remained of the utmost importance that the brothers kept the family secret.

One way to help keep that secret was to present themselves as the ultimate tough guys. The brothers got the chance to prove their toughness in 1954 when they found themselves embroiled in a gangland war with a trio of dockworkers who were known to run Mile End Road.

The outcome of this showdown depends on who's telling the story. According to Charlie Kray, the twins beat the three dockers unconscious and Ronnie would have killed one of them if Reggie hadn't stopped him.[6]

Notable biographer John Pearson, however, tells how the twins arrived at the dockers' pub The Britannia to find their adversaries were already gone – no one was left but a local boy named Terry Martin. According to Pearson, the twins dragged Martin into the street, beat him senseless and left him for dead in the gutter. By luck alone, Martin survived the attack and lived to testify against the twins at Old Bailey.[5]

After the attack on Martin, Ronnie was shipped off to prison (having taken the blame for the near fatal attack), and The Regal was knocked down to make way for low-income housing. In Ronnie's absence, Reggie and Charlie opened The Double R, which was to become a legendary nightclub.

While Reggie ran a reasonably respectable operation out of The Double R, he and his associates – calling themselves the Firm – were building another business the Krays felt was just as valuable to the East End, providing the service of protection.

With all the violent criminals and organised gangs in the vicinity, many businesses were happy to pay the brothers and their associates to keep the peace. If anyone made trouble for one of the Krays' clients, someone from the Firm would deal with the troublemakers quickly and violently.

In his book *Doing the Business*, Charlie Kray described the brothers' method of collecting payment, 'nipping' and 'pension':

> *If you were on the nipping list, the Krays or one of the Firm would nip into the shop or pub and nip out again with a token, consumable payment, such as a crate of gin or carton of cigarettes … Or they might spend an evening in a pub or club, standing drinks for*

everyone and anyone. At the end of the evening, with a word from
the Firm, the bill for the night would be torn up and the evening's
entertainment paid for courtesy of the house.

When cash actually did change hands, it was in the form of a 'loan' the Krays would ask for. In the moment, they would provide a gold cufflink or watch as collateral but eventually the item would be returned and the loan 'forgotten'.[6]

While Reggie, Charlie and the Firm were slowly bullying the East End into submission, Ronnie was going slowly insane in prison. He and Reg had both suffered a serious bout of diphtheria as toddlers, but Ronnie's case was much more serious and many people believed the illness had had lasting effects, one of which was Ronnie's need for constant attention and approval, which he'd always got from his twin. Without Reggie by his side, that attention was gone.

Once in prison, Ronnie became more and more withdrawn. When he learned of the death of his favourite Aunt Rose, with whom the twins had been very close growing up, Ronnie snapped. He was declared legally insane and on 20 February 1958, he was sent to Long Grove Lunatic Asylum.

After several weeks of treatment, however, the doctors at Long Grove dismissed Ronnie's case, calling him 'a simple man of low intelligence, poorly in touch with the outside world'. What they didn't know was that Ronnie Kray was a dangerous criminal afflicted with paranoid schizophrenia.[5]

Once released, it was Reggie's job to look after his brother, so he set up Ronnie at a friend's farm in Suffolk. The Double R was doing so well that Reggie, Charlie and the Firm expanded, opening the Kentucky. While the clubs were attracting respectable crowds and top entertainers like Judy Garland and Liza Minnelli, Ronnie's mental and emotional state continued to deteriorate.

Over the course of the next four years, the Kray empire would continue to grow, branching out from the East End into the more fashionable (and respectable) West End. As the years went by, the Firm installed a number of spies and informers in other crews around town and in the police.

Then, in the summer of 1964, the *Sunday Mirror* printed a front-page story about a Scotland Yard investigation into an alleged affair between a Tory peer and an East End gangster. The story claimed the infamous pair attended homosexual parties and regularly hunted young men.

The story wouldn't be substantiated until decades later when the MI5 files were declassified, but a German magazine had already released the names of Ronnie Kray and Lord Robert Boothby. Within a week, the *Mirror* had a photo of the two men together along with Boothby's chauffeur and lover Leslie Holt.

Though the MI5 files later confirmed the allegations were all true, at the time Boothby denied being gay or having ever attended homosexual parties. Under pressure from the government, the paper paid the peer a record £40,000 out-of-court settlement and printed a front-page apology.[8]

With the Krays apparently involved with top government officials, however, and the media not able to mention the relationship, it seemed no small wonder the brothers were able to get away with murder.

There was much suspicion, for example, that Ronnie Kray was responsible for the death of Francis Shea. On 19 April 1965, the 21-year-old Francis married Reggie Kray. She'd known him for years, and the two had dated since 1960, but the relationship was troubled.

The marriage had only lasted eight months when Francis left Reggie and returned to her family. Then, in 1967, the couple reunited and Francis agreed to go on a second honeymoon with Reggie.

They had just booked tickets to Ibiza when she took an apparent overdose of sleeping pills and died. At the time the death was considered a suicide but at least one source claimed Ronnie Kray murdered her because he was always jealous of her relationship with his twin.[9]

Whether it was because of their high profile connections or their reputation for violence, it was hard to prosecute the twins, even from their earliest days in the criminal underworld.

In documents released decades after the fact, former Detective Superintendent Tommy Butler of the Metropolitan Police told of his frustration in a memo:

Their reputation is already such that persons threatened almost frantically deny visitations by anyone connected with the Kray twins. Not one victim can be persuaded to give evidence against anyone connected with their organisation … and it adds considerably to the victim's undeniable urge to comply with demands made upon him, and to his atrocious memory when questioned by police at any later stage.[10]

This wall of silence would protect the Krays in December 1965 when they helped their friend Frank 'the Mad Axeman' Mitchell escape from Dartmoor Prison. When Mitchell became increasingly violent and difficult to manage, however, he disappeared without a trace. Leonard 'Nipper' Read, who led the investigation against the Krays and the Firm, was certain the brothers killed him, but was never able to gather enough evidence to convict the Krays and eventually, they were acquitted.[11]

'There were other people too, there were a hell of a lot of other murders,' said Read in a later interview. 'I investigated seven murders myself. It was only the fact that we couldn't get enough evidence. It was like the Mitchell case, it was very difficult to charge them. We had no body and they weren't admitting to anything, and at the Old Bailey it was difficult to get anybody to give evidence.'[12]

Shortly after the disappearance of Frank Mitchell, an incident occurred that would lead to the Krays' ultimate demise. It was Christmas 1965 and the Krays found themselves in an altercation with a rival gang from South London, the Richardsons. They were at the Astor Club when one of the Richardson associates, George Cornell, called Ronnie Kray a 'fat poof'.[11]

The use of that particular insult was a huge mistake. According to Charles Clark, with whom Ronnie Kray lived for nine months from the end of 1964, Ronnie was very sensitive about his sexuality. '[Ronnie] once told me the tragedy of his life was that he was the twin who was born the wrong way round sexually. We talked of this for a long time. He said he cried inside himself every day.'[10]

Few people were surprised, then, when Ronnie shot George Cornell in the face the following spring on 8 March 1966 at the Blind Beggar public house on Whitechapel Road. Even fewer people were surprised when no one could recall the events of the days when the police came to question witnesses.[11]

Then, in October 1967, the Krays invited Jack 'the Hat' McVitie to a party in Stoke Newington. Ronnie had paid McVitie £100 to shoot the Krays' financial advisor, Leslie Payne, but McVitie hadn't done the job. In retribution, at the party in front of sixteen people, Reggie stabbed McVitie repeatedly in the face and chest until the hit man was dead. According to one eyewitness, there were two small children in the house at the time of the killing.[5]

In the end, it was members of the Firm who finally cooperated with Nipper Read and the authorities and brought the Kray brothers to justice. Though Read believed the brothers were responsible for several murders, he felt he had the best hope of having them convicted for the deaths of George Cornell and Jack McVitie.

Read's gamble worked and on 4 March 1969, the untouchable Reggie and Ronnie Kray, along with several members of the Firm, were found guilty and sent to prison.[12]

Since their incarceration and subsequent deaths, the Krays have often been portrayed as stylish celebrities in television and film, but the truth is a lot less glamorous. Former Firm associate Chris Lambrianou, who was there the night Jack McVitie was killed and admits to disposing of the body, perhaps said it best in a 2015 interview for which he was not paid:

> [T]he Krays weren't glamorous and they weren't legends... A legend is somebody who does the right things, somebody you can really look up to. The Krays could have been legends, they could have made a difference. But they chose a different path.[13]

CHAPTER TEN

A Case of Mistaken Identity

(1969)

I hear the best thing to do is feed them to pigs ... They will go through bone like butter. You need at least sixteen pigs to finish the job in one sitting ... They will go through a body that weighs 200 pounds in about eight minutes. That means that a single pig can consume two pounds of uncooked flesh every minute, hence the expression 'as greedy as a pig'.

If this chilling monologue sounds like something from a Guy Ritchie gangster film, that's because it is – namely the 2000 dark comedy *Snatch* – but when it happens in real life, there's nothing comic about it.

Arthur and Nizamodeen Hosein grew up dreaming big. The West Indian brothers were born in Dow, a predominantly Muslim village near Port of Spain, the capital of Trinidad. An elder at the local mosque and a tailor, their father taught his son Arthur the family trade, but the brothers wanted more from life than their small Caribbean island had to offer.

Arthur was the first to make his escape, moving to England in September 1955. His first jobs earning £10 a week weren't as lucrative as he'd hoped, so he returned to tailoring, this time in Hackney.

It was a good move for Arthur, and soon he was earning £100 a week as a cutter for some of the best tailors in London's garment district. He loved showing off his wealth especially down at the pub, where he would wave around wads of cash and buy drinks for friends and strangers alike. Few were impressed by him, however, and he quickly earned the nickname 'Nutty Arthur'.

Arthur had been in Britain for just a few years when he was called up for national service with the Royal Pioneer Corps. Whatever industry had led to his success as a tailor did not seem to carry over to his military service. Said one former officer, 'He was the immeasurably the worst soldier it has been my misfortune to have under me.'

Habitually absent without leave, Arthur was finally court marshalled in 1960 and sentenced to six months in prison for desertion.

As soon as he left the army, Arthur married Elizabeth, a German woman ten years his senior, and the couple had two children.[1] Then in 1967, Arthur bought Rooks Farm, a rundown 17th century farm on eleven acres near Stocking Pelham in Hertfordshire. In 1968, Arthur moved with his family to the farm.[2]

Nizamodeen Hosein had always worshipped his older brother Arthur, who had looked out for him when they were children. As Arthur boasted about his success in England, Nizamodeen became even less satisfied with his life in Trinidad. Working as a chauffeur for his father, Nizamodeen was not happy after he left school and his discontent eventually led to violence.

In December 1967, he was charged with malicious wounding when he attacked his brother Charles with a knife, although the charge was later dismissed in court. Then in March 1969, he was charged with assault and battery against his father.

The case never went to court, but two months later, Nizamodeen relocated to England where he first lived with another brother who was already settled. Nizamodeen had only been in Britain for a short time, however, when he went to live with Arthur at Rook's Farm.[1]

Nizamodeen must have been quite surprised to discover that, though his brother had been bragging for years about his successful business and flourishing farm, Arthur was far from being the sophisticated aristocrat he'd made himself out to be.

What Arthur wanted more than anything was to be accepted by his local community, as writer Bill Jones, who has been working on a book about the brothers, explains:

> *Arthur's life in the countryside north of London was the stuff of fiction ... He fantasised about acquiring instant wealth and thereby gaining access to the 'country set' he so envied. In 1967 he had acquired Rooks Farm intent upon entering the 'establishment'. Without success, he tried to join the Puckeridge Hunt. He talked loudly at his local pubs – the nearby Cock Inn and the Raven at Berden – about his secret fortune.*[3]

In reality, the secret fortune didn't exist, but together Arthur and Nizamodeen hatched a plan they thought would bring them the millions they'd always dreamed of.

Since the 1960s, media tycoon Rupert Murdoch has been one man much of Britain hates passionately. Murdoch famously took over two newspapers in his native Australia at the age of 22, increasing their circulation by offering sensational, often tawdry content.

In the autumn of 1968, Murdoch relocated to London where he purchased the Sunday tabloid *News of the World*. The previous year, he'd divorced his first wife and married 23-year-old Anna Tov, a stunning blonde thirteen years his junior. Then, in late 1969, he purchased *The Sun*, revamping it into another sensational rag full of sex, sports and topless page three girls.[4]

In October 1969, Murdoch appeared in a television interview with legendary talk show host David Frost. With his beautiful wife, swank offices and prestigious career, Murdoch presented the image of a fabulously wealthy self-made man – everything Arthur and Nizamodeen Hosein had ever wanted.

It must have seemed obvious to the brothers. The plan was to snatch the television mogul's young wife and demand a hefty ransom from her millionaire husband who would surely be eager to part with a portion of his fortune to get her back.

They had no trouble finding their victim. Her husband drove a distinctive blue Rolls Royce – the brothers had seen it on television – and it was a simple task to follow the car back to the couple's residence in Wimbledon.

The scheme might have worked except for one small problem. The woman who lived at the house in Wimbledon was not Anna Murdoch. In fact, Murdoch did not live in Wimbledon at all.

What the kidnappers didn't know was that the Murdochs were out of town, on holiday in Australia. In their absence, they had left the blue Rolls in the care of Murdoch's colleague Alick McKay, the deputy chairman of the *News of the World*.

On 29 December 1969, 60-year-old Alick arrived home around 7.45pm, expecting to spend the evening watching television with his wife Muriel. What he found instead was his front door standing open, his wife's shoes on the stairs and the contents of her handbag strewn about.

As he called out to his 55-year-old wife, Alick also noticed several objects in his lounge room that did not belong there. One was a copy of the previous day's *People* (a newspaper the McKays didn't read) plus a length of baling wire, an adhesive bandage and a billhook lying on the family writing desk.

Alick quickly surmised that something was very wrong. Muriel was gone but her wallet, keys, handbag and overcoat remained. The vicious looking billhook, a heavy metal tool used for cutting hedges, suggested that Muriel had not been given a choice about her leaving.

Alick discovered further evidence of foul play elsewhere in the house. In the den, the couple's dachshund Carl lay before an open fire. Muriel would never have left the fire blazing without its guard – she always feared a spark or flame would injure the dog. In the kitchen, two steaks sat on a plate, waiting to be cooked.

After a quick look around the garden, Alick called the police from a neighbour's house. They arrived within ten minutes and soon discovered that the McKays' phone was not out of order, as Alick had originally assumed. Instead, its lead had been pulled out of the wall, and the disk that bore the McKays' phone number was missing.

Even more suspicious, £600 worth of jewellery was missing from Muriel's bedroom. Alick was convinced that his wife had been kidnapped.[1]

The authorities were not so quick to jump to the same conclusion. No one had been kidnapped and held for ransom in England since 1192 when Leopold, the Duke of Austria, abducted Richard the Lionheart on his way home from the Third Crusade.

(That kidnapping had actually gone fairly well, with the ransom paid in full and Richard returned unharmed[5] – perhaps Arthur and Nizamodeen thought their plan would work just as well.)

The police, however, first considered other, more plausible theories. Detective Sergeant Graham Birch, one of the lead investigators in the case, was compelled to consider whether or not Muriel had simply left her husband of her own accord, a supposition Alick didn't think was possible.

Birch also briefly looked at Alick as a suspect, but that theory was dispelled less than six hours after Muriel was discovered missing. Using the only advantage he had available to him, Alick had contacted his associates in the media and requested maximum publicity. At 1.00am, the first radio bulletin about the missing woman was broadcast on the BBC. Fifteen minutes later, the McKays' telephone rang.

'This is Mafia Group Three,' said a deep male voice. 'We are from America. Mafia. M3. We have your wife.'

The caller told Alick that they wanted a million pounds in two days' time. The amount, Alick said, was ridiculous. Though he was an associate of Murdoch's and made a comfortable living, the well liked and much respected Alick McKay was nowhere near as wealthy as the despised tycoon.

'You have friends,' said the caller. 'Get it from them. We tried to get Rupert Murdoch's wife. We couldn't get her, so we took yours instead.'

It was obvious to the authorities that they were dealing with incompetent buffoons. The kidnappers had taken the wrong woman and then given themselves an absurd nickname. They'd also had to peel the McKays' phone number off the phone itself, and when they called to make their ransom demands, they had to get the operator's assistance to place the call.

'It seemed clear we weren't dealing with professionals,' said Scotland Yard's Commander Herbert Guiver. 'To them it was more a game of cowboys and Indians.'

It would have been like something from a comedy movie except for that a woman's life was on the line. By all accounts, Muriel McKay was a lovely lady. She and her husband Alick had met in Sunday school as teenagers and had been married for over 30 years. An amateur artist, Muriel had a reputation for being a great cook and an excellent hostess. All her husband and three grown children wanted was for her to come home safely.

At first, it seemed as though Muriel might be released. The kidnappers continued to call and several letters that had been written in Muriel's handwriting arrived at the McKays' house in Wimbledon, the first on 31 December. 'Alick DARLING,' Muriel had written. 'I am blindfolded and cold. Only blankets. Please do something to get me home. Please cooperate or I can't keep going …'[1]

Negotiating with the incompetent kidnappers was not going to be easy – it never is, says crisis management consultants Terra Firma:

> One thing [kidnappings] all have in common is they are always carried out by desperate people. Even the most organized crime syndicates or kidnapping networks are all driven by greed, and fear – and fear is the one weapon they wield most forcefully when they hold someone's loved one captive.[6]

The McKay family understood that the people who were holding Muriel were completely inept. She didn't even have her overcoat, which – in January when the temperature in Britain often hovers around zero – could be deadly in itself.

Hoping to turn up the heat on the kidnappers, Alick and his son-in-law David together decided to print the first letter from Muriel in most of the nation's newspapers on New Year's Day.

As Britain read Muriel's letter in their morning papers, David held a press conference, saying he believed Muriel was alive and asking her captors to contact the family with instructions for paying the ransom. Within a few hours, the kidnappers called the McKay home again then fell silent until 10 January when Stafford Somerfield, editor of the *News of the World*, received a letter from M3.

In the letter to Somerfield, the kidnappers complained that they had not been able to get through to the McKay house, which was not surprising. The line had been bogged down by huge numbers of people calling to offer their help. The letter, which was rife with spelling errors, again demanded the one million pound pay off, threatening that if the money was not paid, Muriel would be 'disposed of'.

Throughout January 1970, Alick McKay continued to receive phone calls from M3 and letters from his wife, but as time passed, the likelihood that she was still alive grew more and more slim. Though the kidnappers claimed to be spending 'a lot' on medical treatment for Muriel, they refused to put her on the phone so that Alick and the authorities could confirm she had not been harmed.

The police began to suspect that the kidnappers had forced Muriel to write several letters early in her captivity and that her captors had waited to post the letters until later, thereby keeping up the ruse that she was alive and well.

As the days went by, the phone calls became increasingly cruel. In one, the M3 caller told Alick that he would be 'responsible for not seeing your wife again … your wife is a lovely person'. After that call, Alick stopped answering the phone and allowed his son Ian, the steadiest of the family, to continue to speak with his mother's captors.

Finally, on 22 January 1970, M3 gave the McKay family instructions for paying the ransom on 1 February. In the intervening days, M3 continued to call and send letters they had dictated for Muriel to write. They threatened to kill the woman if their demands were not met and included with one of the letters bits of material from the clothing and shoes Muriel had been wearing the day she was abducted.

On 26 January, Alick received a final letter from Muriel, begging him to cooperate with 'the M3 gang' and not to go to the police. The envelope also included a note from the captors: 'I am sending you a final letter for your wife's reprieve. She will be executed on February 2, 1970, unless you keep our business date on February 1, without any error. We demand the full million pounds.'

While Alick and his family waited for the date to fulfil the kidnappers' instructions, the police had been at work looking for Muriel and any clues as to who might have taken her.

Several neighbours reported having seen one or two men of Indian descent in the vicinity of the McKays' home on the day of the kidnapping. They also said they'd seen a dark Volvo saloon in the area that didn't seem to belong. An extensive search of the Wimbledon area, however, yielded nothing.

On 1 February, the police were ready for the handover. The Bank of England had printed £500,000 in fake bills specifically for the operation, with the understanding that the notes would be destroyed as soon as the mission was complete.

Hesitant to put the real McKay family members in harm's way, two police officers disguised themselves to carry out the ransom drop off. Detective Sergeant Roger Street shaved his moustache and dyed his hair grey to impersonate Muriel's son Ian McKay and Detective Inspector John Minors acted as a chauffeur.

At 9.00pm, the detectives set off in the Murdochs' blue Rolls Royce. By the time they reached their destination – a telephone booth in Tottenham – 200 unmarked police cars had quietly joined in the convoy.

At 10.05pm, the phone rang and the M3 caller instructed 'Ian McKay' to drive to another telephone booth. At the second booth, 'Ian' was told to follow the instructions the gang had left in an empty Piccadilly cigarette packet on the floor, which directed the officers to High Cross in Herefordshire.

As the captors' instructions had indicated, the detectives found two paper flowers at the drop off point and left the suitcase with the fake bank notes beside them. While the detectives in the Rolls Royce returned to the first phone booth as instructed, Detective Chief Superintendent Wilfred Smith waited in the dark at High Cross to see who would come to collect the case.

At 11.45pm, a dark Volvo saloon with a broken rear light drove past the case. Smith could see two men of Indian descent inside. The saloon drove up to the case, then turned around and drove back in the direction of London. For several hours, police continued to watch the case, but no one came to retrieve it. Finally, the officers collected the case and returned to the McKay home.

On 3 February, the same M3 caller rang the McKays. The caller said 'the boss' had seen cars around the case in High Cross, which explained why they hadn't taken the bait. The caller said he was going to a meeting of 'the intellectuals, the semi-intellectuals and the ruffians' to decide when Muriel would be executed. He promised to make one more plea for the woman, though, because 'I am fond of your mum … She reminds me of my mum.'

The kidnapper soon called back to organise one last drop off attempt on 6 February. This time, he insisted Alick McKay and his daughter Diane take the money. Again, for the family's safety, officers played these roles wearing disguises. Detective Inspector John Minors took the place of Alick and Woman Detective Constable Joyce Armitage played the part of Diane.

As with the previous attempt, M3 led the officers on a tour of London, from phone booths to the train station and finally to a petrol station called Gates Garage in Bishop's Stortford. The 'McKays' were instructed to leave the money at the garage on the ground beside a Mini van. All around, the police lay in wait, ready to apprehend the kidnappers as soon as they arrived for the money, this time in two suitcases.

Just after 9.00pm, two men in a dark blue Volvo saloon with a broken rear light pulled up to the cases. They started to take the cases but when a car horn blew, the men drove away. A short time later, they returned. Three times, the men started to take the suitcases but then left.[1]

The men in the Volvo had just returned for a fourth try at taking the money when a couple called the Abbotts happened to notice the cases. Completely unaware that they were blowing the authorities' careful operation, Mrs Abbott stayed and watched over the cases while Mr Abbott went to fetch the local police, who took the cases to their station, oblivious to the damage they were doing.[2]

The operation had been compromised and by 11.40pm, the officers realised there was no use waiting any longer. The police, however, now had the registration number of the Volvo that had been seen outside the McKays' home and at both ransom drop off points. The next day, they visited Rook's Farm and met Arthur and Nizamodeen Hosein.

Though there was no sign of Muriel McKay, the officers did find enough circumstantial evidence to link the two brothers to the woman's disappearance.

Officers who had been involved with the operation were able to identify the Hoseins as being the same men who had been driving the Volvo the night before. At the farm, they found an exercise book with blue-lined paper that matched the paper on which Muriel had written her letters, plus a piece of paper bearing the registration number of the Mini van from the previous night and the same brand of adhesive bandages that had been found at the McKay home.

They also found Piccadilly cigarettes – and a billhook. When asked why the brothers had the billhook, Nizamodeen said he'd used it to cut up a dead calf that they later fed to their dogs. The police could find no trace of bones to substantiate this claim, and the brothers were taken into custody.

Once at the station, it seemed as though Nizamodeen, the quiet, gawky younger brother, might confess but he never did. Nor did his blustering, arrogant older brother Arthur. (There was no mention of any of their other brothers, although the gang's name 'M3' does seem to suggest that perhaps another Hosein might have been in on the plan at some stage.)

On 14 September, the brothers' trial began. For over three weeks, the high profile case captured the nation's attention. Then on 6 October 1970, the brothers were found guilty of the abduction and murder of Muriel McKay, despite the absence of her body.

One mystery that remains is the ultimate fate of Muriel McKay, who disappeared without a trace, along with her clothing and jewellery. Farmers in the area, however, made one gruesome (yet plausible) suggestion –

that the brothers had used the billhook to cut up and feed her corpse to their pigs.

It happens more often than one might think. In 2013, Italian police reported the case of Francesco Raccosta, a mobster who was beaten with iron bars before being fed to pigs. He was reportedly still alive when his rivals threw him in the sty.

'I didn't see a fucking thing left,' said Simone Pepe, a member of the 'Ndrangheta crime family, whose phone conversations were recorded by police. 'People say sometimes [pigs] leave something … In the end there was nothing left … Those pigs could certainly eat.'[7]

Whatever became of Muriel McKay – a kind and talented much-loved wife, mother and friend – let us hope that the sweet lady will be remembered not for the way she may have died, but for the way she lived.

CHAPTER ELEVEN

The Disappearance of Lord Lucan

(1974)

Hong Kong, South America, Africa, Australia – the list of exotic locales where the dashing 7th Earl of Lucan is said to have landed in the wake of a murderous scandal is long, colourful and entirely unsubstantiated.

Several facts about the infamous lord, however, are known to be true. Richard John Bingham was born in London on 18 December 1934. Though not fabulously wealthy, Bingham grew up in Eaton with his own maid and nanny. During the war, he was sent not to the safety of the country but all the way to America where he stayed with the Brady Tucker family.

With their old money and ancient investments, the Tuckers were incredibly affluent and it was during his time with them that the young Bingham learned to appreciate all the finest things in life. Said one later police officer, 'He didn't know how to be poor', and another, '[Bingham] thought he was entitled to things that he wasn't.'[1]

At the age of eleven, Bingham returned to England where he attended Eton College and developed a taste for gambling.[2] After completing his national service with the Coldstream Guards, in 1955 Bingham took a job with a merchant bank in London.

Despite his modest £500 a year salary, Bingham's moderate income was supplemented by various family trusts, and he lived a lavish lifestyle, travelling and gambling. The debonair playboy looked every bit the part with his dapper suits and stylish moustache. He seemed so much like an elegant spy, in fact, that once he was actually considered to play the role of James Bond.[1]

He hit it big, however, in 1960, winning £26,000 in one night playing Chemin de fer, the original version of the French card game baccarat.

At five times his annual salary, the win was enough (Bingham thought) to set him up for good. 'Lucky' Lucan quit his job and spent some time travelling around the USA golfing, driving his Aston Martin and racing powerboats. When he returned to England, he bought a flat in Park Crescent.[3]

Now a professional gambler, Bingham became one of the first members of the Clermont Club casino, which opened in Berkley Square in 1962. A year later, he met Veronica Duncan, a pretty blonde 26-year-old art student. In November 1963, the two were married. Just two months later, Bingham became the 7th Earl of Lucan when his father died of a stroke.

Now Lord Lucan, the popular earl continued to gamble obsessively. Though he won on occasion, his losses sometimes registered in the thousands of pounds in one sitting, losses that quickly put a strain on Lucan's finances and marriage.

Between 1964 and 1970, Lucan and Veronica had three children – Frances, George and Camilla – and with each birth, Veronica suffered severe postnatal depression. Between her depression and his gambling, it is perhaps no wonder that Veronica didn't make many friends among Lucan's tight circle of aristocrats at the Clermont Club.

'Veronica was a rather sad figure at the Clermont Club,' said James Wilson, a fellow member of the Clermont and friend of Lucan. 'She used to come practically every evening with her husband, who gambled at the tables all night while she sat in the corner just watching him and staring into space.'

More than just sitting and failing to socialize, Veronica was reportedly erratic and even violent on occasion. Wilson recalled one such incident that happened at the Mayfair club:

I was standing next to Veronica and noticed there was a very attractive blonde standing in front of us. Suddenly Veronica started to swing her handbag round and round in front of her ... her handbag hit the back of the head of the blonde girl who fell to the floor, writhing in agony. Lucan, who was standing nearby, looked at Veronica in absolute fury, grabbed her, apologised to the blonde girl and marched Veronica out of the Club.[4]

It's hard to know exactly what went on between Lord Lucan and his wife. He reportedly told her she was insane and that she needed psychiatric treatment. While she wouldn't allow herself to be admitted to a psychiatric hospital (and reportedly ran away from clinics more than once), Veronica did agree to take antidepressant drugs.[1]

The very first antidepressants, however, had only been discovered by accident twenty years previously and were a long way from being a reliable source of treatment.[5] The drugs she took may, in fact, have led to her erratic behaviour and mental instability. They caused paranoia, hallucinations and what we would now call restless leg syndrome, a constant tapping of her foot on the floor.

But Veronica may not have been an innocent victim, either. While it seems as though her husband lied to her about the extent of his gambling debts, she reportedly lied about him, saying that he was violent and abusive. He then countered by lying about her, saying that she would bruise herself on the furniture and threaten to accuse him of assault.

There's truly no telling what really happened in Lord and Lady Lucan's marriage but records indicate that in early 1973, Lucan left the family home at 46 Lower Belgrave Street and moved into a small flat in Eaton Row. Not long after, he moved to a larger five-bedroom flat in Elizabeth Street where he hoped he would be able to live with his three children and a nanny. Now all he needed to do was obtain custody.[1]

While the two younger children were out with their nanny one day, Lucan and two private detectives approached the children's carer. He told her that the children had been made wards of the court and that she was to release them into his custody. Lucan took the two younger children and then collected his oldest daughter Francis when she finished school that day.

When Veronica discovered that her children had been essentially kidnapped, she appealed to the courts for help. Though Lucan had hoped to prove his wife an unfit mother, her doctors instead reported that she was not mentally ill. Lucan instead spent the hearing defending his own actions. In the end, Veronica was granted full custody with Lucan allowed nothing more than fortnightly weekend visitation.[6]

Once again, the gambler had rolled the dice and lost. Now his estranged wife was living in his house with his children and a permanent live-in nanny. Lucan furthermore had paid £20,000 (that he didn't have) in legal fees for a judge to make the arrangement binding.

Desperately hoping for a reversal of the High Court's decision, Lucan became more and more irrational. He made anonymous phone calls to his wife and sat outside her house in his Mercedes, watching her every move. He also hired private detectives to stalk her and report back to him.

Always looking for sympathy from his many friends, he taped telephone conversations between himself and Veronica in which he baited her into violent arguments. Later, he replayed these conversations for friends of the couple, complaining about his horrible wife who had stolen his children.

But Lucky Lucan was losing his glamorous sheen. As his debts grew out of control, his gambling became more erratic and irrational. By late 1974, it was becoming obvious he was never going to get his children – or his money – back.

There has been much debate surrounding the events of 7 November 1974. Veronica's latest nanny, a woman named Sandra Rivett, was meant to have the night off as she usually did on a Thursday. Though she had only been employed with Lady Lucan for six months, the reliable and good-natured Sandra had been just what Veronica had needed and the two women had become good friends.

The women had spent the evening on the top floor of the flat with the children. After putting the two younger children to bed, shortly before 9.00pm Sandra went downstairs to the basement kitchen to make her usual cup of tea for Veronica and her oldest daughter Francis.

After fifteen minutes, Sandra had not returned so Veronica went to investigate. On the ground floor, Veronica noticed the light was not working and called out to Sandra. At this point, Veronica was hit over the head with a blunt object. When she screamed, her attacker told her to 'shut up'. Later she said she recognised the voice as being that of her husband.

According to Veronica, she and Lucan fought until she squeezed his testicles tightly enough to make him release her. She said that he admitted to killing Sandra and that she agreed to help him. As soon as she got her chance to escape, Veronica climbed out the bathroom window and ran to a nearby pub, the Plumber's Arms, where she explained what had happened, still quite shaken and with blood running down her face.[1]

When they arrived at the house on Lower Belgrave, police discovered a large quantity of blood. Most of it belonged to Sandra Rivett. She had been severely beaten in the head with a length of lead pipe that had been wrapped in surgical tape, her body then stuffed in a mail sack. The lead pipe was covered in blood.

They also discovered that the light fixture was not broken. Instead, the bulb had been unscrewed, presumably so that the killer could hide in the darkness. Sandra and Veronica were both petite women, and police quickly formulated the theory that Lucan had come to the house planning to murder Veronica only to kill Sandra in the dark by mistake.

Lord Lucan was certainly at Veronica's house that night. His ten-year-old daughter Francis had seen and heard him – she said he had sent her to bed. He also admitted to having been there in a phone call to his mother.

According to Lucan, it was all a huge misunderstanding. He just happened to be passing by the house, he said, when he looked through the kitchen window and saw a man attacking Veronica. He then used his key to let himself into the house at which point the unknown assailant ran away, leaving him with Sandra's dead body and Veronica, dazed and bleeding.[7]

Lucan's mother said that at around 10.00pm on the night of the murder, her son had called to ask her to go and collect the children. She said that Lucan had spoken of a 'terrible catastrophe' and how he'd tried to rescue his wife, as Lucan's mother later recounted:

> *I asked him what he intended to do and I got nowhere. I also said I had the police with me and would he like to speak to them. He hesitated and then said, 'No. I don't think I'll speak to them now. I will ring them in the morning and I will ring you too.'*[8]

A friend of Lucan's, Madeleine Florman, later reported that a man with a voice like Lucan's had called her house but that she had not spoken to him. Also, someone had knocked on her door that evening but she had not answered. Both Madeleine and Lucan's mother could tell that the calls were not made from public phone boxes, and it has never been established where those two calls were made from.

The last confirmed sighting of Lucan came from Susan Maxwell-Scott, a friend of Lucan's who lived in Sussex. She later reported that Lucan arrived at her house in Uckfield around 11.30pm, asking for her husband Ian. The director of the Clermont Club, Ian was in London at the time. Lucan told Susan the same story he'd told his mother about happening passed the house and rescuing his wife from an unknown attacker.

Shortly after midnight, Lucan called his mother again to make sure the children were safe – she said they were in bed sleeping – then he wrote four letters. Two were addressed to his brother-in-law Bill Shand Kydd, one telling the same version of events Lucan had told his mother and Susan, and the other providing details for repaying certain creditors. The other two letters were addressed to his friend Michael Stoop, only one of which was ever given to police.[1]

It is at this point Lucan's trail goes cold. A few days later, the Ford Corsair Lucan had borrowed from his friend Michael Stoop and had been driving on the night of the murder was discovered in Newhaven. The police discovered a second length of lead pipe wrapped in surgical tape in the boot. Like the one found at the house in Lower Belgrave, this one was also covered in blood.[7]

It's worth noting that, while Lord Lucan had an obvious motive for wanting to kill his wife, Veronica Lucan had just as much motive for misrepresenting the man who had kidnapped her children and made her life miserable.

In a 2012 interview with the *Sunday Mirror*, Veronica's son George indicated that he didn't agree with his mother's version of events because he felt 'the state of her relationship with Lucan at the time clouded her details of fact'.[9]

Then as now, however, there was the morbid desire among the common population to see the aristocracy brought low. The police were quick to brand the wealthy earl a murderer, but several theories have been put forward in connection with Lucan's story about the unknown assailant.

Some of his friends insist he was telling the truth, although this possibility is least plausible. The house at 46 Lower Belgrave Street still stands. The basement kitchen is well below street level and when the lights are off, most people would agree that it's nearly impossible to see in through the window. Also, police found no physical evidence of another man. The only bloody footprints belonged to Lucan.[7]

Another theory is that the killer was actually a hit man who had been hired to kill Veronica. In 2016, Sandra's son Neil Berriman told the *Daily Mirror* that even in the dark, there was no way Lord Lucan could have mistaken the redheaded Sandra (whom he barely knew) for the blonde Veronica (to whom he had been married for twelve years). Berriman also insisted Lucan wouldn't have committed the murder himself as he 'was used to having everything done for him'.[10]

Assuming the killer was a hit man, Lucan is still the person who had the greatest motive for organising the murder, which would make him no less guilty than if he had committed the crime himself.

If he did, in fact, hire someone else to do the job, the question remains – what was Lord Lucan doing at Veronica's house that night? Did he suddenly fear the consequences of getting caught? Did he have a sudden attack of remorse at the thought of leaving his children motherless? Or was it something more sinister?

The discovery of the second bloody lead pipe in the Ford Corsair suggests another reason. Perhaps Lord Lucan simply wanted to be sure the job was done properly.

Whatever the truth of the events, in the early hours of Friday 8 November 1974, Lord Lucan vanished. Later that morning, police searched his flat on Eaton Row and his last known address on Elizabeth Street.

They found his wallet, his car keys and his spectacles. They also found a shirt and suit laid out, his passport in a drawer and his Mercedes out front, the engine cold and the battery flat. In short, there was nothing to suggest that Lucan had been there or planned to come back.[11]

Police suspected Lucan had committed suicide rather than answer for the events of the night in question. They searched the area but nothing was found. Within hours, the world was searching for Lord Lucan.

He had not been found by the time the full inquest into the death of Sandra Rivett began on 16 June 1975. After hearing testimony from 33 witnesses, Coroner Gavin Thurston made a summary of the evidence and presented the jury with their options. In the end, the inquest named its man:

> *I will record that Sandra Eleanor Rivett died from head injuries, that at 10.30pm on 7 November 1974 she was found dead at 46 Lower Belgrave Street ... and that the following offence was committed by Richard John Bingham, Earl of Lucan – namely the offence of murder.*[12]

The jury's decision, as announced by Thurston, was unusual in the extreme. It had been over 200 years since a member of the House of Lords had been found guilty of murder, and it would be the last time a coroner would commit a person to the Crown Court for the crime.

In his final letters, Lucan said that all he wanted was for his children to be looked after and that he couldn't stand for them to see him prosecuted for murder. His disappearance, however, did little to make their lives easy.

As it was, he left his family with substantial debt. In August 1975, it was revealed that Lucan owed £45,000 in unsecured debts and £1,326 in preferential liabilities. The sum of his assets, however, was valued at only £22,632. In March 1976, the Lucan family silver had to be sold for around £30,000 to help offset the debt.[4]

Could he have made it out of England? Many believe it was possible. As soon as they heard of the accusations against him, Lucan's close-knit circle of friends rallied around him, people who had the money and influence to sneak him out of the country if they'd wanted to. As Sandra's mother said after the inquest, 'Lord Lucan has so many friends. There is so much money around.'

Though his friends were generally law abiding, they could also be stubborn. Police described their difficulties in getting information from what they called the 'Eton mafia'.

In the year following his disappearance, there were a thousand 'sightings' of Lucan, placing him in different places around the globe at the same moment, including France, Spain, Scotland and Colombia. Several times, he was reportedly seen throughout Africa, from Mozambique and South Africa to Zambia, Zimbabwe, Kenya, Gabon and Namibia among others.[1]

Other theories place him in Australia. In 2009, 65-year-old Carolyn Campbell of Queensland contacted a BBC reporter after finding medical records among her late father's private papers. Her father, Dr John Watson, had been one of the UK's most eminent plastic surgeons.

After Dr Watson's death in January 2009, his daughter discovered medical records that indicated her father had performed plastic surgery on Lord Lucan's face. The surgery on record had been following a speedboat accident at some point prior to the incident involving Sandra Rivett, but it prompted the question – had Watson performed a similar surgery for Lucan after Sandra's death?

Carolyn Campbell thought it might have been possible, as she explained to the *Sunday Express* and in a BBC documentary:

> *My father and Lord Lucan had got to know each other fairly well. I asked him many times when he was alive if he had carried out more*

work on Lord Lucan's face and he never gave me a straight answer
but I know he was sympathetic to him and I have no doubt that if
my father felt he should have helped him he would have done.[13]

Questions continued to surround Lord Lucan's whereabouts even after
he was eventually declared dead and his probate settled in 1999. There
was enough doubt, in fact, that when his son George applied to inherit
his father's title, his application was denied by then Lord Chancellor
Lord Irvine.[1]

There has not been one confirmed sighting of Lord Lucan since the
early morning of 8 November 1974. Even so, he was not officially declared
legally dead until February 2016 when his son George finally obtained his
father's death certificate after lengthy court proceedings.[14]

Lucan's closest friends, however, would likely say that all the talk of
clandestine escapes and exotic locales is much ado about nothing. They
believe he has been dead for decades. The most common theory is that
Lucan boarded either a ferry or a small boat, weighted himself and drowned
himself in the English Channel.

Speaking forty years after the event, James Wilson didn't deny his
Clermont friend killed his wife – or himself:

Veronica wasn't very well liked, I'm afraid. People would have
understood why [Lucan] wanted rid of her ... I believe that when
he realised he had killed the nanny the remorse, guilt and panic led
him to commit suicide ... He gambled on successfully killing his wife
and being able to hide her body and get away with murder. But
when it went terribly wrong he must have realised he only had two
options open to him; hand himself in or kill himself.[4]

In a more colourful version of events, Lucan met up with his friends
at the Clermont Club shortly after killing Sandra. When he told them
he wasn't cut out for life on the run, one of them handed him a pistol,
which he took into another room and used to shoot himself. The Clermont

crew then took him and fed his dead body to the tigers at his friend John Aspinall's zoo in Kent. No evidence of this story was ever found.

For all the animosity that existed during their marriage, Veronica Lucan has said her former husband killed himself for the sake of the children. Though he left the family in debt, Veronica claimed that if John Lucan had been pronounced dead in 1974, the family would have been responsible for paying death duties, an amount Veronica said would have left the family in a much more difficult financial situation than the debt.

'[If John's body had been found] we would not have been able to pay for the children's education,' Veronica said in a 2012 interview. Instead, when Lucan went missing in 1974, the children became wards of the state. Veronica was named as their legal guardian until 1982 when she lost custody after a mental breakdown, less than a decade after the fatal events.

According to Veronica, Lord Lucan deliberately threw himself off a ferry in such a way that the propellers of the craft would destroy his body and leave no trace for police to find:

> He knew a lot about boats, he would have jumped off close to the propellers that would cut up his body so he could never be found … It was tremendously brave of him to have done that. I think he was thinking of the children and their future.[15]

CHAPTER TWELVE

The Yorkshire Ripper

(1975)

There's no denying that police work is one of the most difficult professions there is, but the Yorkshire Ripper was one criminal that managed to elude the authorities for five long years. Though the authorities would receive much criticism over their failure to catch this Ripper, many factors were responsible for the delay in apprehending him.

The investigation began when the body of 28-year-old Wilma McCann was discovered in Leeds on a freezing cold October morning in 1975, staring up into the sky. The well known party girl and part time prostitute had been out the night before, leaving her four children at home alone as usual.

The post mortem revealed that her killer had attacked her from behind, hitting her twice in the head with something heavy like a hammer. Having shattered her skull, the killer had then slashed Wilma's chest and stomach leaving her with fourteen lacerations.

At first, the motive did not appear to be sexual in nature. Wilma's blouse was open and her bra was pulled up. Her trousers had also been pulled down to her knees, but her underwear was still in place[1] and there was no semen inside her body.

Forensics tests, however, did reveal semen on the back of Wilma's trousers and underwear. Also, Wilma died from the blows to the back of her head, which means she should have fallen forward but when she was found, she was lying on her back. Authorities surmised that the killer had attacked the woman, masturbated and climaxed over her body, then turned her body over and subsequently mutilated her.[2]

The second attack came only weeks later when 42-year-old Emily Jackson and her husband went out for the evening, leaving their three children at home. Like Wilma, Emily was a part time prostitute. She'd only been at the pub for a few minutes when she left her husband to go look for business. Within an hour, someone saw her getting into a Land Rover in the car park.

The following morning, a worker discovered Emily's body sprawled on her back, her breasts exposed and her underwear in place. Her killer has bashed her twice in the head and stabbed her over 50 times in the neck, breasts and stomach. Her back had been gouged with a Phillips screwdriver and her right thigh had been stamped with a heavy ribbed wellington boot.[1]

There were a number of similarities between Wilma and Emily – both bashed in the head, both stabbed, both turned over. Both murders seemed to be somehow sexually motivated but neither woman had been raped.

This sort of thing, however, happened to prostitutes all the time. So when another prostitute, Marcella Claxton, came to police in May 1976, the authorities thought it was just another incident of random violence.

As Marcella told police, on the morning of 9 May 1976, a man approached the twenty-year-old and offered her a ride home. As he drove, he proposed paying her for sex. At Roundhay Park, he hit her in the back of the head eight or nine times with a hammer. Marcella told police that as she lay dying on the ground, he stood over her masturbating.

For whatever reason, the killer didn't slash Marcella but instead drove away, giving her the chance to crawl to a nearby phone box and dial 999. Not only did she survive, she was able to give a detailed description of her attacker to the police. The authorities, however, didn't think to connect her attack to those of the two murder victims.[2]

It wasn't as though the police weren't putting in the effort. As soon as Wilma McCann's body was discovered, Detective Dennis Hoban began putting in twelve-hour days, hoping to find the killer. He soon had a team of 137 officers working on the case.

After reviewing forensic evidence, Hoban made an initial assessment that the killer was most likely a long distance lorry driver. Hoban was also certain the killer was not finished with his dark work, as he said in a statement to the press:

> *He is a sadistic killer and may well be a sexual pervert. I cannot stress strongly enough that it is vital we catch this brutal killer before he brings tragedy to another family.*[3]

Despite the efforts of the police, the killer struck again nine months later. In the early morning of 6 February 1977, the body of 28-year-old prostitute Irene Richardson was discovered behind the sports pavilion at Soldier's Field. Irene was laying face down, and her skull had been smashed in three places.

It was obviously the work of the same killer. Her skirt and tights had been torn off, her neck and torso slashed. Like the others, she had not been raped. It wasn't long before the press drew a connection between these murders and those of another British serial killer who had targeted prostitutes. What better name than the Yorkshire Ripper?

1977 would prove to be a bloody year. On 23 April, 32-year-old Patricia Atkinson went out for the evening. The divorced mother of three was living alone when she met up with her friends at her local pub, The Carlisle.

When Patricia's friends went to her home the following evening looking for her, they found her front door unlocked. Patricia had been attacked as she'd come into her flat. The Ripper had bashed the back of her head four times with a hammer, thrown her on the bed, pulled off her clothes and stabbed her stomach and torso repeatedly.

There was no doubt the killer was the same man who had murdered the others. Police found a boot print on Patricia's bed matching the one they'd found on Emily's thigh.

Now the public was really starting to panic. Patricia was a prostitute, but she had been killed in her own home. The panic became even more pronounced on 26 June 1977 when the body of sixteen-year-old Jayne MacDonald was discovered just a few hundred yards from her parents' home in Chapeltown.

Unlike the others, Jayne was not a prostitute. She was just a nice girl who worked in the shoe department at the local supermarket. She'd been out for the evening with friends and was on her way home when the Ripper hit her on the back of her head. He dragged her from the pavement and hit her twice more before stabbing her in the back and chest.[1]

Now the whole of Yorkshire was in terror. Women were afraid to go out in the evenings, and the police – with few leads and little to go on – advised them to stay at home. 'Do not go out at night unless absolutely necessary and only if accompanied by a man you know,' the authorities formally advised.[4]

With the death of Jayne MacDonald, the investigation took on new life. Assistant Chief Constable George Oldfield of the West Yorkshire Police assumed overall command of the investigation, but his efforts would meet with much disapproval before the killer was caught.[5]

The Ripper continued to evade the authorities. Two weeks after the death of Jayne MacDonald, a drunken Maureen Long (another prostitute) got in a car with a potential customer.[1] She was attacked and left for dead in some wasteland near her home in Bradford. She survived with injuries to her head and abdomen[5] but she was able to give the police a description.

On 1 October 1977, the Ripper left one small clue that could have meant the end for him when he picked up 21-year-old prostitute Jean Jordon in Manchester. He gave her a £5 note as advance payment then took her to the Southern Cemetery where he beat her in the head with a hammer eleven times.[1]

It wasn't until later that the Ripper realized he'd paid Jean with a brand new note from his wages packet. Thinking the note might be traced back to him, the Ripper returned eight days later. Jean's body remained where he'd left her, undiscovered, but he couldn't find her handbag.[5]

Unable to find the note, the Ripper finished his previous work. Using a piece of broken glass, he slashed Jean's body over and over. He tried to cut off her head so that the police wouldn't be able to identify the signature hammer blows that would link Jean's murder to the others. The Ripper finally gave up on decapitating the woman, and with several vicious kicks, he returned to his car and drove away. The next day, Jean's naked body was finally found.[1]

It seemed as though the police had caught a break when the discovery of the brand new £5 note near Jean's body led them to a bank at Shipley, near Leeds, but the lead would soon go cold. One of the 5000 possible suspects they interviewed, however, would eventually come back to haunt them:

Among the workers who were interviewed (twice) was a 31-year-old lorry driver named Peter Sutcliffe, who worked at T & W Clark (Holdings) Ltd, and lived in a small detached house in Bradford … his wife Sonia was able to provide him with an alibi. The police apologized and left …

Just over a month after the police spoke with Peter Sutcliffe for the second time, the Ripper struck again when he attacked prostitute Marilyn Moore on 14 December 1977. He struck her in the head with a heavy metal object when she got in his car, but he drove away before doing any further damage. She survived and gave the police a detailed description.[5]

The Ripper was becoming more proficient and making fewer mistakes that would leave behind survivors. He was also working at a steady pace, though the police wouldn't know it right away.

Eighteen-year-old twin sisters Helen and Rita Rytka thought they were safe working as a pair. The young prostitutes had been working the night of Tuesday 31 January 1978 when Helen arrived at their designated meeting place five minutes early. Thinking she had time to do one more job before her sister arrived, Helen got into a red Ford Corsair with a bearded man and went with him to Garrard's timber yard.

The attack on Helen was unusual in that the Ripper engaged in intercourse with her, but the timber yard was a popular spot for derelicts. When the Ripper saw two men, he carried on with the sexual transaction as if it were his only reason for being with Helen.

Once the other two men were gone, Helen stepped out of the back seat of the car to return to the front seat. It was at this point that the Ripper struck, bashing her in the head a total of six times.

Three months later, the body of Yvonne Pearson, a long time prostitute with wealthy clientele, was discovered on wasteland in Lumb Land. The 22-year-old mother of two had been killed just ten days before Helen Rytka in an especially vicious attack.

Like the others, she'd been bashed in the head with a hammer, but horsehair from a sofa had also been stuffed down her throat and the killer had jumped on her chest a number of times.

It was almost as though the Ripper was taunting the police or even hoping to be caught. Police believed the killer had returned to the scene and moved Yvonne's body to make her more visible. He had also placed a copy of the *Daily Mirror* dated four weeks after her death under one of her arms.[1]

The gesture was an enormous insult to the authorities, which had been lambasted in the press for their failure to capture the killer – and the case was taking its toll. The much-lauded Dennis Hoban died suddenly in 1978 of diabetes. Hoban was one of the first to recognize the series of killings was the work of one man, and there are some who say the case might have been solved sooner if he hadn't died.[6]

Two months after Yvonne was found, on the night of 16 May 1978, Vera Millward reportedly went to the Manchester Royal Infirmary to buy drugs for her chronic stomach pains. The small, frail 41-year-old had resorted to prostitution to support her seven children. Her body was discovered the morning of 17 May on the grounds of the infirmary. She had been hit in the head three times, her stomach slashed.[1]

The killer's elusive nature was maddening, and there was a grave sense of urgency at the highest levels to apprehend him. In an effort to make sure nothing had been missed, Detective Chief Superintendent John Domaille was charged with reviewing all of the information the authorities had gathered to date.

In June 1978, Domaille published a confidential criminal intelligence special bulletin that attributed ten murders to the Ripper (Domaille would later be proven wrong about one). He also named the Ripper responsible for four attempted murders, although later evidence would reveal he'd missed at least two of the killer's attacks. It was at this point that the authorities realized they were dealing with a criminal who had likely killed or tried to kill countless victims.[2]

Though many were quick to point to police incompetence, it's important to note that these crimes were happening at a time when sharing information between police departments was difficult for a number of reasons. The Internet didn't exist and police notes were recorded by hand on index cards. Even the photocopier had only recently been invented.

It's little wonder, then, that officers were often loath to part with their one-of-a-kind paper copies. More than once, files, evidence and interviews obtained through countless hours of tough detective work were loaned out only to be mislaid and never seen again.

There was also a sometimes negative attitude towards sharing information at the time. In early 1979, journalist Nicola Tyler asked why the 'Ripper Squad' hadn't asked for help from Scotland Yard, to which Chief Constable Ronald Gregory of the West Yorkshire Police replied:

> *There is no way I would call in Scotland Yard in this case. This is not to decry the Metropolitan Police in any way ... but a force the size of West Yorkshire [5000 men] has as much and probably more experience than Scotland Yard officers ... When I mentioned the notion of bringing in the 'Met' to Detective Superintendent Dick Holland, head of the Ripper Squad, he said it was a thoroughly insulting suggestion.*

As a neighbouring chief constable put it, many smaller police forces were reluctant to ask for help for fear it would cast doubt on their 'self-sufficiency'.[5]

Despite these issues, the police weren't entirely without the use of technology. One resource they did have available turned up another vital lead. As a result of Domaille's bulletin, in June 1978 officers set up observation points in the red light districts of Leeds, Manchester, Sheffield and Hull.

The authorities believed the Ripper found his victims like many men who did business with prostitutes – by inviting them into his car – so they noted the number plates of 'kerb crawlers' in the four districts they thought the Ripper was most likely to go. Officers at the base would then feed these number plates into the Police National Computer.

Any car noted as having been in two of the four areas was flagged for questioning. One was a red Ford Corsair belonging to Peter Sutcliffe. In August 1978, the officer who interviewed Sutcliffe was the same officer who had interviewed the lorry driver in connection with Jean Jordon's £5 note. Again, Sutcliffe had a tidy explanation. Again, he was released.

None of the officers working the case seemed to notice how much Sutcliffe looked like the descriptions that had been given by the women who had survived the Ripper's attacks, but Sutcliffe was masterful at misleading the police. At every interview, he seemed like nothing more than a typical married man.

Though Sutcliffe was giving nothing away, there were also problems within the police force. In September 1978, an internal audit of only 10 per cent of the Ripper Squad's completed inquires revealed a number of substantial errors and omissions. In the wake of the audit, two detectives quit the force and thirteen more saw disciplinary action.[2]

For all their mistakes, it seemed as though the police were beginning to move in the right direction. It may have been for this reason that, after Vera Millward, the Ripper stopped targeting prostitutes.

Later, he would plead insanity, saying that God had told him to cleanse the earth of these women, but six of his twenty known victims – none of whom would ever be mistaken for prostitutes – would disprove his claim.

After a tense eleven-month lull, the Ripper struck again, this time 19-year-old Josephine Whitaker. On the night of Wednesday 4 April 1979, Sutcliffe attacked Josephine as she walked across Savile Park playing fields in Halifax, smashing her in the back of the head and then dragging her into the nearby bushes.[1]

The vicious attack on the young bank clerk showed a distinct sexual motivation. The Ripper left bite marks on her left breast and he repeatedly stabbed her in the vagina with a screwdriver.[2] In his bid to convince the court he was insane, the Ripper would later say his attacks were not motivated by sexual desire, but Josephine's injuries, plus the evidence of semen found on earlier victims, suggested otherwise.

Shortly after the death of Josephine, the search for the Yorkshire Ripper was thrown for a loop when a series of letters came into play. There was some evidence to suggest that the writer of these three letters was the real killer, but that evidence was far from conclusive.

Then came a cassette tape with the voice of a man with a Geordie accent taunting Chief Constable George Oldfield, who had been leading the investigation for over two years. 'I reckon your boys are letting you down, George,' said the singsong voice, 'ya can't be much good, can ya?'[7]

The tape was released to the press and suddenly the nation was in a frenzy. Everyone was terrified, so everyone wanted to help. The tape was played over and over again in pubs, shopping centres and working men's clubs in the hopes that someone would recognise the voice.[4]

While the rest of Britain feverishly looked for a Geordie serial killer, in late July 1979, Detective Constable Andrew Laptew was taking a closer look at Peter Sutcliffe. It was the fifth time Sutcliffe had been called before the police in the course of the investigation, and there was a lot to see.

Laptew noticed that Sutcliffe looked very much like the description Marilyn Moore had given of her attacker, and the lorry driver also had a gap between his teeth that was the same as whoever had bitten Josephine Whitaker. Sutcliffe also had the same shoe size as the boot that had stomped both Emily Jackson and Patricia Atkinson, and he had once been arrested for 'going equipped to steal' – in other words, he'd been carrying a hammer.

It was enough that Laptew thought Sutcliffe warranted further investigation, but his superiors dismissed his suspicions. Sutcliffe didn't have a Geordie accent like the man on the cassette tape and his handwriting didn't match that of the letters the police had received. Laptew's report was filed and nothing more was said about it.[7]

Only weeks later, on 2 September 1979, twenty-year-old student Barbara Leach was walking with a group of friend outside the Mannville Arms in Little Horton. Just past 1.00am, she moved away from the safety of the group. The Ripper struck just 200 yards (182 m) from the pub and then pulled Barbara into the darkness to stab her eight times.

There was another eleven month lull – during which Peter Sutcliffe was interviewed by police four more times – before the Ripper killed again, this time 47-year-old Marguerite Walls. On 18 August 1980, the civil servant was on her way home from work when the Ripper bashed and strangled her. It was two days before her body was found.

Then on 17 November 1980, twenty-year-old student Jacqueline Hill was murdered within sight of her residence hall at the University of Leeds. It was a ghastly attack. In addition to her other injuries, the Ripper also stabbed Jacqueline repeatedly in her eye.[1]

By now, the Home Secretary had intervened, setting up an advisory body of scientists and police under Scotland Yard Commander Ron Harvey. They had begun to doubt the authenticity of the letters and cassette tape, which in fact were fakes, although it would be 2006 before the man responsible for the hoax would be found guilty.

There had also been brutal attacks on two more women, 34-year-old Dr Upadhya Bandara and nineteen-year-old student Theresa Sykes. Despite thousands of hours of investigation, it seemed as though the police were no closer to catching the Ripper.

Then, on 2 January 1981, Peter Sutcliffe picked up 24-year-old prostitute Olivia Rievers. He asked the girl to get into the back seat of his car but she refused, a decision that probably saved her life.

As they sat in the car, a police cruiser pulled up and arrested Sutcliffe for having stolen number plates. At first, Sutcliffe seemed like just another punter but this time his answers to the police's queries were suspicious enough to prompt a blood test. The test revealed that his blood type was the same as the elusive killer's.

After two days of questioning and further investigation, Peter Sutcliffe finally confessed to being the Yorkshire Ripper.

Four months later, on 29 April 1981, Sutcliffe's trial began. The prosecution and the defence had come to an agreement. Rather than admitting to murder, Sutcliffe would plead guilty to thirteen counts of the lesser charge of manslaughter. He couldn't be held fully accountable for his crimes, his defence claimed, because he was suffering from paranoid schizophrenia.[2]

Mr Justice Sir Leslie Boreham, however, the judge presiding over the case, was not so convinced. In the end Sutcliffe stood full trial and was found guilty of thirteen counts of murder and seven counts of attempted murder. He was sentenced to incarceration for the remainder of his life. In 2009, that sentence was reiterated when the High Court ruled that he was never to be released.

Journalist Joan Smith, who covered the Yorkshire murders from 1978 to 1981, agreed with the High Court's 2009 ruling for good reason:

> *This is a man who hated women so much that he smashed their skulls with a hammer to disable them, then slashed and mutilated their bodies. I don't believe that anyone – doctor, lawyer or anyone else – can ever say with confidence that he no longer poses a threat to women.*[7]

CHAPTER THIRTEEN

Taken Too Soon

(1993)

At the time of this writing, a person in England must be at least sixteen years old before they can legally have sex (even consensual sex) with another person. The age to join the armed forces is also sixteen, and if you want to buy cigarettes or alcohol, get a tattoo or vote, you must be at least eighteen – but you only have to be ten years old to become a criminal.

The age of criminal responsibility has come up for debate several times in recent years. One report by the Centre for Crime and Justice Studies at King's College, London, suggests that setting that age too low can actually encourage a life of crime. 'A court appearance can, in certain cases, confirm an adolescent's deviant identity both in their own eyes and those of others,' the study contends, 'thereby extending rather than curbing a delinquent career.'[1]

Every so often, however, a young person commits a crime so horrific that the current age of responsibility seems justified.

On 12 February 1993, two-year-old James Bulger was out shopping with his family when Jon Venables and Robert Thompson lured him away from his mother. What the pair did to the toddler at a nearby railway track was enough to horrify the nation – and Venables and Thompson were only ten years old.

The real question, though, is how responsible can we hold these two boys for their actions?

There is no denying that Jon Venables and Robert Thompson were products of the environments in which they were raised. Born within ten days of each other in August 1982, both Venables and Thompson grew up in the North Liverpool suburb of Walton, a place long famous for unemployment and low-income families.

Jon Venables' parents Susan and Neil lived a mile apart from each other, sharing custody of Jon and his two siblings. The children stayed with their mother during the week and their father on the weekends.

The three Venables kids were reportedly a handful at best. They attended three separate schools, Jon's brother and sister each at different specialist schools to address their learning difficulties. Jon was described as hyperactive and was always getting into trouble at his school.[2]

It's perhaps not surprising that Jon acted out at school. His mother displayed many characteristics of a classic narcissist and seemed much more interested in her many boyfriends than she was in looking after her children.[3]

On one occasion in January 1987, for example, the police were called to Susan Venables' home when it was discovered that her three children – aged seven, five and three at the time – had been left alone for three hours.[2]

In spite of what transpired in February 1993, Jon Venables' mother would later insist that she had done nothing in the way of neglectful parenting that might have led to his criminal behaviour, as she said in an interview with the press:

> *I don't think we went wrong at all. He has had the love and attention that any boy would. He has had more love and attention than a lot of children I know. He has been educated. He has never really been a truant. He has had his holidays like everyone else. He has had Christmas presents. He is not a little urchin boy. He is*

far from it. He has had security with loving parents and a loving brother and sister.[2]

Many would disagree with Susan's assessment of her success as a mother. She suffered from a number of mental health issues, mainly depression, and had attempted to commit suicide.

Those mental health issues carried over into her relationship with her children. Jon was reportedly afraid of his mother, the harsher of his two parents. She would threaten him to the point that he would hide under chairs. Jon also dealt with his fear of his mother by self-harming, cutting himself with knives.[3]

In the same way Susan's issues spilled over onto her son, Jon subsequently took out his issues at school and in his neighbourhood. He was known to frequently punch and kick his classmates, once attempting to throttle another boy.[2]

Robert Thompson was no stranger to violence, either. When his father wasn't openly beating Robert, he often intimidated the boy or one of the other six children in the family.[3]

Robert was only five years old when his father left his mother Ann to raise her rambunctious mob on her own. An overweight alcoholic, Ann didn't manage the job well and often left the children to fend for themselves while she spent the day in the pub drinking herself into oblivion.

According to an NSPCC case conference on the Thompson family, things were out of control at the Thompson household, as author Blake Morrison (who saw notes from the conference) described:

> *The Thompson report is a series of violent incidents, none of them in itself enough to justify the kids being taken into care but the sum of them appalling. The boys, it's said, grew up 'afraid of each other'. They bit, hammered, battered, tortured each other.*

On one occasion, Ann took her third son Philip to the police station when he threatened his older brother Ian with a knife. The situation was so bad that the fifteen-year-old Ian asked to be taken into care. When he was returned home, he attempted suicide by taking an overdose of painkillers. Such was life at the Thompson house that at least three members of the family tried to kill themselves.[2]

From these two broken homes emerged Jon Venables and Robert Thompson. By the age of ten, each of them had already earned a bad reputation. Regularly truant, they were known to shoplift and fight. Many people said they were often cruel to animals. The boys would shoot pigeons with air rifles or tie rabbits to the railway tracks to be obliterated by the passing trains.[3]

The boys' mistreatment of animals was particularly worrisome. In the 1970s, the FBI began using behavioural profiling to look for common traits in serial killers and rapists, psychopaths characterized by impulsivity, selfishness and lack of remorse.

The FBI identified three adolescent behaviours they called the 'Homicidal Triad' that were most common to these offenders – cruelty to animals, bed wetting and obsessive fire setting.[4] (It is perhaps bizarrely coincidental that, a week after his father left the family home, Robert Thompson's house burned to the ground in an accidental fire.[2])

Given the circumstances of their upbringing, there are many who have felt varying degrees of sympathy for Jon Venables and Robert Thompson. The two have been cast as victims themselves, barely accountable for what happened that grim Friday in February 1993.

At the same time, Venables and Thompson were two of thousands of children born and raised under very similar conditions. While Thompson had been diagnosed with a learning disorder, neither of the boys was mentally incapacitated and they both understood what they were doing. Nor was the boys' crime some momentary act of impulse. Its planning and execution took hours.

The boys had skipped school that Friday and headed to The Strand, a popular two-storey shopping centre in Merseyside's Bootle. There, they'd spent the morning stealing an assortment of odds and ends – batteries, a clockwork soldier and some blue Humbrol model paint.[5]

There's no way of knowing what inspired the boys to steal a child, although there's a fair chance neither of the boys would have done it on his own. It is also true that both boys had firsthand knowledge of extraordinary violence.

Thompson and his brothers were used to perpetrating violence on each other. They had been beaten, burned with cigarettes, their eyes blackened. One of Thompson's brothers had locked another in the garden shed and left him for hours. Another had convinced a younger brother to skip school and then abandoned him beside a canal. Like cruelty to animals, cruelty to children was a way of life for Robert Thompson.

Venables had also learned many lessons in brutality, although in a different way. While Venables' father seemed to be a loving parent, in the weeks following the incident, it came to light that Mr Venables had rented over 400 movies in the previous few years, many of which contained extremely violent or pornographic material, such as the infamous *I Spit on Your Grave* in which a woman is brutally gang raped and then exacts her revenge by killing her attackers in one graphic murder after another.

The last video Mr Venables rented prior to the infamous incident involving his son was a horror film called *Child's Play 3*, in which a demonic toddler-sized doll named Chucky comes to life. In the film, Chucky tries to kill a young cadet by throwing him under the wheels of a train. In the end, Chucky is splashed in the face with blue paint and horribly mutilated.[6]

Mr Venables would deny that his son ever saw the film, but the events of 12 February would tell another story.

Around midday, the boys took their first crack at luring a child out of the shopping centre. They convinced one toddler to follow them a short distance out of the department store TJ Hughes on the upper floor, but the child's mother soon realised her little one was gone and came running to the rescue.

Going downstairs, the pair found James Bulger standing in the doorway of AR Tyms, a butcher.[5]

James Patrick Bulger was born on Friday, 16 March 1990 at Fazakerley Hospital in Liverpool. He was the second child born to Ralph and Denise Bulger. His older sister Kirsty had been stillborn two years previously, and his parents had been devastated by her loss. The birth of James, however, brought them closer together and cemented their new marriage into a loving family.

Named after Ralph's father, James was the centre of the Bulgers' world with his bright blue eyes and blonde hair. Even as a baby, he was active and boisterous, always on the go. As his father recalled in his memoir *My James*, the little boy's laughter was infectious, and everywhere he went, people loved him.[7]

Knowing his fun loving personality, it's no surprise that Venables and Thompson were able to lure him away – James probably thought they were playing.

James had been in the shops with his mother, his cousin and his auntie for hours. They'd been to The Photo Expert, Marks & Spencer and Tesco already. His mother, 25-year-old Denise Bulger, was buying chops for dinner when she found herself distracted by the clerk for just a moment.[5]

A few people would later claim that Denise should never have let go of James' hand, but the truth is that every parent in the world knows the panic of turning around and finding their child is not where they should be. Most of the time, that panic lasts a few seconds, a few minutes at the most. For Denise, that moment of panic was just the beginning of her worst nightmare.

There are several accounts of the events that happened next. Hundreds of news articles make vague reference to the torture and murder of James Bulger, and often times, there is little value in recalling the specifics of that afternoon.

Much time has passed, however, since that day and it is worth remembering exactly what Jon Venables and Robert Thompson were capable of doing, the conscious choices they were capable of making.

Though James was willing enough to go along with the boys at first, the excursion would have quickly stopped being fun for him. Witnesses – believing the toddler to be in the care of his older brothers – reported seeing Venables and Thompson pull and drag James the two and a half miles (4 km) towards the railway line at Walton Lane, sometimes hitting or kicking him for encouragement.

When the boys arrived at the desolate railway yard, the assault began in earnest. In his later post mortem examination, pathologist for the Home Office Dr Alan Williams reported that, by the end of it all, Venables and Thompson had inflicted 42 separate injuries on the little boy, including 22 bruises, splits and grazes to James' face and head and another twenty wounds to the rest of his body.

Using bricks, stones and a 22-pound (10kg) iron bar, Venables and Thompson beat James repeatedly, during which time the child suffered a number of internal and external injuries. They beat his head so severely that they cut his forehead to the bone, fracturing his skull from his jaw across the whole of his head.

They also removed his trousers and underpants, during which time the boy sustained a number of injuries to his legs. While the child was half naked, the boys also performed at least one act of sexually indecency on their victim. When his body was discovered, James' foreskin had been forcibly retracted.[8]

There was also reason to believe that the boys inserted batteries into James' rectum, a detail that the police were unable to prove at the time but would become relevant in years to come.[9]

After kicking and stomping on James' head and body, the boys splashed blue paint in the toddler's eyes and laid him on the train tracks. They covered his body with stones and then left him for the train to kill him as they had done so many times before with rabbits.

Dr Williams' post mortem revealed that little James was still alive when his killers placed him on the tracks but that he had died before a speeding train severed his body in two.[8]

For two days, James body would lie hidden on the tracks, but the alert had already been sounded. Gaynor Davis, who worked at The Photo Expert, recalled being called back to work the night James went missing to see if perhaps he'd been locked inside the shop by mistake.[5]

James' mother described what they were looking for – his Noddy t-shirt, his hair (ready for cutting), his eyes (blue with a brown streak in the right eye), a full set of baby teeth. She mentioned how he loved anything to do with trains.[10]

The day after James' disappearance, one shop manager at The Strand suggested his CCTV camera might have caught an image of the boy. Detective Phil Roberts remembers seeing the footage:

> *It showed James hand in hand with what we thought was a teenager. There was another boy in front – we thought he was about thirteen. That was a surprise, that two youths had apparently taken him. We immediately started combing records of anyone between the ages of twelve and eighteen who might be involved. We brought in several boys but as soon as I started questioning them, I knew they weren't involved.*[11]

Then, on Sunday 14 February, a group of boys came upon what they thought was a broken doll laying shattered on the railway tracks. To their horror, they discovered it was not a doll. Moments later, they rushed down the embankment, screaming what they had found to the Walton Lane Police Station only a few hundred yards away.[5]

'It was as if he had been put into a concrete mixer with two great big heavy cement blocks,' said Detective Roberts. 'The level of trauma was beyond belief. I never saw photos – I didn't want to. That list [of injuries] was enough.'

The authorities thought they must have been dealing with an adult psychopath. Almost no one could believe it when their inquiries began pointing to a pair of ten-year-olds who were always making trouble.

When Detective Roberts first went to question Thompson, he was struck by how small the boy was for his age:

> *I had to get on my knees to address him. I told him why we were there and that he would have to come to the station. He started to cry, but there were no tears. In all the time I spent with him I never ever saw him shed a tear. It was always pretend crying.*[11]

Thompson, in fact, would never show any real remorse. As his solicitor Laurence Lee would later recall, Thompson remained detached throughout the entire ordeal. 'Thompson was the coldest child I've ever seen,' said Lee.[12]

The same could not be said of Venables. At first, he denied having been anywhere near The Strand that day, but when officers compared what he said with the statement Thompson had given, Venables finally burst into tears and wailed, 'OK, we did go to The Strand but I never grabbed a kid.'[12]

While it seems Thompson and Venables had a very clear understanding of the pain they were inflicting on their infant victim, it didn't seem to occur to the boys until long after the fact that there might be consequences for their actions.

One consequence was that they were deemed capable of criminal intent and thus tried as adults, sent to Old Bailey to stand in a special dock purpose built just for them.[5] Much would be made of their later prosecutions. They would be portrayed as two small, scared boys, traumatized by the ordeal of standing trial in an adult court.

But were the boys really capable of understanding what they'd done?

Criminologist Gwyneth Boswell says no. 'What you have to look at really is each individual according to intellectual and emotional maturity,' says Boswell, a professor at the University of East Angelia. 'I don't think children of ten have developed sufficiently to know the difference between right and wrong.'[5]

There is also research to support that children like Robert Thompson who grow up in an abusive environment may experience delays or damage in brain development.[13] The American Psychological Association further says that watching violent movies like Jon Venables did may cause children to become 'less sensitive to the pain and suffering of others' and 'more likely to behave in aggressive or hurtful ways toward others'.[14]

Others disagree. Looking at the extent of the wounds the boys inflicted on little James and the length of time it took for them to execute the crime, many believed that unless they'd had a severe mental disability, there was no way Thompson and Venables couldn't have known that what they were doing was wrong, even at the age of ten.

Albert Kirby, for example, thinks ten is a perfectly appropriate age of criminal responsibility.

'In this country we're streets ahead by having an age of ten. And now there is even stronger evidence to suggest that boys of that age have the ability to become involved in some quite serious sexual perversions,' says Kirby, who was the head of the Merseyside Police Serious Crime Squad at the time of James' murder.

The issue came up for debate a few years after Venables' and Thompson's trial and, as they did in 1993, the government again maintained that ten was an appropriate age:

> We believe that children aged ten and over can differentiate between bad behaviour and serious wrongdoing. We do not intend to raise the age of criminal responsibility. It is not in the interests of justice, of victims, or the young people themselves, to prevent serious offending being challenged.[15]

Perhaps unjustly (and perhaps not), the boys were tried as adults and found guilty. Their minimum sentences of eight years were raised to fifteen the following year when Home Secretary Michael Howard received a petition from James Bulger's family signed by 278,000 people who all believed Venables and Thompson should never be released.

Throughout the trials, the boys' identities had been kept secret. They were called simply Child A and Child B.[10] When they were found guilty in November 1993, however, the judge determined that the boys should be publically identified.[5]

After the trial, Mr Justice Morland said the moral responsibility of children belonged to the parents and that a public debate about the parenting and family background of Thompson and Venables was required:

> In my judgement, the home background, upbringing, family circumstances, parental behaviour and relationships were needed in the public domain so that informed and worthwhile debate

can take place for the public good in the case of grave crimes by young children.[2]

He had a point. If the public had known, for example, that Robert Thompson had once watched his father beat his mother so badly that she'd miscarried, they might have understood what had driven him to act the way he did. How many people knew his mother was usually so drunk by the time he came home from school that she couldn't stand up, much less walk home from the pub?

Both of Jon Venables' siblings went to specialist schools for their learning disabilities, but no one had seemed to notice that Jon needed just as much attention. After his parents separated, he seemed disturbed, throwing tantrums and acting strangely. Said one teacher, 'He would sit back and hold his desk and rock backwards and forwards, moaning and making strange noises.'[6]

Thompson's mother was so absent from his life that, most of the days he appeared in court during the trial, she didn't bother to turn up. Police told members of the press that Susan Venables actively inhibited her son's confession – they were horrified that she was 'constantly repairing her make-up'.[2]

Most of the public, however, either didn't know or didn't seem to care about any of those details. All they remembered were the details of what the boys had done to little James.

Though some felt the boys should have been tried as juveniles, no one believed any good could come of returning Venables and Thompson to their unsatisfactory home environments. As it was, the public hatred for the two boys was so comprehensive many believed there was no way they could ever be truly rehabilitated.

Unable to tell anyone of their true identities, the boys spent the next eight years in secure care, playing video games and lying about who they were. In his case notes, Venables frequently asked if the people of Liverpool still wanted to 'get' him.

While in care, Venables often agonised about the events of the day, recalling how James seemed to have trusted him. It was his hand James held. James even allowed Venables to carry him for a while on the miserable trek to the railway yard, but none of that trust would save the little boy. Venables was haunted by nightmares and how he could not undo what he had done.

The system appears to have served Robert Thompson. Released in 2001, his identity was changed and he was given a new start in life. Though reports vary, he seems to be a very different person today than the troubled little boy he was in 1993.

Though given the same rehabilitation, new identity and opportunities at a new life as Thompson, Jon Venables didn't manage nearly as well. He began drinking soon after his 2001 release and in 2008 he was arrested for fighting outside a nightclub. He didn't cope well on his own, reportedly 'living like a teenager' and barely able to hold down a job.

Then in 2010 he was arrested again, this time for possession and redistribution of child pornography, including images portraying penetrative sex with children as young as seven and eight years old.[9] Whatever good might have come from his being separated from his family at the age of ten was clearly not enough.

CHAPTER FOURTEEN

The House of Horrors

(1994)

By 1994, Britain had come to know some truly terrifying psychopaths – husbands who had murdered their wives, serial killers who had murdered and mutilated dozens of young women, gangsters who had murdered anyone who stood in their way. Even more disturbing were the killers who had abducted little children, torturing and slaughtering them. Some of those killers were only children themselves.

So when police arrived at 25 Cromwell Street on 24 February 1994 with a search warrant, the people of Britain thought they'd seen it all. Then the bones started turning up and, bit by bit, a story unfolded that was almost too horrific to believe.

Like others before them, Fred and Rose West had abducted young women. Like others, they had raped, mutilated and murdered them. They had even tortured and raped children. What set the Wests apart from the criminals who had come before them, however, was that these were not just any children – these children were their own sons and daughters.

Fred Walter Stephen West was born on 29 September 1941 into a poor farming family in Herefordshire's Much Marcle.[1] The eldest of six surviving children, Fred was described as 'a nice boy'. As a neighbor would later recall, there was nothing special about him as a child:

> He was just an ordinary little lad, nothing that would stand out in your mind. He was small with a crop of curly hair and was very like his mother to look at. He was a cheerful lad. He was a bit cheeky, a bit mouthy, but that was the way these kids were. I would say that he was probably naïve and easily led.

On the outside, his family seemed quite normal. His parents were regarded as decent and hard working in their community.[2] According to West, however, there was more going on that the neighbours didn't see.

West would later claim that his father had incestuous relationships with West's sisters, something that was accepted as part of the household, and that his father taught him to engage in bestiality. The one rule was 'don't get caught'.

In November 1958, at the age of seventeen, West was involved in a serious motorcycle accident, a head-on collision[3] with an oncoming car that fractured his skull and broke his arm and his leg.

For eight days, he lay in a coma and when he woke, he was reportedly a different person, now prone to fits of rage and unable to control his emotions. Not long after the accident, he fell from a fire escape at a local club during which he suffered another head injury that caused him to lose consciousness for 48 hours.

The change in West's behaviour after the two accidents suggested he'd sustained serious brain damage, the type that several studies have linked to criminal behaviour. One such study found that twelve out of sixteen death row inmates had a history of similar brain damage.[1]

It wasn't long before West had become a nuisance with the local police with a string of petty crimes. In 1961, things took a turn for the worse when West was accused of impregnating a thirteen-year-old girl. It was to be the first of a long line of accusations.

Now a construction worker, he lost his job when he was caught stealing from his employers and having sex with under aged girls. At the age of twenty, he was convicted of rape, but escaped a jail sentence when he was able to persuade the court he'd acted under the influence of his head injuries. Convicted of the lesser charge of child molestation, he was nonetheless disowned by his family.[4]

In September 1962, West became reacquainted with a former girlfriend, a Scottish prostitute known as Rena Costello, who was pregnant by a Pakistani man at the time.[1] In November 1962, West and Rena married.

'We didn't know Fred was getting married until afterwards ... only [his brother] John knew about the wedding,' said Doug, another of West's siblings. 'That was Fred all over. If he decided to do it he just went ahead and did it. He was a bit secretive. He would go and do things without thinking and that was that.'[2]

Rena's daughter Charmaine was born in March 1963, followed by Rena and West's daughter Anne Marie only sixteen months later in July 1964. Now living in Glasgow, West worked as an ice cream truck driver, a job that gave him access to a number of young girls. It was around this time that West and Rena met Anne McFall.[4]

On 4 November 1965, West was involved in a case of vehicular manslaughter when he accidentally ran over and killed a four-year-old boy with his ice cream truck. Later that year, fearing for his safety in the wake of the accident, Fred took Rena – along with their nanny Isa McNeill and Anne McFall – and moved to Gloucestershire with the children.[1]

The family moved into the Lakeside Caravan Park in Bishop's Cleeve and West took a job in an abattoir. Some researchers later said that while working this job, West developed a fascination with death, mutilation and dismemberment.

It is perhaps no small coincidence, then, that the Gloucestershire area saw eight reported incidents of assault during the time that West lived there, and in every case, the attacker's description matched West's.[4]

At the same time, West's relationship with Rena was becoming more and more unstable, and he was beginning to show sadistic sexual tendencies. To escape him, Rena and Isa returned to Glasgow. Anne McFall, however, had become infatuated with West, so she and the children remained with him. Still married to West, Rena regularly returned to the caravan to visit the children.

When McFall became pregnant with West's child in early 1967, she begged him to divorce Rena and marry her. In August, now eight months pregnant, McFall disappeared, but she was never reported missing.

A month later, Rena returned on a regular visit to see her two children Charmaine and Anne Marie. Finding McFall gone, Rena moved back into the caravan but left again the following year, once more leaving her children in West's care.[1]

Fred West was only half of the equation. The other was the woman who was to become his partner in life and in crime. On 29 November 1968, Rose Letts turned fifteen years old – the same day, she met Fred West. Though West was still married to his estranged wife Rena, it was to be a portentous encounter.[4]

One of Bill and Daisy Letts' seven children, Rosemary Pauline Letts was born in Devon in 1953. Both of Rose's parents were mentally ill and while she was pregnant with Rose, Daisy suffered a mental breakdown for which her doctors prescribed a course of electroconvulsive therapy. Perhaps as a result, Rose exhibited unusual behaviour as an infant:

> [E]veryone commented on how beautiful the new baby was but noticed her strange behaviour. She rocked her head for hours on end and the older children complained as she rhythmically bashed her head against the cot at night. As she got older she continued to swing her head for long periods of time, inducing a trance-like state. At other times her eyes were said to look vacant and lost in her own world.

Though it is unknown what impact Daisy's electroshock therapy may have had on Rose, there is no doubt her father's treatment of her would have had a profound effect. A paranoid schizophrenic, Bill violently abused everyone in the family.

When her father began sexually grooming Rose, she learned that she could use sex as a way to avoid the beatings. By the age of thirteen, she'd begun sexually abusing her two younger brothers and it wasn't long before she was looking for satisfaction beyond the family home.[5] Then, at age fifteen, Rose met Fred West.

What to other girls her age might have seemed sadistic perversion was more like sexual experimentation for Rose. She and West seemed made for each other. Around the same time, Rose's mother left her father. At first, Rose went to live with her mother but she returned to live with her father shortly after she began her relationship with West.

Rose's father was livid and balked against his daughter's relationship with the 27-year-old West, twelve years her senior. He tried to get social services to intervene and even threatened West directly but nothing worked.[4] On her sixteenth birthday, Rose moved in with West and soon fell pregnant. On 17 October 1970, she gave birth to West's daughter Heather. Two months later, West went to prison for theft.[1]

Now living in a flat on Midland Road in Gloucester, Rose was responsible for looking after Rena Costello's half-Pakistani daughter Charmaine, Rena's daughter by West Anne Marie and Rose's newborn Heather. Just a teenager herself, Rose reportedly did not manage the job well. She was given to fits of rage and, according to one source, she would beat the older girls and tie them to the bed at night.[5]

In June 1971, eight-year-old Charmaine went missing while her father was still in prison.[4] Days later, West was released on 24 June.[1] When Charmaine's mother Rena came looking for her, she too went missing. Up to this point, West had been legally married to Rena. With Rena now gone, he was free to marry again and in January 1972, he and Rose were joined in a secret ceremony in Gloucester.

In June 1972, Rose and West had their second child. Now with three children – Anne Marie, Heather and baby Mae – the family moved into 25 Cromwell Street, a home large enough to take in lodgers to help with the rent.

The house would also serve as a brothel. In addition to the extra income from the lodgers, Rose worked as a prostitute.[4] Lodgers who had rented rooms at Cromwell Street would later testify that men and women were always drifting in and out of the house. One said that girls were often brought back to the house and 'shared around'.

Another lodger, Liz Brewer, recalled how Rose had her 'special room' where she spent a lot of time having sex. 'Rose had her boyfriends and Fred his girlfriends,' said Brewer. 'They were quite happy … they seemed to have a bond between them.'

The lodgers also described 'thumps, crashes, wails and shrieks' coming from Rose's special room. They said the noises were the sounds of sexual excitement but not necessarily of pleasure. They didn't know what was going on, they said, only that it happened late at night when male visitors went into the room.[6]

At the time, most of the lodgers weren't bothered by it. The idea that the Wests might have been running a raunchy sex club was not a huge scandal. This was the 70s and for the first time, sex was everywhere. *The Joy of Sex* was sitting on everyone's bookshelf covering topics like 'foursomes and moresomes'. Page three girls had recently hit the newsstands and *Debbie Does Dallas* was showing in the theatres.[7]

It wouldn't be long before Cynthia Payne's famous brothel with the Mirror Room and the Group Sex Room would be making front-page news. The loveable mistress, often pictured in a negligee or dominatrix leathers, was often seen as a sympathetic character rather than a lewd degenerate.[8]

What most of the lodgers of 25 Cromwell Street probably didn't know was that, unlike at Cynthia Payne's brothels, the things that happened in Rose's special room were not happening between consenting adults.

Fred West would later be classified as a sadistic rapist, someone who gains sexual satisfaction through the suffering of his or her victim:

> *These offenders use excessive force, such as bondage, torture, rape with objects, sexual mutilation and, in extreme cases, murder. In addition, they may perform other acts of degradation, such as cutting hair [and] burning with cigarettes … [T]he attacks*

of sadistic rapists are carefully planned and preventative against discovery ...[1]

To this end, West and Rose had fitted out their special room in the basement with a number of implements to use for bondage and torture. The first person to be subjected to this room was eight-year-old Anne Marie, the daughter Fred West had had with Rena Costello (who had by now been missing for several months).

The abuse the little girl suffered was gruesome in the extreme. Bound and gagged, she would lie helpless while her stepmother used a vibrator on her and her father then had intercourse with her. Such was the hold the couple had on the child that she was too afraid to ever repeat a word to anyone – and the abuse would only get worse.[9]

The first person to notice that something seriously wrong was going on with Anne Marie was Caroline Owens. The seventeen-year-old was hitchhiking through Gloucestershire in 1972 when Fred and Rose West picked her up. Caroline thought they seemed nice and soon took a job working for them as a nanny.

It was while she was living at the house at 25 Cromwell Street that she noticed how West would grope his young daughter Anne Marie, often touching her in inappropriate ways. Even more unsettling, however, were the comments he would make to Caroline, as she said in a later interview:

> *He seemed to brag about really strange things, like he told me, 'If you ever get pregnant don't you worry because I can do abortions, I've done them before.' But it wasn't until about a week before I left there that he mentioned Anne Marie, who was eight. He said that she wasn't a virgin, and Anne Marie was in the room at the time and I saw her head go down and then I thought, 'I think maybe there might be some kind of abuse going on.'*

The Wests tried to get Caroline to join in with their sex circle, but by now she was so disturbed by what she had seen that she quit her job and moved out.

Less than a month later, Caroline was out hitchhiking again when the Wests saw her walking along the side of the road. This time, they did not invite her into the car. Instead, they abducted her and knocked her unconscious.

When she awoke, Caroline found herself naked, bound and gagged in the front room of the first floor of the house on Cromwell Street. It was to be the beginning of a horrific ordeal. For twelve hours, the couple sexually and physically abused Caroline, who later said she felt like she was 'about to be operated on' the whole time.

West told her that when they were finished with her, they were going to take her to their basement room where they would let their friends take turns with her. 'When we've finished with you,' West told Caroline, 'we're going to kill you and bury you under the paving stones of Gloucester. There's hundreds of girls there – police haven't found them and they aren't going to find you.'

After hours of torture, the couple agreed to release Caroline if she would return to work for them as a nanny again. Caroline said that she would and they let her go. Instead of returning to them, however, she went straight to the police, who were less helpful than Caroline had expected them to be:

> *The detective that was brought in was not at all compassionate. I felt like he kept saying to me, 'Well you slept with this guy, then you slept with this guy – surely you were up for it. Maybe it got a little bit too rough.' He made me feel like it was all my fault.*[10]

After her experience with the police, who didn't believe her and made her feel responsible for the attack, Caroline was unwilling to undergo being questioned in open court. When the case against Fred and Rose West finally went to trial in January 1973, the charge had been dropped to indecent assault. The couple was found guilty of two offences each and fined £100.[11]

Though it seems unbelievable – considering the terrifying attack against Caroline and the appalling lack of justice thereafter – she was one of the lucky ones. Between 1973 and 1979, a further eight girls went missing including twenty-year-old Lynda Gough in April 1973 and fifteen-year-old Carol Ann Cooper later that year.

Lucy Partington disappeared after spending Christmas with her family in 1973. She was 21, just a little younger than 22-year-old Therese Siegenthaler, who was hitchhiking when she disappeared in 1974. One of the youngest known victims was fifteen-year-old Shirley Hubbard, who also disappeared in 1974.

Juanita Mott and Shirley Robinson were both lodgers at 25 Cromwell Street when they disappeared. The eighteen-year-old Juanita had moved out when she went missing in 1975. Nineteen-year-old Shirley had written to her father that she was in love with Fred West. She was eight months pregnant with his child when she disappeared in 1978. Seventeen-year-old Alison Chambers disappeared in August 1979.[12]

Throughout this time, the Wests continued to have children of their own, a total of eight in all, although it is believed that some of Rose's children were not fathered by Fred West but by clients of the brothel. Many of these children fell victim to their parents' sadism, and it was the abuse of these children that would eventually be the Wests' undoing.[4]

At the age of fifteen, Anne Marie – who had suffered severe abuse for so long – finally left home to live with her boyfriend, having never spoken a word of what went on at 25 Cromwell Street to anyone.[8] With Anne Marie gone, West and Rose turned their attention to the next girls in line, Heather and Mae, both the biological children of the couple.

Heather did not cope with the abuse as well as her older sister had and in June 1987, she told a friend about what had been happening to her. After telling the family secret to her friend, the sixteen-year-old promptly disappeared.[4]

Heather was soon missed, however, and it seemed highly suspicious that her parents had never reported her disappearance. When the police questioned the Wests, Rose said that Heather had left home of her own accord. Rose assured the authorities that she had spoken with her daughter on the phone.[13]

The authorities, not satisfied with Rose's explanation, continued their investigation and in 1992 Detective Constable Hazel Savage led a search of the house that uncovered pornography and clear evidence of child abuse, including that of Anne Marie. There was also enough evidence to pursue the disappearances of both Heather West and Charmaine, Rena Costello's daughter who had disappeared in 1971.

Fred and Rose West were both arrested, Fred for the rape and sodomy of a minor and Rose for assisting with the rape of a minor. Though the case against the Wests began to deteriorate when two key witnesses decided not to testify, all of the West children were taken into protective custody.[4]

While they were in care, the West children made a number of worrisome jokes about their missing sister Heather and how she was 'under the patio'. The jokes were enough to alarm their social workers, who passed on their concerns to the authorities.[14] Police finally obtained a search warrant and on 24 February 1994, they returned to 25 Cromwell Street.

Two days later, the bones began to turn up. Heather West had been decapitated and dismembered, as had Carol Ann Cooper and Lucy Partington. The remains of nine women were eventually discovered buried on the Wests' property, many still gagged, most dismembered, several buried in a circle in the cellar.[13]

Shirley Hubbard, the youngest of the victims at fifteen, must have suffered tremendously in her final hours. When her body was discovered, her head had been completely wrapped in tape with nothing more than a rubber tube inserted through the seal and into her mouth to allow her to breath.[10]

On 25 April 1994, the search extended from the house on Cromwell Street to the ground floor flat on Midland Road in Gloucester where the Wests had lived previously. There, authorities discovered bones and a skull experts later identified as belonging to Charmaine who had died at the age of eight in 1971.[13]

Nearly two months later, in June 1994, the body of Anne McFall was discovered buried near Lakeside Caravan Park in Bishop's Cleeve where she had lived with Fred West almost thirty years before. The remains of her eight-month-old foetus lay beside her.[1] In the same area, authorities found the body of Rena Costello. The fingers and toes of McFall, little Charmaine and Rena had all been removed.

With an overwhelming amount of evidence stacked against him, Fred West was taken into custody at Winson Green Prison in Birmingham on 13 December 1994 charged with twelve counts of murder. Within a month, he'd hung himself with a bed sheet to avoid answering for his crimes.

Throughout the investigation, Rose West denied all knowledge of the murders and, prior to his suicide, Fred West absolved her.[4] It would slowly be revealed however, that Rose had been every bit as involved as her husband had been.

The testimony of Anne Marie West was especially damning. Rose, apparently, was not the only prostitute working at the Cromwell Street brothel. The girl told the court how she had been raped not only by her parents but also by numerous clients who had come to the brothel. These clients included her own uncle, Fred's brother John West, who had raped her more than 300 times. John later committed suicide while awaiting trial.[8]

Despite her claims of innocence, Rose gave herself away during her trial when it was established that she murdered West's stepdaughter Charmaine while he was still in prison. The couple then mutilated and moved the girl's body together after his release.

Once she'd let slip the information that would mark her as Charmaine's killer, the house of cards Rose had built around herself came tumbling down. On 22 November 1995, Rose West was found guilty of ten separate counts of murder for which she received a life sentence, which was then extended to a whole life sentence.[4]

Though the pair were held accountable for twelve murders between them, it remains widely believed that they were responsible for the abuse and deaths of a far greater number.

Through it all, it seems Rose's second daughter Mae may have said it best in a 2011 interview: 'I just don't know why Mum bothered having us. Why would you subject more and more children to that?'[14]

Truly, no one will ever know.

CHAPTER FIFTEEN

The Dunblane Massacre

(1996)

Prior to 13 March 1996, there had been a lot of warning signs that something was seriously wrong in the mind of Thomas Hamilton. Though the authorities were aware that they were dealing with a dangerous man, they were powerless to detain him within the confines of the law – until he walked into a primary school one quiet Wednesday morning and opened fire.

The massacre at Dunblane remains one of the deadliest attacks to target children in history. Since Dunblane, only three primary school shootings – Beslan in Russia 2004, Sandy Hook in the USA 2012 and Peshawar in Pakistan 2014 – have resulted in more deaths. The events of that fateful day in Scotland, however, would prompt legislation that would lead to a safer Britain.

The quaint little town of Dunblane, situated a short distance north of Stirling, is believed to have been founded in 602 AD by St Blane, a Celtic missionary. Centred around Dunblane Cathedral, a magnificent Gothic edifice dating back to the 13th century, the village is also home to Leighton Library, the oldest private library in Scotland.[1]

On the morning of 13 March 1996, children made their way to school as usual. The third term was in full swing and the students were looking forward to the Easter holiday less than a month away.

After settling her 29 students and calling the role, 44-year-old Gwenne Mayor took her P1 class to the gymnasium. Wiggly and excitable, the P1 children were all either five or six years old. While the children were listening to the instructions of their PE teacher Eileen Harrild, Thomas Hamilton was walking steadily towards them.[2]

Many people who knew the chubby, nondescript 43-year-old thought he was a little strange and more than a little creepy. Born 10 May 1952 and abandoned by his father at birth, Hamilton was raised by his grandparents, believing his birth mother to be his sister.[3]

There is no indication that Hamilton was mistreated when he was young. As a child, he did well in school, and as a teenager, he joined a rifle club and the Boys Brigade. By the age of twenty, he'd risen to the rank of assistant leader of his local Boy Scouts club.[4]

It's obvious that Hamilton valued his work with the Boy Scouts because he was quite devastated when he was dismissed from his position as assistant leader after only one year.

The reason for the dismissal was fairly obvious. In 1973, Hamilton took a group of eight boys on a camping trip to Aviemore in the Highlands. He'd told parents that the children would be staying in a hostel but nothing had been booked. Instead, the boys spent a miserable night sleeping in the back of a freezing cold van. On a second trip, the boys were made to dig holes in the snow.

The parents of the boys complained to Comrie Deuchars, who was responsible for organising the Scouts in Stirling at the time. Though Hamilton would later claim he'd been wrongly dismissed for sexual misconduct, Deuchars always insisted that he'd quietly told Hamilton to leave the Boy Scouts on the grounds that Hamilton was an incompetent leader.[3]

The following year, at the age of 22, Hamilton learned that the woman he'd always thought was his sister was actually his mother. In his book *Understanding Dunblane and Other Massacres*, police officer and forensic psychotherapist Peter Aylward argues that, for Thomas Hamilton, learning the truth about his family situation had a profound impact on him.

According to Aylward, Hamilton felt as though his family had been taken away from him. At the same time, Hamilton had also formed a sort of surrogate family with the children he'd come to know through the Boy Scouts. The loss of both families (in his mind) combined with a possible gene disorder to create the turning point for Hamilton that may have ultimately caused him to kill.

To compensate for the intense loss he felt, Hamilton tried to build another family by organising boys' clubs. The purpose of the clubs, Hamilton said, was to give boys something to do and keep them off the streets. Kids could do with a little exercise and discipline, he believed.[5]

Aimed at boys aged between the ages of seven and eleven, the clubs met at gymnasiums in local schools or halls, sometimes at community sporting grounds, where Hamilton ran a programme of gymnastics, sports skills and fitness.

At the clubs, Hamilton's nickname Mr Creepy was, it seems, well earned. The boys said he would discipline them or make them do things that made them feel uncomfortable then give them presents to keep them quiet.[6]

Parents often worried about what went on at the boys' clubs, as outlined in the 1996 Cullen Enquiry:

> *Parents were particularly concerned about Thomas Hamilton's insistence that for gymnastics the boys wore black (and ill fitting) swimming trunks which he provided and that they changed into them in the gym rather than in the changing rooms ... Another matter which was of concern to parents was his practice of taking photographs of the boys posing in their black trunks ... [The parents'] overriding impression was that there was something unnatural. The boys did not seem to be enjoying themselves but appeared silent and even frightened.*[5]

Despite these criticisms, Hamilton was also very good at gleaning support. One mother, Penny King, had heard rumours about Hamilton, but when she went to speak to him, she found him very reassuring. 'He told me that people had been talking behind his back for years,' she said. 'He left me feeling ashamed for believing tosh. My son was happy playing with his friends and in the end I did not see why I should stop him.'[3]

During another incident in the early 1980s, Hamilton was threatened with losing the use of the hall at Dunblane High School. He rallied the troops and managed to obtain 30 letters of support from parents who were pleased with the work he was doing.

He also secured 70 signatures on a petition of support which included this favourable epitaph: '[W]e are all proud to have Mr Hamilton in charge of our boys: he has a most activated, excellent quality of leadership and integrity and is absolutely devoted to his lads: above all he cares.'[5]

It wasn't just parents who felt Hamilton was sometimes the victim of gossip and unsubstantiated rumour. Hamilton also found support from gun shop owners and gun club managers, councillors, policemen who had granted his gun certificates and the local government ombudsman for Scotland.

Though he was never convicted of sexual misconduct, as time went on, more and more red flags seemed to be going up around Hamilton.

For one, he was a loner who had never married and didn't have any close friends. He wasn't close to any of his family and he seemed to have a way of rubbing people the wrong way. If kids thought he was creepy, adults thought he was weird and called him 'Spock' behind his back.

But it was more than what one acquaintance called his 'oily' manner. George Robertson, the Shadow Secretary of State for Scotland at the time, took his son Malcolm out of Hamilton's boys' club when he saw a session for himself:

> *There were lots of little boys there all stripped to the waist and Tom Hamilton and his cohorts all swaggering around. It was like something out of the Hitler Youth. I took Malcolm away.*

Though most parents could point to nothing more specific than a gut instinct, the recollections of Colin Louden, who once attended the boys' clubs, lends those instincts a bit more credibility:

> *There were some boys [Hamilton] was very familiar with, his favourites if you like who we would call 'teacher's pet'. They would go off on camps with him and seemed to be sworn to secrecy when they got back.*[3]

At these camps, the boys were not allowed to contact their parents. One camp on Inchmoan Island didn't even have a telephone.[5]

According the National Society for the Prevention of Cruelty to Children, kids are more likely to be sexually abused by someone they know, especially someone in a position of trust, and these predators will go to great lengths to coerce their victims into keeping the abuse a secret.[7] If Hamilton encouraged his boys to keep secrets, that would be highly suspicious in itself.

Of particular concern were the activities that happened at Lake Lomond. One mother was so troubled that she compiled an entire file of information, which she took to police. Though the authorities did not reveal their investigation, there was evidently cause for further scrutiny.

Even more suspicious were the photos and videos Hamilton took of the boys, which he obtained without the knowledge or permission of the children's parents. Though he openly admitted to taking the photos and videos, many people felt the images were inappropriate, not the least of which were the photography shops in Stirling charged with developing the film.

By the early 1990s, in fact, these shops began to refuse to develop Hamilton's photos, saying the images were 'obscene'. The police said that the images were not obscene enough for them to prosecute, but Hamilton was now on their radar.

In 1992, Hamilton was banned from Fife Council surrounding concerns over films he had made of young boys. In 1993, Hamilton was the subject of two more police inquiries, and Central Regional Council warned

CRIMES THAT SHOCKED BRITAIN

teachers to contact its legal department before dealing with Hamilton. The following year, Hamilton was caught behaving indecently with a young man in Edinburgh – he was cautioned by police and sent on his way.[3]

Hamilton, of course, continued to deny all allegations against him, but as time went by he found less and less support in the community. By September 1995, the popularity of his boys' clubs had gone down dramatically.

In response, Hamilton sent several circular letters to the parents of Dunblane accusing the Scouts of spreading false rumours about him having been dismissed under sinister circumstances. In the letters, he claimed he had left the Scouts (over twenty years previously) of his own accord.

Then, on 26 January 1996, Hamilton sent another letter to a councillor and copied it to all local schools, pointing an eerie finger at the community of Dunblane:

> [A]t Dunblane Primary School, teachers have contaminated all the older boys with this poison ... that I am a pervert ... that has led to losses of attendance at my club, my public standing and capacity to earn a living ... [These rumours have resulted] in a death blow to my difficult work with children as well as my standing in the community.[5]

Hamilton's behaviour was becoming increasingly worrisome, but then police had been worried about the odd loner for a long time.

On 11 November 1991, Detective Sergeant Paul Hughes submitted a report asking that the department seriously consider withdrawing Hamilton's firearms certificate. Hughes believed Hamilton to be 'a scheming, devious and deceitful individual who is not to be trusted'.

Hughes had been prompted to write the report when he discovered Hamilton owned a 9mm Browning pistol and a .357 Smith and Wesson revolver. Hamilton also had permission to acquire a .22 rifle and a deadly 7.62 rifle. This, to Hughes, seemed a disquieting amount of hardware for a man with an unstable personality and an unhealthy interest in young boys.

Hughes' report went to Detective Superintendent Joseph Holden, who attached a note to the report: 'Sir, it is a difficult situation. I would agree with Mr Hughes' appraisal of Hamilton. Do we have any latitude for progress on respect of revocation of his certificate?'

Holden passed on the report to his superior, Detective Superintendent John Miller, who argued against revoking Hamilton's firearms certificate. Hamilton had no criminal convictions, Miller pointed out, and it seemed likely the fiscal at Stirling was going to reject charges against Hamilton in connection with one of his summer camps for boys.

With this information, on 18 November 1991, Deputy Chief Constable Douglas McMurdo stamped the report 'No Action' and in 1992, Hamilton's firearms certificate was renewed without any hesitation.[8]

In the months leading up to 13 March 1996, however, the people who knew Hamilton knew better than to trust him. One gun club refused to let Hamilton join. Two members knew him and said the club should have nothing to do with him.[3]

Hamilton himself sent a fairly direct notice of his intentions six days prior to his attack on Dunblane Primary School – a fourteen-page collection of letters and circulars dating as far back as March 1992 addressed to the Queen, his MP, a local councillor, the Assistant Scout Commissioner for Stirling, local head teachers and parents.

In one letter to the Queen, he complained of the damaging rumours the Scouts had spread about him and how the Scouts were jealous of all he'd accomplished with his boys' clubs. In his letter to Secretary of State Michael Forsyth, he cited the murder of James Bulger as an example of why his boys' clubs were so important.

The letters, also addressed to BBC Scotland and *The Scotsman*, painted him as the victim of a 'sinister witch hunt', entirely unwarranted.[3] Hamilton wrote, 'I turn to you as a last resort and am appealing for some kind of intervention in the hope that I may be able to regain my self-esteem in society.' With the benefit of hindsight, his warning is glaringly obvious.

On the morning of 13 March 1996, Hamilton could be described as 'a loner, unmarried, living in a ground floor council flat, unemployed, on benefits, with significant debts.' Though frequently questioned by police, he had never been arrested. He didn't drink, he didn't smoke and as far as anyone can tell, he had never done drugs.[9]

Whatever else was going on in his mind, he felt himself the victim of an enormous amount of persecution and today, the town of Dunblane was going to pay.

As the children of Mrs Mayor's P1 class were getting into their PE lesson, Hamilton walked through the school gates, into the corridors and towards the gym. At some point, he put on the noise-cancelling ear protectors he'd brought with him – he'd probably worn them before in the gun club gallery.[2]

At 9.30am, he burst into the gym, his arm outstretched with his gun in his hand, and started shooting almost immediately.

His first victims were the adults. Hamilton shot PE teacher Eileen Harrild in the chest. When she put up her arms to shield herself, he shot her another three times in the arms and hand. 'He walked straight towards me,' she wrote in a later statement. 'He did not pause or speak, he just continued walking straight towards me, looking at me. He pointed his gun at me and shot me.'[11]

Next, Hamilton shot Harrild's advisory assistant Mary Blake in both of her legs and her head.[10]

Gwenne Mayor stood over her students, trying to shield them.[2] The mother of two was shot in the head six times, including through her right eye. She died almost instantly.

With the adults dispatched, Hamilton turned his attention to the children.

Later in the day, eleven-year-old Dunblane student Steven Hopper described what happened out outside his classroom:

> *I looked over and saw the gunman. He seemed to come out of the gymnasium and he was just firing at something. He was coming towards me, so I just dived under my desk when he turned and fired at us. The firing was very fast, like someone hitting a hammer quickly. Then there was a few seconds of a pause and he started again.*[12]

Within moments of Hamilton's entrance into the gym, everyone in the school was aware of what was happening. Teachers took measures to keep their students safe, instructing the children (including future tennis star Andy Murray) to hide under their desks and keep quiet to avoid attracting the gunman's attention.

Police praised head teacher Ronald Taylor – who reportedly contacted emergency services moments after the shooting began – for his quick thinking and steady hand in helping to keep the 700 students of Dunblane Primary calm.[12]

Shortly after 9.35am, Hamilton left the gym. He shot out several windows, then put the barrel of one of his automatic weapons in his mouth and pulled the trigger.

Later that morning, an ambulance paramedic found Hamilton's body. A veteran of the Lockerbie bombing, the paramedic was no stranger to catastrophe, but the sight of the dead killer filled him with rage:

> *I saw the gunman lying there and a handgun by his side. For the first time in my life I had this overwhelming desire to mutilate that corpse – I know that sounds terrible. I had to really force myself not to kick him as I walked by.*[2]

Paramedics found fifteen children and one teacher dead on the scene, another twelve students and two teachers seriously injured. One of the injured children would later die in hospital, bringing the total to sixteen dead. With one exception, all of the children were only five years old; the other was six.

Senior consultant paediatrician Jack Beattie, who arrived with the medical team, said it was the worst carnage he had witnessed in his nineteen years as a doctor:

> *We saw a large number of dead and injured children when we arrived in the gymnasium. They were distributed within the room in various positions, the dead with the injured … The children were very quiet. They were in shock both because of the injuries and because of the psychological shock.*[12]

Authorities later determined Hamilton arrived at the school with two semi-automatic pistols and two Smith and Wesson revolvers, with 743 rounds of ammunition. They believed he went directly to the gymnasium hoping to disrupt the morning assembly (at which the entire student body of the school would have been in attendance) but was held up by traffic.[10] Had he carried out his plan as he'd intended, the final outcome could have been significantly worse.

In the days following the massacre, messages of condolence, cards and flowers poured into Dunblane from around Britain and the world. Two days after the incident, political rivals John Mayor and Tony Blair visited Dunblane side by side, together pledging the money to demolish and rebuild the gymnasium where the children of P1 and their teacher were killed.

Later that night, mourners of all faiths put aside their religious differences to come together for prayers and a vigil at Dunblane's ancient cathedral. Eight clergymen representing Dunblane's five major religions were in attendance. The following Sunday, the Queen and her daughter Princess Anne attended a memorial service honouring the victims on the occasion of Mothering Sunday.[10]

Despite the enormity of the tragedy, some good would come of it. Within a year and a half, Parliament had banned the private ownership of all handguns in mainland Britain, giving the country some of the toughest anti-gun laws in the world.

Before the ban, there had been around 200,000 legally registered handguns in Britain – Hamilton had owned all of his guns legally – but the new tougher laws resulted in the surrender of thousands of firearms and rounds of ammunition.

Gill Marshall of the Gun Control Network told CNN that the massacre at Dunblane was a leading factor in the ban. 'It was one of the most shocking things that has ever happened in this country,' Marshall said, 'and it united the country in a feeling that we had to do something.'[13]

Though the new legislation has undoubtedly saved countless lives, it came too late for Victoria Clydesdale, who loved gym class and begged to go to school that fateful day even though she had a rash. It came too late for the lively, charming Emma Crozier who was baptized – and buried – alongside her best friend Joanna Ross, with her sweet blonde fringe and big blue eyes.

Melissa Currie, who had just moved to Dunblane from Braemar, will never get a chance to grow up, nor will her best friend Charlotte Dunn, also newly arrived from the West Midlands. The two had a joint memorial service. Kevin Hasell, with his soft little chin and dimples, will always be five years old. So will the apple-cheeked Ross Irvine with his gorgeous smile.

David Kerr loved to run and play. His fun loving spirit shined in his eyes. His headstone reads, 'May he run, skip and play forever.' Mhairi McBeath was a stunning little girl. She had just lost her father to a stroke. Best friends Brett McKinnon and John Petrie loved nothing more than riding their bikes together.

Abigail McLennan had just returned with her family to Scotland from living in the Far East. Her long straight blonde hair was the polar opposite of Emily Morton and her mop of dark curls. Sweet little Sophie North was only two when her mother died of breast cancer. She had become very close to her father, who set up a memorial fund in her honour.

Hannah Scott, with her infectious smile, was deeply loved by her parents, as was Megan Turner, who was always running and jumping. As her mother said, 'Megan stood on her head more than she stood on her feet!'

For all the young lives that were lost that day, one life that must be remembered is that of Gwenne Mayor. When emergency services arrived, it was evident that she had died trying to shield her students. In 1997, she received the Queen's Commendation for Bravery in the Birthday Honours.

Said her mother-in-law, 'Gwenne's life was rich and she enriched the lives of all who knew her. Her final act was a positive, caring one for the young children who were placed in her charge.'[1]

CHAPTER SIXTEEN

The Soham Murders

(2002)

You would have been hard pressed to find two girls sweeter than Holly Wells and Jessica Chapman.

Affectionate and creative, Holly was every bit the golden girl who worked hard and had lots of friends. The talented little blonde loved to sing and dance and would spend hours making cards and keepsakes for her friends and teachers – before the school year ended, she had made a 'thank you for teaching me' card for her form teacher, Ms Pederson. She'd also performed as a majorette and played the cornet.

Holly's best friend was the cheeky dark haired Jessica, a loveable tomboy in her football kit and ponytail. She played for the Under-11 Soham Town Rangers, following in the footsteps of her idol David Beckham.[1] She had been on the winning Junior Superstars team the previous year and was looking forward to defending the title.[2]

The two girls were just as clever as they were likeable, and Ms Pederson had planned to recommend them as house captains for the following school year:

They were bright girls, slightly above the average of what you would expect of a Year Five pupil. They got on well with the other pupils. You could give them messages and know that they would be passed on. They were very conscientious. They always treated their schoolwork seriously.[3]

There's little surprise that the girls were well mannered and personable. They came from loving families who treasured their daughters. Holly lived with her two parents and her older brother on a quiet street in the sleepy middle England town of Soham.

Though not extravagantly wealthy, she and her family were well off and she had few worries. The same could be said for Jessica, who lived with both of her parents and her two teenaged sisters not far from Holly near a beautiful pond.[1] Both of the girls' families were involved in their daughters' educations and were supportive of their school, St Andrew's Primary.

Though they were only ten years old, the girls were both competent and capable. Their teacher described them as 'mature in a sensible way'. They had taken self-awareness classes that included lessons on sex education, the dangers of drug abuse and risks in school and elsewhere.[3]

All in all, the girls were living what might be called charmed lives in their comfortable homes and secure community – until Sunday 4 August 1994 when their young lives were shattered.

It was nearing the end of the summer holidays and the girls had enjoyed another fun weekend. On Saturday night, another of Holly's friends, a girl named Natalie Parr, had come round for a sleepover. Holly and Natalie had gone shopping for sweets on Saturday afternoon, then stayed up late that night as little girls do, snacking and giggling. Sunday morning saw them lying in, listening to Holly's favourite band S Club Juniors.[1]

Around midday, Natalie returned home and the Wells prepared for yet another weekend barbeque. Holly was excited because Jessica was coming over. Jessica had just returned home the night before from a two-week holiday in Menorca.

When Jessica arrived at the Wells' home, she presented Holly with a present – a necklace she'd bought for her best friend, exactly the same as one she'd bought for herself.

When Holly's mother Nicola suggested taking a picture, Holly insisted the girls wear matching outfits. Jessica was wearing her beloved Manchester United jersey with Beckham's number seven on the back, so Holly grabbed her brother's Man U jersey (exactly the same as Jessica's) and put it on just in time for her mother to click the camera. The photo was time stamped exactly 5.04pm.[2]

Within days, the photo of the two girls – standing arm in arm, side by side, wearing their matching red football jerseys and their matching necklaces – would become grimly famous.

There were several people at the Wells' house that afternoon enjoying the barbeque, and Holly's parents were distracted. At the end of the evening when the guests were leaving, Nicola called for the girls:

> *We shouted, 'Come and say good bye' and there was nobody there. I shouted several times and then popped up just to check they could hear me. They weren't there. I just thought perhaps they had popped outside, but as we stood with our friends they weren't anywhere to be seen. At a quarter to nine, I phoned Jessica's mum and asked if they were around there, which they weren't.[4]*

Nicola found Holly's mobile upstairs. Jessica's mobile had been switched off. Though it made no sense, the girls were simply gone. It just wasn't like them, so at 9.55pm, the Wellses phoned the police and reported the girls missing.[5]

The police began where the girls had last been seen – in Holly's bedroom on her computer. At 5.11pm, the girls had switched on the computer and accessed the Internet for 24 minutes. The police would not say if they had been in a chat room or online with someone else but they were smart girls, after all, and would have known all about Internet safety.

Then again, they had been told to never leave the house without telling someone, and evidence would soon prove that they had blatantly broken that rule.

At 6.17pm, less than an hour after the girls logged off the computer, a CCTV camera captured the image of two girls walking across the car park of Ross Peers Sports Centre. The girls' parents would later confirm it was definitely Holly and Jessica. In the footage, the girls looked happy and carefree. Someone suggested the girls might have gone looking for sweets like Holly had done with her other friend Natalie the previous afternoon.

Whatever the reason, the girls had changed out of their shorts and into long pants then left the house without permission and without telling anyone, all of which was completely out of character for them. The last known sighting of the girls was at 7.20pm when a woman who knew them both well saw them in the High Street.[6]

At first, the Wellses and Chapmans held their breath, hoping that the girls had just wandered off on a lark. Throughout that long night, the two families prayed Jessica and Holly would come home any moment, but with every tick of the clock, that hope became more distant.

As hours turned into days, it became more and more clear that something had happened to the girls, and people turned out in droves to search. Hundreds of volunteers stood alongside the girls' friends and families to help the authorities comb the wetlands, marshes and rivers of the Soham area. No trace of the girls turned up.

It wasn't long before authorities were forced to admit what no one had wanted to believe. By the middle of the week, Detective Superintendent David Hankin, who was leading the inquiry, said, 'From the outset we thought this might be a prank or an accident, but now sadly we have to seriously consider abduction.'[2]

Clinging to the hope that the girls were still alive and being held captive, the police and their families made a number of appeals to their captors to return the girls. Even David Beckham went on national television to make a plea on behalf of the little girl who had loved him so much.[7]

The search would be confounded by several well-meaning reports of sightings that would later prove to be false. One vital clip of CCTV footage previously thought to have placed the girls on the outskirts of town wasn't dismissed until almost a week after the girls had gone missing.[2]

Believing the girls to have been abducted, the police began a massive house-to-house search of the little village. One of their first stops was the home of Ian Huntley, the caretaker at the local college. He'd been spotted in some of the CCTV footage chatting with the girls, who'd asked about his girlfriend Maxine Carr.[5]

Maxine, in fact, knew the girls quite well. She had been Ms Pederson's teaching assistant in previous school years, and she had become friendly with a group of children that included both Holly and Jessica. Ms Pederson thought Maxine was a little too close to the students and that her assistant's behaviour in class was sometimes 'inappropriate'.[3]

When police first went to 5 College Close where Maxine lived with her boyfriend, Huntley told the authorities that he'd seen the girls at 6.00pm. The officers on the scene quickly checked his house and, finding nothing suspicious, moved on.

Detective Chief Superintendent Chris Stevenson would come under fire for the officers' failure to notice what some considered to be obvious clues, but in reality, the officers couldn't have known how close they had come to solving the case. There were so many sightings, Stevenson's men just couldn't follow up on every one, as he later explained:

> *There were loads of people who could have been the last ones to see them alive. What do I do? I mean, a member of the public is driving down the road and they see two girls and they report it. Do I seize his car and forensically search [it] because he might be the one?*[5]

In fact, the police put in a colossal effort. More than 250 detectives worked 24-hour days using special equipment to search hedgerows, dykes, drains, rivers and sewers. Garbage collections were cancelled so officers could sift through the refuse for any clues. When every one of the 3000 homes of the Soham area had been visited, the search was extended to outlying areas.[6]

At the same time, police began investigating more than 300 known paedophiles in Cambridgeshire and Suffolk. By the second week of the investigation, the most likely explanation was that the girls had gone in a car with someone they knew. Working on that supposition, the police began working their way north and east following leads based on possible sightings of the girls, looking for male child sex offenders.[5]

A major breakthrough in the case finally came on Thursday, 15 August. The girls had been missing for eleven days and the police had so far come up with nothing when telephone technician David Bristowe provided a vital piece of information that would narrow the search area to a pinpoint.

Bristowe was an expert on triangulation. According to Bristowe, Jessica's mobile phone 'disengaged itself from the network' at 6.46 the night the girls went missing. Using signal data from surrounding transmission masts, he was able to determine where Jessica's mobile phone had been switched off – in a hot spot generated from 5 College Close.[8]

At first, the authorities were not convinced. Ian Huntley had no prior convictions, and his partner Maxine Carr was friendly with the girls. He'd even joined in the search for the girls and had approached Holly's father to offer words of sympathy.

Over and over, he'd told police and journalists how the girls had come by his house 'happy' and 'giggly' and then walked away again.[9] The authorities would soon learn, however, that the mild mannered school caretaker was not what he appeared to be.

Ian Kevin Huntley was born on 31 January 1974 near the coastal town of Grimsby. His early childhood was fairly uneventful, but a change of secondary schools and a chronic case of asthma saw Huntley bullied by the other kids.

Things got worse for Huntley at the age of thirteen when he discovered his father's infidelity with the family babysitter. Huntley' relationship with his father – which up to that point had been loving and supportive – deteriorated quickly.

Huntley's parents separated for a short time, but their eventual reconciliation was not enough to repair the damage done. Following the affair, Huntley's father began drinking heavily and violently abusing his teenaged son Ian who in turn began bullying other kids around him.

At the age of sixteen, Huntley left school. Working only basic factory jobs, he suffered from depression and drank heavily. He blamed all of his problems on the state of his parents' marriage and soon earned a reputation for lying to try to impress people. He loved to say he'd been a RAF pilot or a store manager.

In reality, he was growing more and more unstable. On a number of occasions, he attempted suicide, twice in June 1994. Five months later he met Claire Evans, a seventeen-year-old Grimsby girl with whom he got very serious very quickly. A month later they were married at the registry office in a romance so hushed her family didn't even know about it. Within days, however, she'd left him.

The tipping point came for Huntley when, in the wake of his failed marriage, his younger brother Wayne stepped in and took his place. Devastated by the betrayal, Huntley flew into a rage, swearing he was going to 'kick his brother's head in'.

Mid-1995 saw Huntley in trouble with the authorities when the parents of a fifteen-year-old girl contacted social services and reported him for sleeping with their daughter. Preying on under aged girls was to become a habit with Huntley, many of them fourteen and fifteen years old.

Over the next few years, nine complaints were brought against Huntley for having sex with under aged girls, but despite investigations by Humberside police, Huntley managed to escape conviction every time.

As time went by, however, Huntley's behaviour became more serious as the allegations turned to that of rape. Between the spring of 1998 and the summer of 1999, he was accused of the offence four times. Only once was he charged and that case collapsed.

In July 1999, Huntley finally granted his ex-wife Claire a divorce and she and his brother Wayne were immediately married. By now, however, many people in Grimsby had begun to see through Huntley's slick veneer, calling him a paedophile. He'd had his flat attacked, his windows smashed and his front door broken down.[5]

It was during this time that Huntley met 22-year-old Maxine Carr. Together, the two moved to Soham in 2001 where Maxine took a job as a teaching assistant at St Andrew's Primary School. Because he'd never been convicted of sexual misconduct, Huntley had no criminal record, so despite his long history of sex with under aged girls and allegations of rape, he was awarded a position as caretaker at Soham Village College.[10]

Around the same time David Bristowe was working out the triangulation of Jessica's mobile phone, Amanda Marshall was watching the national news in Grimsby. When the mother of two saw Ian Huntley giving an interview with news reporters, she picked up the phone. 'The man I have just seen on the television has been in court for rape,' she told the authorities in Soham.

After sending officers to confirm the allegations against Huntley, Detective Stevenson found himself in a delicate position:

> *It was extremely borderline. The determining factor was the possibility, albeit remote, that Huntley had got Jessica and Holly secured somewhere. If I arrested him and spent three days questioning him, I effectively would have been signing their death warrant.*

Now, however, more and more evidence was pointing to Huntley as the killer. When asked where she'd been the night of the disappearance, Carr said she'd been upstairs in the bath, giving Huntley a tidy alibi, but after seeing her on television, several people called to say they'd seen her out in Grimsby on the night in question.

The couple were taken in for questioning to two separate locations in Ely, a city near Soham. By now well versed at lying, Huntley stuck to his story – he had been brushing his dog outside when the girls walked by and Carr had been in the bath upstairs. At a station across town, Carr told the same story.

While officers questioned Huntley and Carr, police began a thorough forensic search of Huntley and Carr's house. It had now been two weeks since the girls had disappeared, however, which had given Huntley and Carr plenty of time to disinfect the house. Within that time, Huntley had also scrubbed his car inside and out and replaced his tyres.

What police did find, however, were the keys to a storage hangar at Soham Village College. At 11.30pm on 16 August, a sergeant discovered the burned remains of Holly and Jessica's clothes in the garbage bins at the storage hangar where Huntley worked. The following morning, at 4.20am Huntley and Carr were both arrested under suspicion for murder.[5]

Only hours later, at 12.15pm on 17 August 2002, a gamekeeper and his girlfriend were out walking in Thetford Forest Park near Lakenheath United States Air Base near Mildenhall in Suffolk when they noticed a foul odour. The bodies of Jessica Chapman and Holly Wells – naked, burned and badly decomposed – were soon discovered in an overgrown ditch.[11]

In the months following the discovery of the girls, Huntley would admit to nothing. Despite Huntley's efforts to sanitise his house and car, police experts would uncover an overwhelming amount of forensic evidence linking him to the girls' deaths.

Huntley's hairs, for example, were found mixed in amongst the girls' burned clothing. Fibres from Huntley's carpet were found on Holly's shirt. Chalk from the area where the girls' bodies had been found was discovered on the underside of Huntley's car. Hundreds of pieces of evidence would link him to the crime.

Maxine Carr immediately sought to distance herself from the entire affair. While Huntley awaited trial, she admitted to police that she had lied. She had actually been in Grimsby, she said, with a rugby player she'd been seeing on the side on the night the girls had died.[12]

She claimed that she'd lied to the police because she felt sorry for Huntley. She said he'd been wrongly accused in the past and it had caused him to have a nervous breakdown. When she learned he'd been the last person to see Jessica and Holly alive, she didn't want to put him through the anguish of being wrongly accused again.

Though Carr would break all contact with Huntley within weeks of her incarceration, phone calls Carr made from Holloway Prison hours after the couple's arrests would record her telling Huntley's mother how she had discussed lying with him the day after the girls' disappearance. It would quickly come to light that she had known within hours what he had done and had helped him cover up his crime from the outset.[13]

But what, exactly, had he done? That question remains unanswered. It wasn't until he took the stand on the twentieth day of his trial that Huntley deigned to tell his version of the events. According to Huntley, he was outside cleaning his dog Sadie when Jessica and Holly came walking by his house. As he was chatting with the girls, Holly had a nosebleed – Holly had a history of nosebleeds, a fact of which Maxine Carr was likely aware.

Huntley explained how he took the girls upstairs into the bathroom so he could help Holly staunch the flow of blood. While she was sitting on the edge of the bathtub, Huntley said he accidentally bumped her and she fell backwards into the tub, which had been filled so that Huntley could wash the dog.

When Holly fell into the water, Jessica started screaming 'you pushed her', at which point Huntley panicked and put his hand over her mouth to silence her. Huntley said that while he was accidentally suffocating Jessica, Holly was accidentally drowning in the bathtub.

The rest – taking Jessica's mobile out of her pocket (so that her body could not be traced back to it), cramming the girls' bodies into the boot of his car, dumping them into the ditch, cutting off their clothes and setting the clothes on fire – were all the acts of a desperate man who feared he would once again be misunderstood.[9]

The court was not convinced. While there was no denying the girls had died at 5 College Court, Dr Nathaniel Cary, senior pathologist for the Home Office, said that Huntley's explanation of how the girls had died was 'implausible, unlikely and contrary to common sense'.

If Holly had fallen into the bath by accident, Cary reasoned, it would have taken Huntley no more than a moment to rescue her. Also, Jessica's death was unlikely to have been a momentary lapse of judgment:

> [Jessica] was a fit, conscious young girl. In my view the only way in which she could have been smothered to death would have been through forced restraint against vigorous struggling.[14]

Though Cary admitted the bodies were too badly decomposed to positively determine the cause of death, he said it was most likely that the girls had been asphyxiated.[13] He was unable to determine whether or not the girls had been sexually assaulted, but he said he could not rule it out.[14]

The prosecution believed that what happened at Ian Huntley's house was no accident. 'These were not two little babies,' said QC Latham. 'They were two fit ten-year-old girls, and ten-year-old girls just do not drop dead.' He told the court that Huntley's actions were not those of 'a confused man but the workings of a careful and deliberate man'.

For her part, said Latham, Maxine Carr told a number of 'persistent, devious and detailed lies' from the very beginning, lies that were meant to mislead the police and hinder their investigation.[13]

Sentenced to only three and a half years in prison for conspiring to pervert the course of justice, Carr was given a new identity upon her release, compliments of the British taxpayers. She is one of only four criminals to ever receive a new identity from the British government.[15]

In the end, Huntley never admitted to anything more than perverting the course of justice, but there's still time for him to come clean. Huntley was found guilty of murder and given two life sentences. Maybe someday, the real truth about what happened that night will finally be revealed.

CHAPTER SEVENTEEN

The Milly Dowler Case

(2002)

Bob and Sally Dowler have been through more than any two people should ever have to bear.

After suffering through the disappearance of their daughter Milly and the controversial trial that followed, they had to watch her name became the focal point of a scandal that brought down one of the most notorious publications in Britain. Now the couple is back in the national spotlight once again, thanks to the man who dragged them there in the first place almost fifteen years ago.

It's no secret that teenaged girls are emotional, and thirteen is a turbulent age at the best of times, but as Milly Dowler made her way home from school that bright sunny Thursday afternoon, she was probably more than a little distracted. She had recently made an accidental discovery – to her father's horror – that had thrown her into emotional turmoil.

The thirteen-year-old had lived a fairly typical life up to that point. Born on 25 June 1988, Milly (what she preferred to her given name Amanda Jane) was a Year Nine student at Heathside School in Surrey's Weybridge.

Shortly after 3.00pm on 21 March 2002, she left school and got on a train with her friends.

At Walton-on-Thames, Milly and her friends got off the train and shared some chips at the station café.[1] At 3.47pm, she called her father Bob from her friend's mobile phone to say that she would be on her way home soon – her own phone was out of credit. Eighteen minutes later, she set off for home, a one-mile walk away in broad daylight down Station Avenue, a busy street.[2]

As Milly left the train station, Katherine Laynes was sitting at a bus stop near the station on the opposite side of Station Avenue. A friend of Milly's older sister Gemma, Katherine knew Milly and for a moment, the two girls made eye contact. Katherine boarded her bus and, once seated, she looked for Milly again but did not see her.

Katherine would be the last person to see Milly alive.

At the Dowler house, Milly's father Bob was distracted with other things including a series of 'stressful' phone calls and the family's plans for the evening. When his daughter called to say she'd deviated from her usual route and would be half an hour late coming home, he told her that was fine.

At 5.21pm, realizing Milly had not yet come home, Bob rang his youngest daughter's mobile and left a message. At first he was annoyed (he later admitting yelling out, 'Where the fuck is Milly?'), but when he realised what time it was, he became alarmed. The walk from the train station should have taken no more than ten minutes.

After driving the route and the surrounding area looking for Milly, Bob called the local hospitals and Milly's friends, now very worried. By 7.00pm, Bob and Sally were certain something was wrong and at 7.07pm, they called the police.[3]

What followed was the largest investigation in the history of the Surrey police, involving over 100 officers at an estimated cost of £6 million. Codenamed Operation Ruby, the investigation saw officers make 3500 house-to-house inquiries, searching more than 350 sites and taking 5600 statements.[4]

At first, the case was treated as a missing persons inquiry. No one had reported seeing a teenaged girl struggling as she was abducted from busy Station Avenue on the afternoon in question, so authorities thought she must have run away.

Milly's best friend from school Hannah MacDonald, however, could have told them they were looking in the wrong direction, as she said told the press shortly after Milly went missing:

> *She definitely hasn't run away but I'm keeping my hopes up that she has. She has no boyfriend, no secret boyfriend and no secret friends. I'd have known about it if she had. On Friday night there was a gang of us going to a disco … [and] she was going to tell the boy she fancied there how she felt about him … She was really looking forward to it.*[3]

The police would come under intense scrutiny for the direction in which they initially focused their investigation but it would later come to light that they had good reason for following their first instincts. In fact, the authorities helped to protect the privacy of the Dowler family by keeping those reasons confidential for as long as they could.

What the police didn't reveal in the first stages of Operation Ruby in 2002 was that, on the day Milly disappeared, Bob Dowler had at first lied about his movements earlier in the day. The IT consultant hadn't wanted to tell police that, instead of coming directly home, he'd actually stopped at a Fleet petrol station to look at a pornographic magazine.

The omission was just the beginning. When the police went to search the Dowler home, Bob told them what they would find – a collection of fetish porn magazines and videos featuring hard core bondage, plus a box of bondage equipment including a rubber hood and a ball gag.[5]

Bob also had to admit that his daughter Milly had accidentally found one of his magazines in a bureau drawer while she'd been looking for an article of clothing. Though none of the extreme material the police uncovered was illegal, it was difficult to explain to his young daughter and, subsequent to the police's discovery, his wife.[6]

Even worse, the police found notes and poems that Milly herself had written, notes that sounded very much as though she intended to run away – or worse:

> *Dear Daddy and my beautiful Mummy, by the time you find this letter I will be gone, up there or down below you ... I am sorry, you deserve a better daughter so I have left. If anything, you should be happy now, you can concentrate on lovely Gemsy [her sister] now without me getting in the way. You should have had an abortion or at least had me adopted ... It's nothing you have done. I just feel I had to go ... I am sorry but goodbye. Lots of love, as always, your little disappointment, Amanda.*[5]

Considering how often child murder cases are perpetrated by the parents, and in light of the unsavoury evidence the police had found at the Dowler home, the police rightly pursued Bob Dowler as a suspect.

There were some, however, who believed the level of attention the Surrey force focused on Bob was more than necessary. For months, he was the target of intense surveillance as his house, car and phone were all bugged. Police listened to the details of every deeply private conversation between Bob, Sally and Gemma as they waited for news of Milly.

While the police were fixated on Bob, they failed to follow up on one key incident that had been reported the day before Milly went missing. On 20 March, twelve-year-old Rachel Cowles was walking home from school in Shepperton, just a few miles from Walton-on-Thames, when a man with a 'chubby head' in a red car tried to lure her into his vehicle.

Rachel refused and thirty minutes later, her mother Diane reported the incident to the police. Because no crime had been committed, the exchange between the girl and the man in the car was logged simply as 'suspicious behaviour'. When a report was sent to the local intelligence officer covering Shepperton, he never passed it on to the Dowler team as he didn't think the report was 'relevant' to the case.

A similar incident also failed to catch the authorities' attention. A month before Milly disappeared, an eighteen-year-old girl was walking down

Station Avenue when a man walked up behind her and dropped his pants. She immediately reported what had happened to the police, describing the man – a big guy, tall, dark hair, balding.

Within 24 hours of Milly's disappearance, the report of the man exposing himself had been passed along to the Dowler team, but two months later, the officers of Operation Ruby ruled out the suspect because the flashing victim was five years older than Milly.[7]

Despite the mistakes in the investigation, which the police later admitted, the Operation Ruby team put in thousands of hours searching for the lost teenager. Eventually, Bob Dowler was cleared of suspicion and efforts were concentrated elsewhere.

It was a massive effort. Well-meaning members of the public called in with 70 sightings of the girl from as far away as Fiji.[8] Fifty registered sex offenders living within a five-mile radius of Walton-on-Thames were interviewed and eliminated.[4] Numerous appeals were made to the public by the authorities, the family and celebrities including *My Fair Lady* actor Jonathan Pryce and *Pop Idol* winner Will Young.[3]

Though the authorities had admitted that it was highly likely Milly had been the victim of a 'chance abduction'[2], one theory police explored was the possibility that Milly had gone in a car with someone that she knew.

Milly's best friend Hannah, with whom Milly had shared a secret diary that even their parents hadn't known about, offered an interesting insight one month after Milly's disappearance:

> *She wouldn't get into a car without knowing the person unless she was grabbed. She would have been too scared to put up a fight ... Milly never once said that she was going to run away – and she wouldn't because she hates the dark ... She's scared there might be a bogeyman under the bed.*[3]

In fact there was a bogeyman haunting the streets of Walton-on-Thames, a massive balding former body builder with dark hair who stood over six feet tall, a man named Levi Bellfield. Though police had received 93 reports linking the man to sexual assaults, threats, obscene phone calls and physical attacks between the years of 2000 and 2002 alone, he would somehow slip through the cracks of the Dowler investigation.[8]

Born on 17 May 1968 in nearby Isleworth, Bellfield was inordinately proud of his Romani heritage, in later years boasting of his 'pure' gypsy blood. Growing up in a West London council estate,[9] Bellfield had two brothers and two sisters. His father died when Bellfield was ten.[10]

Bellfield first became a criminal at the tender age of thirteen. Motoring offences, possession of an offensive weapon and assault were just the beginning. By 23, he'd already been in prison for hitting a police officer.[9]

Bellfield lived his entire life in the Hounslow, Hanworth and Feltham areas southwest of London. Until 2002, Bellfield had worked as a bouncer, supervising the doors of a number of bars and nightclubs in Uxbridge, Watford, Ealing and Sunbury.[10] A massive man, Bellfield was known to use steroids and even as a young man had weighed as much as 224 pounds (101 kg).

Bellfield was reportedly bizarrely close to his mother Jean, a dominant woman whom he visited nearly every day once he moved out of the family home at the age of 22. During his stretches in jail, he would call his mother up to four times a day and she would bring him pork scratchings on visiting days.

There's no telling how Bellfield developed his attitude toward women – his relationship with his mother, his sense of racial superiority, a feeling of entitlement or something else – but as he grew into adulthood, Bellfield seemed to view women as objects, possessions at best. As he told one cellmate, 'You feed them and keep them, you can do what you want to them.'[9]

What he wanted often wasn't very nice. Detective Chief Inspector Colin Sutton of the Metropolitan Police came to know Bellfield fairly well. According to Sutton, Bellfield could come across as friendly and jokey, 'but he's a cunning individual, violent. He can switch from being nice to being nasty, instantly.'[10]

It was a pattern with which his former girlfriends were well familiar. A notorious womaniser, Bellfield was involved in a number of relationships. He was believed to have eleven children by five different women. He often had several lovers at the same time, and sometimes two women would be pregnant by him at the same time.[9]

Bellfield seemed to feel no compulsion to remain faithful to any of his lovers and often treated them badly. Detective Sergeant Jo Brunt spoke with several of Bellfield's former girlfriends. 'He was lovely at first, charming, then completely controlling and evil,' said Brunt. 'They all said the same.'

Bellfield would reportedly take his girlfriend's phone and trade it for another phone that contained only his number. He would forbid her from seeing any friends or family and would monitor her every movement. One girlfriend spoke of an argument she had with Bellfield after which he told her to sit on a stool in the kitchen. He instructed her to not move while he went to bed for the night.

'We asked her what she did about going to the toilet and she said she would rather wet herself than have moved from that stool,' said Detective Sergeant Brunt. 'That shows how frightened [his girlfriends] were of him.'[10]

As Bellfield got older, his tastes turned towards younger girls. By 2002, he'd taken employment as a wheel clamper. One of his colleagues was a man named Ricky Brouillard, who was acquainted with Bellfield at a time when Bellfield was dating what Brouillard described as a 'naïve' teenaged girl whom Bellfield didn't treat very well.

'Her sister was a tiny girl, fourteen years old,' said Brouillard. 'He told me he had sex with her. I remember being disgusted. I met her on one occasion and he asked me, "Do you want to buy her off me?"'[9]

Bellfield's oldest daughter Bobbie-Louise said her father was a violent man who raped and beat her mother Becky Wilkinson. She also said he used to leer at schoolgirls during the school run. 'He was always beeping at girls walking down the street,' said Bobbie-Louise. 'They were clearly in uniform. He would shout "Oi! Oi!" and things like that.'[11]

Ten times in the two years following Milly's disappearance, police visited Bellfield's address. On every occasion, no one was home and the officers carried on with their investigation.[7]

For months, the Dowler family waited, not knowing what had happened to their daughter. Then, on 18 September 2002, six months after Milly's last day at school, a breakthrough came.

Richard and Bogumila Wislocki had been out picking mushrooms in Yateley Heath Woods in Fleet, Hampshire when they came upon the scattered remains of a corpse. The body had been left naked and exposed, and wild animals had torn it apart. There was little left but the mutilated skeleton. Dental records confirmed that it was Milly Dowler.[3] Due to the level of decomposition, pathologist Hugh White was unable to determine the cause of death, but he was able to exclude natural causes.[12]

While police continued their investigation, Bellfield prowled the streets west of London. In February 2003, nineteen-year-old Marsha McDonnell was walking home from the cinema when she was hit over the head with a lump hammer. She'd just got off the 111 Bus and was only yards from her door when the attack happened in her quiet, residential road. She died in hospital the following day.

Just over a year later, in May 2004, eighteen-year-old Kate Sheedy had just got off a bus in Isleworth when she became suspicious of a vehicle parked in a side road. The white Toyota Previa ran her over then reversed back over her again. Though she suffered several life threatening injuries, Kate survived the attack.

Only three months after the attack on Kate Sheedy, 22-year-old Amelie Delagrange was murdered in August 2004 when she was hit over the head with a blunt object while crossing Twickenham Green. The French national had just got off the bus after a night out with friends when the attack happened. A police officer found her lying in a pool of blood.

Dubbed the bus stop killer, Bellfield was finally arrested in 2004, and in 2008 he was found guilty of the murders of Marsha McDonnell and Amelie Delagrange and the attempted murder of Kate Sheedy.[13]

By now, police had begun to put the pieces together. As soon as he was arrested in 2004, they began to see several ways in which Bellfield could have been linked to Milly's disappearance. To begin with, he'd been living just yards away from where she was last seen on Station Avenue at an address in Collingwood Place. Milly looked very similar to his other victims – young, slim and blonde – and she was very near a bus stop when she was grabbed.

There was also a chance Milly might have known Bellfield. He'd lived in Walton-on-Thames between 1996 and 1997, and Milly had gone to primary school with the daughter of one of Bellfield's former girlfriends. She could have met him then.

When police looked at CCTV camera footage again, they noticed a 'red splodge' coming out of Copenhagen Way and into Station Avenue about 30 minutes after Milly was last seen. The splodge turned out to be a Daewoo like the one Bellfield's girlfriend drove.[7] The evidence against Bellfield was mounting rapidly and would continue to grow.

Though Bellfield was finally a suspect, it would be several more years before the police were able to compile enough evidence to bring Bellfield to trial for Milly's murder. Finally, in May 2011, the trial began.

It was to be a gut wrenching experience for Bob and Sally Dowler. All the family secrets the police had kept confidential nine years before were now laid bare for the whole world to see. While Levi Bellfield sat smug in the dock, Bob Dowler was forced to sit through cross examination, explaining the pornography he'd used, the notes he'd written alongside ads for kinky services in contact magazines.

It was almost too much for Milly's mother Sally, who taught maths at her daughters' school, to bear. When it was her turn on the stand, Sally had to reveal in open court how she'd had words with Milly over her young daughter's email account with the user name 'sexmeslow'. She was forced to discuss Milly's dark poetry and letters in which the girl spoke of how miserable she was at school, how she believed her family hated her and how much she hated herself.[14]

In June 2011, Bellfield was found guilty of Milly's murder and, as in 2008, he was given a whole life sentence. He is believed to be the first person to received two whole life sentences.[15]

The Dowlers had been given less than a month to heal when they found their daughter's name once again splashed across the front page. In July 2011, *The Guardian* reported that journalists from Rupert Murdoch's controversial *News of the World* had hacked into Milly's mobile phone in the early days of her disappearance.

It was initially believed that the reporters, working with a private detective, had hacked into the phone's voicemail so that they could listen to her private messages. Then, when the mailbox was full, they deleted earlier messages so that the phone could continue recording.[16]

Six months later, *The Guardian* printed a correction, stating that it was unlikely that the reporters had deleted the messages, but by then the damage was done. Within a month, *News of the World* closed amidst a flurry of litigation. Whether they'd deleted messages or not was irrelevant. The fact that the reporters had hacked the phone at all was enough.

What the scandal did reveal, however, was that, while the reporters of *News of the World* likely didn't delete the messages in question, someone did.

A report written by Scotland Yard detective DCI John MacDonald found evidence of an unidentified person who had hacked into Milly's phone prior to 10 April, which was the first date on which the *News of the World* reporters were known to have accessed her phone. MacDonald concluded that the real culprit will probably never be identified.[17]

As if the disappearance of their daughter, murder, trial and phone hacking scandal weren't enough, Sally and Bob Dowler are now in the spotlight once again. In May 2015, the police informed the Dowlers that Bellfield had spoken of his crimes to a fellow inmate who was set for release. The authorities wanted the Dowlers to be privy to the information in the event that the inmate in question went public with what Bellfield had told him.

For eight months, the Dowlers kept quiet while the police conducted an investigation into an alleged accomplice to Bellfield's crimes. When the suspect was finally cleared due to lack of evidence, Bob and Sally came forward with a statement in January 2016 revealing what they knew.

Bellfield told police that, after abducting Milly, he assaulted her at his flat in Collingwood Place. He then drove her to his mother's house where he raped her in the driveway and to another location where he continued to rape and torture her for a number of hours before strangling her to death and dumping her body.[18]

Whatever Bellfield has told the police, it's worth remembering that he is also a known liar. A month after the Dowlers made their statement, his solicitor sent a letter to Surrey police denying his confession.[19] While

Bellfield is certainly guilty of Milly's murder, any inglorious details that come from him should be taken with a clear understanding of the source. We are left to wonder how much of what he said was true and how much was prison bravado exaggerated for the benefit of his cellmates.

The name Milly Dowler has become associated with so many things that have nothing to do with the girl herself, it's easy to forget the person she was before she hit the headlines, a good student and a lively musician with lots of friends.

As her mother said, 'Milly was in the school orchestra and the saxophone group. It was something very dear to her. When Milly was at home, she was always making up little dance routines with her friends and her sister Gemma. She also adored singing and loved karaoke.'[3]

Milly was a bright, sweet girl who was loved by many. She was always moving, always dancing, always smiling. Let's hope she can be remembered that way.

CHAPTER EIGHTEEN

A Hammer and a Frying Pan

(2004)

In the 1991 thriller *Silence of the Lambs*, FBI agent Clarice Starling says of the monstrously creepy Hannibal Lecter, 'They don't have a name for what he is,' but in reality, they do.

For all the ways one human can do evil to another, there are few that make the skin crawl more than the concept of cannibalism. It seems unthinkable that a person would want to eat the flesh another person, but British serial killer Peter Bryan did exactly that. According to Bryan, he wanted his victims' souls.

Peter Bryan was born in London on 4 October 1969. He was the youngest of seven children, three of whom (including Peter) suffered mental illness. Though Bryan never lived there, Bryan's parents were natives of Barbados and Bryan visited the island at least once as an adult.[1]

Not much is known about the heritage of Bryan's parents but a little of the history of Barbados seems relevant to his story. The earliest known settlement of the easternmost Caribbean island dates back to 1623 BC and the peaceful Arawak tribe, which were mostly farmers and fishermen.

The Arawak lived in relative isolation until around 1250 BC when the Carib tribe arrived. The taller, stronger Caribs were much more violent and prone to war. They were also known for their rituals during which they ate human flesh to 'gain control over dead enemies or acquire the qualities of dead ancestors'.[2]

Despite his Barbadian background, Peter Bryan would not prove himself to be a noble warrior. As a child, Bryan struggled in school. He would later recall that he had few friends and was unhappy as a primary school student. He was not diagnosed as being dyslexic until the age of 33.

Bryan compensated for his poor academic performance by bullying other children, especially those he saw as being weaker than himself. At the age of twelve, he was running with a gang of classmates, shoplifting and carrying weapons that he used for mugging people on the street. Not yet a teenager, he was already smoking marijuana and skipping school.

Bryan left school before the legal age at either fourteen or fifteen. Upon leaving school, Bryan took a job working as an assistant in a retail clothes shop run by the Sheths, a family from Pakistan.

Despite his regular employment, he continued to sell drugs, mug people and steal from his employers. Since his employers paid him in cash, he also illegally signed up for unemployment benefits. An expert at manipulation, Bryan excelled at telling people what they wanted to hear and getting what he wanted out of them.

Bryan became more heavily dependent on drugs and, by the age of 23, he was spending all of his income on marijuana. He would often miss work for days, sometimes weeks, at a time due to his drug use.

Remarkably, for all his criminal activity, his only conviction was for possessing a controlled drug for which he received a conditional discharge for one year in October 1992.

During this time, Bryan continued to work as a sales assistant for the Sheth family at their clothing stops in Shaftesbury Avenue and King's Road in Chelsea. It was while he was working at these shops that Bryan met the shop owners' daughter, a girl three years his junior named Nisha Sheth.

According to Bryan, Nisha had been in an intimate relationship with him but the two had never had sexual intercourse. According to her family, the two were never in a relationship.[1]

Whether or not the two were ever romantically involved, Bryan was finally caught stealing and fired from his position in March 1993. A week later, on 18 March, the 23-year-old Bryan returned to the shop where he found Nisha and her younger brother Bobby. Bryan knocked the twelve-year-old Bobby to the floor and then turned to Nisha who had been talking on the phone.

In a brutal, sudden attack, Bryan beat Nisha in the head with a claw hammer. Before the ambulance arrived, she had already died.[3]

An hour after the attack, Bryan went to a building in Battersea where he jumped from a third floor balcony. He landed on his feet, suffering a number of severe fractures to his lower legs and ankles. He later said he'd intended to jump headfirst and commit suicide but had second thoughts at the last moment. Charged with murder, he was sent to Brixton Prison.

When police spoke with Nisha's mother Rashmi, Mrs Sheth spoke of Bryan's erratic behaviour over the previous four months. She described his violent mood swings and how he would vacillate between scrubbing himself with disinfectant and failing to wash for days.

Sometimes he wouldn't respond when spoken to. Sometimes he would wander around muttering to himself in a language she could not understand, repeating one word over and over again. Often he would carry around a hammer and leave it lying around.

Two weeks before the incident, he'd come into the shop saying he felt like killing someone. Rashmi said she was afraid of him. He would taunt her and threaten her, but when her husband was around, Bryan was always polite to the point that her husband didn't believe her when she expressed her concerns.

While in Brixton Prison, Bryan began exhibiting the same erratic behaviour he'd shown before Nisha's murder. On two occasions, he attacked other inmates without being provoked. Nurses from the department of forensic psychiatry found him to be paranoid and thought he had the potential to turn violent towards others.

In light of the nurses' assessment, Bryan was referred to the consultant forensic psychiatrist at Hackney Hospital, who spoke with Bryan for two hours. According to Bryan, Nisha had been teasing him for five or six years. She would kiss and touch him, Bryan said, but whenever he responded, she would become frigid and run away.

Bryan said that on the day of the murder, he'd gone to the shop and Nisha had asked him to have sex with her. 'Make me … rape me' were the words she'd used, Bryan said. He had been shocked, he told the psychiatrist.

He went on to say that Nisha had given him the impression that she'd wanted him to kill her and that she hadn't shouted but had rather stood there and taken the beating. Witnesses who saw the attack, however, reported that Nisha had screamed 'in a terrified manner'.

Throughout the two-hour interview, Bryan remained polite and cooperative, so much so that the psychiatrist characterised him as a 'quiet and withdrawn man'. It would become a pattern that would fool many healthcare professionals in the years to come.

During the session, Bryan spoke of his interest in traditional voodoo practices, specifically the use of a voodoo doll. According to one Bachelor of Liberal Arts in Religious Studies candidate at Harvard University, voodoo is traditionally practiced throughout the Caribbean, including Barbados. Though voodoo beliefs vary, one common theme is the juxtaposition of the physical world and the spiritual world and how the two can become entwined.[4]

Bryan described lighting candles and sticking pins into his voodoo doll. He would write the names of Nisha's mother Rashmi and others he felt were against him on pieces of paper that he would then burn, a process that gave him a 'quickening'.

He spoke of 'turning the warheads', the movement of the plates of the earth and how the chemicals in the warheads were oozing – he knew because he felt pain in the veins of his body. He said his voodoo kept nature in its proper pattern.

Bryan spoke of dead souls listening to his conversations and hurting him when he was alone. As he spoke to the psychiatrist, the pain in his legs became worse. Bryan said he believed the pain might be a sign from the spirits telling him not to say any more.

He said that he sometimes felt like others were 'thinking out of his head for him' and that his actions were not his own. The murder of Nisha Sheth, he claimed, had been entirely beyond his control.

At the end of his two-hour interview, Bryan was diagnosed as suffering some form of paranoid psychosis and possible schizophrenia. The psychiatrist recommended Bryan for further assessment at Rampton High Security Hospital.

Bryan saw a second psychiatrist at Brixton Prison in November. He again expressed feelings of paranoia. He said that prior to the murder, he believed his neighbours had been conspiring to annoy him by copying his every movement and that his brother's girlfriend had been harassing him. He felt like he didn't fit anywhere, England or Barbados.

He gave a similar account of his family background and his reasons for killing Nisha Sheth – that she had been leaving him sexually frustrated for years, that she had asked him to rape her and that, in the end, she'd wanted him to kill her.

In the end, four psychiatrists consulted each other regarding Peter Bryan and what to do with him. All of them found his mental state 'hard to assess'. While they all agreed he suffered from a 'psychotic illness', the symptoms were difficult to define and 'impossible' to diagnose.[1]

Bryan admitted killing Nisha but was only charged with manslaughter on the grounds of diminished responsibility. As a result, he was remanded to the Rampton maximum security psychiatric unit 'without limit of time'.[3]

From his earliest days at Rampton, Bryan was able to fool his caretakers. By May 1994, staff at Rampton noted that Bryan did not appear to be developing any signs or symptoms of schizophrenia. Three months later, his psychiatrist determined he was showing no signs of mental illness at all.

He was not, however, doing as well as his doctors thought. At the end of April 1995, he was transferred to Hawthorn Villa and within weeks, his behaviour began to deteriorate. In July, he was seen exposing himself to female staff and making threats to other staff. On one occasion, he burned a male nurse with a cigarette and then walked away laughing.

On numerous occasions over the next few months, Bryan made comments about killing people and became violent, getting into fights and stealing things. He refused to participate in any treatment and was described as being poorly motivated. Eventually, thought, he began to settle down.

In April 1997, the first two psychiatrists who had ever seen Bryan prepared a comprehensive 36-page report on their patient. The two professionals met with Bryan during twelve sessions between January and March 1997, during which Bryan appeared well dressed, punctual, polite and cooperative. The report concluded:

> *Mr Bryan's ward behaviour appears to have been within the normal range, with some incidents of inappropriate behaviour and a degree of boisterousness with fellow patients. Overall, Mr Bryan has posed no significant management problem.*

Following this assessment, Bryan seemed to undergo a complete turn around and by September 1997, it was like he was a different man. A report from the Further Education Centre said that Bryan interacted well with everyone and that he'd particularly enjoyed studying literature, especially *Macbeth* and *Tom Sawyer*.

In his maths lessons, he applied himself in 'a constructive, sociable and pleasant manner' and in a social skills group on the ward, he was reportedly a 'lively contributor'. Employment services said that he'd started an upholstery workshop and had attended four sessions a week for four months. He worked hard, accepted criticism and showed no signs of mental illness.

After more therapy, Bryan was again reassessed in January 1999. This time, the praise was glowing. Though he was still described as immature, the nursing staff reported that he was very popular with both staff and patients. They called him a 'pleasure to have on the ward'. They said he had an 'infectious smile and sense of humour' and that, even though other patients sometimes teased him, he didn't 'rise to the bait'.

After much consideration, Peter Bryan was moved from Rampton to the John Howard Centre where he was admitted to the Colin Franklin

Ward on 12 July 2001. Here, he continued to give psychiatrists and social workers all the right answers – he felt 'terrible' for killing Nisha Sheth, he'd had problems in the past with violence and drugs but he was now keen to move forward.

On 14 August 2001, on the recommendation of his latest psychiatrist, Bryan was granted an interview with the managers of Riverside House, a hostel with 24-hour supervision on Seven Sisters Road in London.

As the staff at the John Howard Centre told the managers he would be, Bryan was pleasant and friendly. He assured them he would stay away from drugs and would continue to take his prescribed medication. The managers agreed that they had a place for Bryan on the condition that he continued his treatment and abided by the rules of the house.

In February 2002, Bryan moved into Riverside House, but within a month, he was complaining. The members of the staff were watching his every move, and he was unhappy that he was not allowed to take female guests back to his room. He said he was being treated like a child.

By August, the managers of Riverside were growing concerned. Bryan had begun to drink on occasion and make threatening remarks. In one confrontation, he'd held a large kitchen knife and his eyes had 'glazed over'.

Bryan also gave indications of becoming more and more paranoid. These concerns were noted and in November, Bryan was considered to be a 'moderate risk' for becoming violent. Despite these concerns, he remained at Riverside.

Bryan himself thought he was cured. He couldn't understand why he needed to stay at Riverside. He'd done his time, he said, and he was ready for his own flat. If he'd gone to prison for manslaughter, he argued, he'd have been released years before.

Bryan also repeatedly insisted he no longer needed medication. As far as he was concerned, the only factor that might possibly trigger a psychotic episode in him was the use of illegal drugs like marijuana or cocaine. As he was using neither of those, he had no cause for concern.

In July 2003, all care of Peter Bryan was assigned to one social worker, a professional who had been working as part of a team for several months overseeing Bryan. When the social worker was given the solo role, Bryan claimed he had not seen the person in several weeks.[1] This social worker would later be described as 'very inexperienced' with no training in mental health.[5]

In November, Bryan got his first job in a decade working for a cleaning agency fifteen hours a week. It was the first step towards true independence. The second was that Bryan was to start self-medicating. He had been attending a drug-counselling programme and had not missed a dose in all the time he'd been on the prescription.

It seemed like he was moving in the right direction, but his social worker and the managers at Riverside had seen a number of unsettling relapses. Bryan was constantly complaining, and he'd become very secretive – he hadn't told anyone, for example, that he'd found the job or bought a car. He was also drinking more heavily and didn't always follow house rules.

Even so, a report dated 5 December 2003 noted that Peter Bryan did not show signs of becoming a danger to himself or others. His social worker even recommended he move to a less secure facility.

In early 2004, however, Bryan began to show signs of paranoia. He believed money had been stolen from his room and that he'd been singled out for persecution at the hands of the Riverside managers. According to the managers and the social worker, there was no evidence for his claims.

A further worrisome sign was that he was no longer cleaning his room. One manager described the state of his room as being so filthy it was a 'healthy and safety issue'. When the staff offered to help him clean the mess, he refused. He was also seen talking to himself. In light of these concerns, Bryan's social worker and the Riverside managers decided Bryan was no longer capable of self-medicating.

Then, in February 2004, Bryan was involved in a critical incident involving a seventeen-year-old girl. On 6 February, Bryan went to visit the girl, with whom he had been acquainted for nearly two years.

The girl said that, once Bryan had confirmed that her father was not home, he had sexually assaulted her, slapping her and fondling her breasts and private parts. Bryan denied the incident. He claimed the girl had invited him inside her flat to watch DVDs. He admitted to 'blowing raspberries' on her stomach but nothing more.

Shortly after the incident, two carloads of men arrived at Riverside reportedly intending to take Bryan away in the boot of one of the vehicles and murder him in retaliation for his treatment of the girl.

In light of the threats against him, Bryan's social worker immediately sought to remove him to hospital for his own safety. For this reason alone, on 10 February 2004 Bryan was admitted as an informal patient of Topaz Ward, a general psychiatric ward for adults at Newham Hospital.

There was no suggestion that he was being admitted due to any relapse of his mental illness, only as a safety measure to keep him out of the hands of the men who had threatened him. It was also recorded in his admission file that, if he wanted to leave, he was to be allowed to do so the same as any other informal patient would be.

Between 10 and 17 February, Bryan behaved calmly, giving none of the staff at Newham any cause for concern. The nurses described him as well settled and presenting no problems. Despite his calm demeanour, something was not right with Peter Bryan, however, as his carers would soon learn.

Sometime between 3.00 and 4.00 on the afternoon of 17 February 2004, Bryan left Newham Hospital. At 4.22pm, he purchased a claw hammer, a Stanley knife and a screwdriver then got on a bus to Walthamstow.[1]

Sometime after 6.00pm on the evening of 17 February, Bryan arrived at the flat of a man named Brian Cherry. Bryan was acquainted with Cherry through a girl named Nicola Newman that Bryan had come to know during his time living at Riverside.

The 43-year-old Cherry was described as a 'nice man, lonely with no friends'.[3] He had given Nicola money on a number of occasion to support her drug habit, expecting nothing in return. According to Nicola, Cherry thought he was her boyfriend, even though the two had never been intimate.

Around 7.30pm, Nicola arrived at Cherry's flat. When she rang, she could hear movement inside but no one answered so she pushed the door open (the door had been damaged previously and it didn't shut properly).

Upon entering the flat, Nicola noticed the unusual smell of disinfectant. Moments later, Peter Bryan came out of the front room, stripped to the waist and sweating. Disturbingly, he had a blade in his hand. When he told her to go away, Nicola asked him where Brian Cherry was. Bryan told her, 'Brian Cherry is dead.' Nicola promptly left and alerted the authorities.

Less than an hour later, the police arrived. Bryan seemed startled to see them. He was covered in dried blood and in the next room, the body of Brian Cherry lay on the floor, cut into several pieces. The authorities later surmised that, when Cherry had first opened his door to Bryan's ring, Bryan had bashed Cherry in the head with the hammer and then dismembered him, distributing his arms and legs around the room.

Even more shocking was Bryan's revelation, 'I ate his brain with butter. It was very nice.'

The police were not sure if they should believe him as they were clearly dealing with a madman, but when the officers went into Brian Cherry's kitchen, they found something that looked to be human flesh with hair coming out of it sitting on a plastic plate.

It also looked as though Bryan had recently been cooking some sort of white substance with a yellowish tinge in a frying pan on the stovetop. Beside the cooker was an open tub of Clover brand margarine. A later DNA analysis confirmed that the substance in the frying pan indeed belonged to Brian Cherry.

As they waited for the police van to arrive, one officer reported that Bryan said, 'I wanted his soul.' Later, Bryan would say that Cherry had told him 'make me', a chilling echo of what Bryan claimed Nisha Sheth had said.

Following the murder, Bryan was said to be 'quite calm' and showed 'no signs of psychotic illness'. He seemed so sane, in fact, that a forensic psychiatrist deemed him fit to be interviewed by police and not in need of hospitalisation.

Bryan was charged with murder and sent first to Pentonville Prison and then to Belmarsh Prison on 23 February. Bryan's mental state, however, continued to deteriorate and by 8 March, he was becoming agitated, violent and unpredictable.

On 15 April 2004, Bryan was transferred to Broadmoor Hospital. Upon his arrival, Bryan was placed in seclusion but after three days, he managed to fool his carers yet again. Thinking he had 'settled', they released him from seclusion and placed him under 'general observation', which allowed him to mingle with other patients.

One week later, he attacked Richard Loudwell, a 60-year-old fellow patient[1] who had sexually assaulted and murdered an 82-year-old woman in 2002. Nine staff members were on duty when Bryan attempted to strangle Loudwell with a trouser cord in an unobserved dining room.[5] Bryan then bashed Loudwell's head repeatedly into a table and on the floor. Loudwell later died of his injuries.[1]

According to Joanne Fisher, registered mental health nurse and team leader on the ward, the attack on Loudwell was no sudden impulse. As she described, 'Mr Bryan said he had been thinking about it for a few days. He also said, "I wanted to eat him."'[6]

Two independent inquiries into Peter Bryan's mental health care found a number of 'systematic failures' that contributed to his being given the opportunity to kill again after his initial attack on Nisha Sheth. His symptoms, however, were deemed to be so unusual that even experienced psychiatrists could be fooled by him.[5]

With any luck, Bryan won't get that chance again. Following the deaths of Brian Cherry and Richard Loudwell, Bryan was given to two life sentences and returned to Broadmoor. Authorities say it is unlikely he will ever be released.[1]

CHAPTER NINETEEN

The Cumbria Shootings

(2010)

The British government has traditionally been quick to respond to gun violence. Following the Hungerford massacre in 1987, during which sixteen people were killed, Britain introduced the Firearms Amendment 1988 which made registration for owning shotguns mandatory and banned both semi-automatic and pump-action weapons. Within eighteen months of the Dunblane massacre in 1996, private ownership of all handguns was also banned in mainland Britain.

Both tragedies resulted in the surrender of thousands of firearms and rounds of ammunition throughout the nation.[1] Despite having some of the toughest anti-gun laws in the world, Britain would have to face the fact that – under the system in place – not all gun violence can be prevented.

Unlike Thomas Hamilton, who had given a number of signs that something was amiss prior to the Dunblane massacre, Derrick Bird had lived a fairly unremarkable life until 2 June 2010. Born in Cumbria in 1957, Bird and his twin brother were the youngest children of Mary and Joe Bird, who also had an older son, Brian. The Birds were well respected in their community and described as a good family.

Bird attended the local school where he met Linda Mills, a girl several years younger than he who would eventually become his partner and the mother of his two children, sons Graeme and Jamie.[2] Upon leaving school, Bird took a job as a joiner working for an undertaker in Whitehaven then went to work at the famed nuclear plant Sellafield, the largest employer in the area.

Bird might have made a real career for himself at Sellafield, but in 1990 he was fired when he was found stealing decorations from his employer, for which he was given a six-month suspended sentence. Losing his job at Sellafield was a serious blow for Bird, who found it difficult to find full time employment following the conviction. At this point, Bird put his passion for cars to work and became a self-employed taxi driver in Whitehaven.

Bird excelled at his job as a driver. He got to know his regular customers on a first-name basis and had such a thorough knowledge of West Cumbria that he was able to act as a handy tour guide for visitors to the region.

In early 1994, Bird and Linda split and, while it was common knowledge they had not parted on good terms, Bird maintained healthy loving relationships with his boys. Shortly after the split, Linda moved with the children to the nearby town of Lamplugh where Bird would often visit.

While Bird was able to make a living as a taxi driver, it was not a lucrative one. In contrast, Bird's twin brother David had done well for himself. David's business and property ventures had paid off and he was living in a large farmhouse on four acres of land on the outskirts of Lamplugh, a far cry from Bird's rundown pebble-dashed cottage in Rowrah.

Bird was far from destitute, though. He had lots of friends and travelled regularly. Most years, he would take a trip abroad to go scuba diving in Thailand – his favourite destination – or trekking through Egypt. There were photos of him with his cabbie friends or friends from his diving club sunbathing on the deck of a motorboat in Lanzarote, Tenerife or Croatia.[3]

There had, of course, been difficult moments in his life. According to one friend, when Bird's partner Linda fell pregnant with his second son Jamie, Bird had wanted her to have an abortion. Bird and Linda had never married and shortly after Jamie was born, the two were separated.

If it is true that Bird wanted Linda to abort Jamie, that fact did not seem evident in Bird's relationship with his son. The same friend went on to say that, as Jamie grew up, Bird spent a lot of time with the boy.

There was quite an age gap between Bird's son Jamie and his older brother Graeme who was born in 1982. Jamie was only three years old when Graeme, aged 25, was charged with driving a car without insurance in February 2007. He was fined £200 plus another £35 in court costs.[2]

Graeme's minor indiscretion seems to be the only trouble the kids ever caused their father, and his later accomplishments (including as a motor cross motorcyclist, about which both father and son were passionate) would more than make up for the incident.

Derrick Bird also made the local newspapers later in 2007 when he was the victim of an attack by a passenger who didn't want to pay his fare. When the teenager and three of his friends jumped out of Bird's taxi without paying, Bird challenged the youth. The 50-year-old Bird was knocked unconscious and two of his teeth were broken in an assault that left him 'nervous and anxious'.[4]

But for the most part, life had treat Bird well. From the outside, Derrick Bird looked like a calm, average man. Sylvia Bridges, who lived down the street from Bird, described him as 'a placid lad', perhaps 'a bit of a loner' but 'quiet'. James Campbell, another neighbour, agreed: 'He was a good lad as far as I knew, and a good neighbour. He was a private person, but he was well respected.'

Bird was never known to be a heavy drinker. On occasion, he would pop round to The Stork Hotel in Rowrah or perhaps The Hound Inn in Frizington. 'He was just a normal bloke, a nice guy,' said Michelle Haigh, landlady at The Hound. 'He would come into the pub, have a couple of pints of lager, have a chat with his friends and go home.'[2]

Nearly everyone said the same – Derrick Bird was just your typical harmless bloke. He had never been to prison, he'd never been in contact with any mental health agencies and he wasn't taking any medication.[5]

But Bird had been hiding a secret. In May 2010, he received a tax form indicating that he was to be investigated for undeclared income.

According to Bird's closest friend Neil Jacques, the form was cause for considerable concern:

> *He said he received a form and he was bothered because he had too much savings and he had to declare it. He had not paid any tax for fifteen years and they were going to find out if he filled the form in … [H]e thought he was going to go to prison.*

As it turns out, Bird had failed to declare over £60,000 in earnings, an offense for which he had good reason to be worried.[7]

Neil Jacques knew Bird very well. The two had been friends since secondary school and they lived only a few houses apart in the same street in Rowrah. Neil said that Bird had been 'very distressed' about the form.[6]

Bird saw a respite from his concerns on 22 May. He became a grandfather when his oldest son Graeme and his wife gave birth to their first son Leighton. Bird was reportedly 'chuffed to pieces',[3] but the arrival of baby Leighton would only give Bird a moment of peace.

Sometime during the week of 25 May, Bird and his two brothers saw their mother's will. Until he saw the will, Bird had believed that when his ailing 87-year-old mother Mary died, he and his two brothers would split their father's estate. It is believed he'd been counting on the inheritance to help solve his growing financial problems.

When he saw the document, however, he learned to his dismay that even though he'd been caring for his mother, the amount he would be receiving was much less than what he'd anticipated. He also learned that prior to his death in 1998, Bird's father had given Bird's twin brother David £25,000.

When the will was drawn up in 1987, Bird's father had stipulated this amount was to be subtracted from David's share of the inheritance. The rules of probate, however, stated that, since Bird's father died before his mother, everything went to Mary Bird and the £25,000 would not be subtracted from David's share when she died. In effect, Derrick Bird would end up receiving less than his wealthy twin.[7]

Between 30 May and 1 June 2010, Bird visited his friend Neil several times. His behaviour was erratic and he was 'shaking and petrified', Neil later said. Bird was convinced he was going to go to jail for tax evasion. Bird also believed that his twin brother David and his solicitor, a man named Kevin Commons, were 'in cahoots' against him.

On 1 June, Bird visited Neil at lunchtime. He gave Neil his Winchester automatic ejector shotgun and asked his friend to look after it. Bird had mentioned taking his own life, and although Neil had not taken his friend seriously – he'd told Bird 'Don't be so daft' – Neil took the gun for Bird's safety.[6]

Sometime that day, Bird went round to visit his new grandson Leighton. He gave his son and daughter-in-law a 'financial gift' for the baby and held the newborn in his arms for a while.[3]

Around 6.00 that night, Bird returned to Neil's house. He seemed paranoid and he kept saying over and over how his brother and his solicitor had 'stitched him up'. Bird claimed his brother had taped him over the phone. Neil told Bird he was just being paranoid.[6]

At some point on the evening of 1 June, Bird reportedly had an argument with a few of his fellow Whitehaven taxi drivers. According to one source, the altercation was about queue-jumping.[5] Another driver said, 'There are so many new drivers out there and not a lot of jobs. There have been fights over fares, and accusations that some drivers are coming in from Preston and Blackpool to take jobs.'[4]

Much is unknown about Derrick Bird and what motivated him. What is known is that, in the early morning hours of 2 June 2010, sometime prior to 5.15am, Bird climbed into his silver Citroen Picasso and drove to his brother's farmhouse in Lamplugh.

Though he had given one of his weapons to his friend Neil Jacques the previous day, on the morning of 2 June, Bird took two others with him – another shotgun and a .22 rifle fitted with a telescopic viewer and a silencer. At 5.30am, he walked into his brother's unlocked house and into the bedroom where his twin lay sleeping.

There, he shot David at point blank range with the .22 rifle. Bird used the silencer and, coupled with the fact that the farmhouse was so remote, David's body would not be found for several hours.

At some point after leaving the farmhouse, Bird went by Mowbray Farm in Frizington, the home of his solicitor Kevin Commons. Iris Carruthers, who had gone to school with Bird and knew him well, was out walking her dogs when she saw Bird coming down the lane.

Assuming Bird had dropped a fare at the solicitor's house, she stopped to say hello, but Bird did not respond. '[H]e didn't speak,' she later recalled. 'He seemed dazed, as if he was in another world. He kept looking straight ahead.'

Around 9.30am, a neighbour saw Bird cleaning his car. The neighbour said 'hello' and Bird replied with a calm 'good morning'. Nothing in his demeanour indicated that he had just committed murder four hours before – or that his rampage had only just begun.

At 10.00am, Bird was seen driving in the direction of Frizington. When he arrived at Mowbray Farm for the second time that morning, Bird parked in front of the house and waited.

At 10.20am, the 60-year-old solicitor emerged from his house. Bird shot Commons in his driveway, again using the rifle. This time, Bird did not use the silencer. Police were alerted to the sound of gunshots in the area within moments – Bird passed the patrol car on the road – but officers would not find Commons' body until several hours later.[3]

After killing Kevin Commons, Bird returned to the home of his good friend Neil Jacques and asked to have his Winchester shotgun back. After a two-minute conversation, during which Neil refused to hand over the gun, Bird left[8] and continued on to Whitehaven and the taxi rank in the town centre where he'd worked.

Arriving at 10.30am, he sought out Darren Rewcastle, a fellow taxi driver who Bird wrongly believed to have had an affair with his ex-partner Linda Mills. Rewcastle had also been involved in the queue-jumping argument of the night before. At 10.33am, Bird called out, 'Darren, here, I want you.' When Rewcastle turned, Bird shot him in the face, killing him instantly.

With Rewcastle dead, Bird got out of his car. Former Royal Marine Dan Williamson saw Bird walking around the town with a shotgun in his hand. It appeared to Williamson that Bird was not in a hurry and that he was looking for someone.

Not finding who he was looking for, Bird returned to his car. As he drove, he took a shot at Don Reed, another Whitehaven driver, who managed to dive out of the way, sustaining only shrapnel wounds. When Bird called over Paul Wilson, the cabbie at first thought his good friend was having a laugh by pointing a gun in his face. Wilson pulled back just in time to walk away with a graze on his cheek.

At this point, it seems as though Bird's reasoning became irrational. Driving up Scotch Street, he called out to fifteen-year-old schoolgirl Ashley Gastor, someone he didn't know at all. She dodged a shotgun blast that came so close to hitting her it whistled past her ponytail.

By now the police were onto Bird, but the Cumbria force was a small operation and most of the officers had already been dispatched in response to the shots that had been fired in Frizington. The only officer left had no weapon or vehicle. Commandeering a taxi, he and the driver went in pursuit of Bird. Eventually, two other unarmed policemen also joined the chase.

The policemen watched as Bird pulled up alongside cabbie Terry Kennedy and his passenger Emma Percival sitting beside him. Bird shot at Kennedy through the window. Though they both survived, Kennedy sustained injuries so severe he lost his right hand and Percival was injured in her neck, arm and side.

Stopping to tend to Kennedy and Percival, the police fell far behind Bird who turned south along the coast. Cutting through the town of Egremont, he passed Susan Hughes, a mother of two, at 10.55am struggling with her shopping. When he saw Susan, Bird stopped the car, got out and shot her twice in the stomach. She was dead within minutes.

Five minutes later, Bird came upon retired soldier Kenneth Fishburn at Bridge End. Bird shot the 71-year-old in the back, killing him, and then drove off through the village firing his gun in the air.

Over and over, Bird called his victims over to his vehicle, many who later said they assumed he was asking for directions, only to find him pointing a gun at them. In Egremont, he tried this ploy with handyman Les Hunter who narrowly avoided taking both barrels in his face. Hunter survived with 39 pellets in his back.

Though several of Bird's victims were strangers to him, his next target was not. Jason Carey was an instructor at Bird's diving club who had incurred Bird's wrath when Carey reprimanded him for taking a novice diver into deep water. Now Bird went looking for him.

When Bird banged on Carey's door, Carey was still in bed, having just worked the night shift the previous evening. Carey's dogs actually saved his life. They were barking so much that his wife had trouble restraining them. By the time she could get to the door, Bird was walking away.

Bird had worked with his next victim Isaac Dixon, a 65-year-old mole catcher, during his time at Sellafield, but authorities could not establish if the two men had ever known each other. At any rate, Bird shot and killed Dixon as he drove away from Jason Carey's house.

By now, every available police officer in the area was pursing Bird, but with his extensive knowledge of the area, the taxi driver managed to elude them in the isolated country lanes. At 11.05am, he came upon 65-year-old Jennifer Jackson. When he sounded his horn to get her attention, she turned towards him and he shot and killed her.

Moments later, Bird killed Jennifer's husband Jimmy who had been walking down the road to meet her. He'd stopped to talk with two neighbours, Steve and Christine Hunter, at whom Bird also shot. Steve managed to pull Christine out of the way and, though she sustained a collapsed lung, she survived.

Minutes after killing the Jacksons, Bird came upon 31-year-old rugby player Garry Purdham who was out trimming hedges on his father's farmland. Bird got out of the car and shot Purdham, killing him.

By now, there seemed to be no rhyme or reason to Bird's actions. Driving towards Seascale, Bird encountered 23-year-old real estate agent Jamie Clark driving back from a viewing. Bird shot into Clark's vehicle, causing Clark to crash and overturn his car. He would not survive.

At 11.25am, Bird arrived in Seascale and shot into another vehicle, this time a Land Rover belonging to pub owner Harry Berger. In a move that saved his life, Berger instinctively put up his arm at the last moment, sustaining serious injuries but surviving.

Less than 30 seconds after shooting Berger, Bird took the life of his next victim, 64-year-old Michael Pike, another former Sellafield employee who had been out riding his bike. Bird first shot out the back tyre then shot Pike in the cheek.

Just a few yards beyond Pike, Bird encountered Jane Robinson. The 66-year-old had been delivering catalogues when Bird called her over to his car. Like with so many others, he shot her in the face at point blank range, ending her life.

Driving away from Seascale towards Lake District National Park, Bird would continue to take shots at random strangers. Jacqueline Lewis, Fiona Moretta, Nathan Jones and Samantha Christie would all survive their injuries, but Derrick Bird had not yet taken his last life.

For hours, police had been tracking Bird, but a number of factors had confounded their efforts to catch him. For one, the tiny Cumbria police force, already spread thin, had had to contact the RAF and the Lancashire force to obtain the use of a helicopter.

Then at Seascale, Harry Berger's Land Rover had blocked the one road into town, preventing police vehicles from pursuing Bird. As Bird drove away from Seascale, CCTV footage would show that the police vehicles were just not fast enough to make up the time and catch Bird's Citroen.

By the time Bird reached the national park, he knew the police were closing in and his driving had become erratic. The Citroen had lost one tyre in a crash and the others were shredded. Eventually, Bird rammed his vehicle into a wall on a quiet country lane and walked into the woods. At 1.30pm he shot himself, ending his reign of terror and his life.[3]

The immediate response to the incident was absolute shock. Most of the people who knew Derrick Bird were flabbergasted. They just couldn't imagine that someone so mild mannered could commit such a horrific crime. It wasn't until the inquest into the incident months later that the details of Bird's financial difficulties, the only motivation that seemed plausible, came to light.

Unlike other mass shootings that had happened previously, this one did not lead to a major change in firearms legislation.

According to British law, prospective gun owners must obtain a certificate from the police prior to purchasing any firearms or shotguns. Applicants must meet a number of criteria to obtain a certificate, one of which is providing a good reason to possess the weapon in question. Self-defence or a simple desire to have the weapon isn't considered to be a good reason. The applicant must also be able to prove secure storage for the weapon, among other conditions.[9]

An independent report released in November 2010 found that police had no grounds to deny Bird certificates for any of his guns. Bird had acquired his first weapon, a shotgun, at the age of sixteen. As he purchased more weapons, the reasons he gave for needing the guns were clay pigeon shooting and vermin control on local farmland.

After the Cumbria shootings, some would claim that Bird should never have been given his certificates due to his 'criminal record', but prior to 2010 he had hardly been a hardened criminal.

His record consisted of one £100 fine and a one-year ban for drink driving he'd had at the age of 25 and the six-month suspended sentence he'd been given for stealing from his employer in 1990. Police were called once in 1998 after he'd had an argument with his girlfriend and in 1999, he was arrested after an argument over a taxi fare, neither of which led to prosecution.

Chief Constable for Cumbria Craig Mackey, who commissioned the report, said, '[W]e could not have used our Firearms Licensing process to identify him as a risk or prevent the tragic shootings in West Cumbria.'[9]

The report, led by Assistant Chief Constable Adrian Whiting, called for a 'strengthening' of firearms laws. It also proposed more compulsory liaison with mental health services, GPs and other family members before the granting of firearms certificates. In reality, though, none of these measures would have stopped Derrick Bird, who essentially gave no warning of what he meant to do.

Short of severely restricting gun ownership or banning all guns completely, there is little the government could have done to prevent the tragedy of 2 June 2010. As Director of Firearms for the British Association for Shooting and Conservation Bill Harriman said, 'The UK's firearm's laws are among the strictest in the world. Sadly, you cannot legislate for the moment when a switch flicks in someone's head.'

CHAPTER TWENTY

King Jimmy

(2012)

There was a time when the name Jimmy Savile was synonymous with quirky humour and iconic British entertainment, but as far back as the 1970s, there were rumours that the peculiar performer was not all he appeared to be.

It would take nearly six decades, however, before it would come to light just how many top officials in some of Britain's most prestigious institutions knew what Savile was up to – and how many of those officials allowed him to operate unchecked.

James Wilson Vincent Savile was born into acute poverty in Leeds on 31 October 1926. The youngest of seven children, he left school at the age of fourteen and took a job as an office boy. At the start of the Second World War, he was sent to work as a Bevin Boy in the mines where he was seriously injured.

With a love for music and a collection of popular records, Savile took his turntable and started putting on shows at local parties and pubs. In 1948, he organised his first disco, a gig that would eventually turn Savile into a Mecca dance hall manager. By the late 1950s, he was in charge of the entertainment at 45 Mecca ballrooms throughout the nation.

Savile first came into the public eye in the early 1960s as a DJ for Radio Luxembourg, but it was as the very first host of *Top of the Pops* on BBC Television that Savile would begin his rise to fame.

Over the course of 300 episodes in twenty years, the British people came to know Savile's signature style – standard tracksuit (sometimes in gold lamé), chunky gold jewellery and his customary gigantic cigar that served as a handy prop. Despite his odd persona, he became truly legendary in his role as 'miracle worker' on *Jim'll Fix It*, a BBC programme he developed and presented on which he granted wishes to children from 1975 to 1994.[1]

If Savile was famous for his work as an entertainer, he was equally well known for his charity work. In his lifetime, he ran over 200 marathons and raised over £40 million for various charitable organizations, including the National Spinal Injuries Centre at Stoke Mandeville Hospital in Aylesbury, for which he raised £20 million alone in 1983 following a storm that caused considerable damage to their facilities.[2]

Savile was so devoted to his charity work that he actually lived on site at Stoke Mandeville and Broadmoor Hospitals, the better to entertain and bring joy to the patients. In 1988, he was chosen to head a Department of Health task force to advise on the running of the hospital for the criminally insane and reportedly ended up all but taking over operations.[1]

Savile was the picture of generosity, paying 90 per cent of his approximate £250,000 annual income into two charitable trusts and keeping just enough for himself to guarantee his personal independence.

The famous philanthropist earned the admiration of a number of high profile figures from the royal family to show business and political heavy weights. In 1971, he was awarded the OBE, followed by a papal knighthood and a knighthood from the Queen in 1990.[3]

For all his fame and glory, however, most people thought Jimmy Savile was more than a little odd. He'd made his mark with catchphrases like 'howzabout that then' and 'now then, now then', and his bizarre clownish blonde hair coupled with his distinctive yodelling to create a character that no one would forget.

His was more than just an act put on for an audience, though. For one, he seemed to have a strange attitude towards personal relationships. Though he had many acquaintances, he had very few close friends and no wives or girlfriends.

Not only did he never marry, he never appeared to have any romantic liaisons at all. When asked why not, he said that sex was 'like going to the bathroom' and that he'd rather devote himself to his career.[3]

If his romantic attitude towards women was strange, his relationship with his mother was even more bizarre. Savile was extremely close with his mother, whom he called the Duchess. When his father died in 1953, Savile brought his mother to live with him. She was often seen with him at film premieres and on holiday at the Imperial Hotel in Torquay.

When she died in 1973, Savile isolated himself with her corpse for five days. He later said they were the 'best five days of my life … she looked marvellous. She belonged to me. It's wonderful, is death.' In the years following his mother's death, Savile kept her room exactly as it had been when she was alive, even having her clothes dry-cleaned once a year.[1]

There were rumours that Savile was more than just a harmless oddball, though. In 1983, he told *The Sun* that he'd been violent in his younger days. 'The people who work for me call me the Godfather, and nobody messes with the Godfather. He is the boss. The big man.' As a telling footnote, he added, 'Some of the hairy things I've done would get me ten years inside.'[3]

The worst rumours about Savile, however, were not to do with his heavy handed treatments of drunken brawlers at dance halls but rather his handling of children and teenaged girls.

Savile always denied these claims and in fact went to great lengths to insure that he gave no appearance of impropriety. If children knocked on his door to ask for an autograph, he would refuse to answer and pass the scraps of paper through the letterbox.[1]

'Never in a million years would I dream of letting a kid, or five kids, past my front door,' he told *The Sun*. 'Never, ever. I'd feel very uncomfortable.' He also wouldn't allow a child to ride in his car without having one of their parents along because 'you just can't take the risk'. He was that worried about being accused.

One a few occasions, television presenters brought the rumours into the open and asked him the question more or less directly. In 1990, journalist Lynn Barber interviewed him for *The Independent on Sunday*.

It was in that interview that Savile suggested that the knighthood he'd just received was 'a gi-normous relief' because it got him 'off the hook'. The comment was his response to Barber's question about tabloid journalists and their quest to find enough proof of the 'skeletons in his closet' to print the story, something no one had ever been able to do.

Finally, Barber presented the topic more as a statement, opening the closet door and inviting Savile to reveal any skeletons that might be lurking inside. 'What people say,' Barber offered, 'is that you like little girls.'

Savile's evasive response, hesitant at first, neither answered Barber's question nor denied the allegation:

> *Ah now. Sure. Now then. Now then. First of all, I happen to be in the pop business, which is teenagers – that's number one. So when I go anywhere it's the young ones that come round me ... I know the people they love, the stars, because they know I saw Bros last week or Wet Wet Wet. Now you, watching from afar, might say, 'Look at those young girls throwing themselves at him', whereas in actual fact ... I am of no interest to them.*[4]

Ten years later, Louis Theroux again brought up the topic in the first episode of his documentary series *When Louis Met*. Theroux asked Savile why he would tell people he hates children and asked Savile if it was to stop tabloids questioning if he was a paedophile:

> *Jimmy: Yes, yes, yes. Oh, aye. How do they know whether I am or not? How does anybody know whether I am? Nobody knows whether I am or not. I know I'm not, so I can tell you from experience that the easy way of doing it when they're saying 'Oh, you have all them children on Jim'll Fix It', say 'Yeah, I hate 'em.'*

Louis: Yeah. To me that sounds more, sort of, suspicious in a way though, because it seems so implausible.

Jimmy: Well, that's my policy, that's the way it goes. That's what I do. And it's worked a dream.[5]

In 2007, Irish radio presenter Orla Barry revisited the issue once more, this time asking directly. Savile denied having ever heard so much as a rumour:

Oh … Never heard of it in my life … Now you see when you get a documentary like [Louis Theroux's], what they do is they keep prodding you and … what they hope is that you will fall out with them. And then they think that makes good television.[6]

Despite Savile's denials, the allegations against him would become more serious. In 2007, three former students from the Duncroft Approved School for Girls came forward to say that Savile had sexually abused them when they were teenagers years before.

Surrey police questioned Savile under caution about the incident, but the case was dropped when the authorities were unable to find enough evidence to confirm the allegations.[7] The only evidence they had was the word of the victims – and one throwaway comment Savile had made on Louis Theroux's documentary.

When Theroux asked if Savile used to be a wrestler, Savile quipped, 'Still am. I'm feared in every girls' school in Britain.' When asked what he meant, Savile called the comment a 'pleasantry', just a 'J – O – K – E'.[5]

Former Duncroft head teacher Margaret Jones later said she knew nothing of the abuse at the time. '[The alleged victims] should've reported him,' said Ms Jones in an interview with the *Daily Mail* several years after the incident. 'They knew if they reported him to me I'd report him to the police.'

In the same interview, Ms Jones – who reportedly allowed Savile to sleep overnight at the school and take the girls on unsupervised rides in his Rolls

Royce – also called the claims of her former students 'wild allegations by well known delinquents'. The victims said they did, in fact, tell Ms Jones at the time of the abuse, only to be dismissed.[8]

The following year, Savile was implicated in a scandal at the Haut de la Garenne Jersey Children's Home, where it was revealed that residents of the home had been victims of abuse for decades. In 2008, police took statements from 192 alleged victims at the home. Savile's name came up as one of several people accused of perpetrating sexual abuse against the children.

Shortly after the scandal broke, *The Sun* published several articles linking Savile to the affair. In response, Savile began legal proceedings to sue the paper in March 2008, claiming he had never been to the home.

A short time later, a photo surfaced picturing a smiling Savile in sunglasses and jacket surrounded by about thirty children on the grounds of Jersey Children's Home, one of whom holds a sign: 'Jim fixed it for us'. Savile tried and failed to have the photo suppressed.

He finally admitted that he had been a regular visitor to the home, but despite Savile's dishonesty, there was no evidence to connect him to any abuse and the case against him was dropped.[9]

Police again interviewed Savile in 2009, this time at his office at Stoke Mandeville Hospital. In the interview, the police asked Savile – whom they casually called 'Jimmy' – about allegations that he had touched a girl 'over her clothes'. Savile dismissed the accusations, saying he always had 'women looking for a few quid … coming up for Christmas'.

During the interview, Savile told police that throughout the years, he'd found the best way to deal with anyone who accused him of sexual impropriety was to threaten to sue. He said he'd never had to actually sue anyone because 'my people can book time in the Old Bailey so my legal people are ready and waiting. All they need would be a name and an address, and then the due process from my angle would stop.'[10]

His ploy – to threaten put his accusers on trial – worked well. For years, the burden of proof had been on victims to prove what had happened to them. If the only case to be made was one word against another, who could afford to stand up to the venerable Jimmy Savile, who had devoted so much of his life and career to charity? The answer was nobody.

When Savile died in 2011 at the age of 84, he was remembered with honour and dignity. Prince Charles released a statement from Clarence House expressing his condolences.[2] Adam Sweeting of *The Guardian* called him 'an impossible act to follow'.[3] The writer for *The Telegraph*, perhaps somewhat less kind, summed him up as 'simply an odd chap'.[1] In other words, no one really knew what to think of Jimmy Savile, but now he was well and truly off the hook.

The world finally took notice of the rumours against Savile on 3 October 2012 when ITV released its documentary *Exposure: The Other Side of Jimmy Savile*. A year in the making, the programme included interviews with a number of women who said they had been in their teens when Savile sexually abused them during the 1970s.

One of the victims was Katrina Rose. In the documentary, she explained how she had been fourteen years old and very naïve when Savile invited her to see a studio at the BBC before stopping at his flat. It was there that the assault took place, she said.

When the assault happened, she reported it but she was also told that she needed to be 'prepared for the media circus' it would cause. Unwilling to have 'press camped out on [her] doorstep', Rose chose not to pursue the matter, a decision she said she later regretted.[11]

Following the documentary, Scotland Yard opened a formal criminal investigation. Called Operation Yewtree, the investigation sought to examine the allegations of what Commander Peter Spindler called a 'staggering' number of victims who had come forward after seeing the programme, saying Savile had abused them as well.

By the end of October 2012, the operation had already identified 200 potential victims, most of whom had been abused as children. It had also identified abuse that had happened at the hands of 'other individuals' in addition to Savile.

John Cameron of the Nation Society for the Prevention of Cruelty to Children called Savile a 'well organised, prolific sex offender' who had used 'his power, his authority and his influence to procure children and offend against them'.

When asked why the victims had not spoken out before, Cameron said he was not surprised it had taken so long for the allegations to surface:

> *It's very difficult for children … when they're being victims of sexual abuse from people that they know, to speak out. So you can imagine what it must be like for young children who are being abused by people in significant power, like celebrities.*[12]

The authorities began a massive operation looking into dozens of police reports involving accusations against Savile. There were hundreds from across the nation, dating as far back as 1955 when Savile was a dance hall manager. In 1960, he reportedly seriously sexually assaulted a ten-year-old boy in his hotel room. In 1965, there were reports of abuse at the BBC, Leeds General Infirmary (where Savile volunteered), Stoke Mandeville and Broadmoor.

In 1966, Savile began a period of extensive abuse. In 1970, there were reports of his abuse of the girls at Duncroft Approved School for Girls. In 1972, he was reported for groping a twelve-year-old boy and his two female friends at *Top of the Pops*. In several reports, Savile assaulted young women in a caravan he kept parked on the premises at the BBC and elsewhere. The reports went on and on.[13]

During the course of the investigation, Operation Yewtree also looked into other potential sexual predators. Paul Francis Gadd, also known as Gary Glitter, was famously convicted of one count of attempted rape, four counts of indecent assault and one count of sexual intercourse with a girl under the age of thirteen. Rolf Harris was also found guilty of twelve counts of indecent assault against four girls, the youngest of whom was just eight at the time of the assault.

The investigation also turned into something of a witch hunt. Dave Lee Travis was convicted of one count of indecent assault, but it would take two more trials to clear him of another fourteen counts.

Freddie Starr was arrested four times as part of Operation Yewtree but was never charged. Jim Davidson, DJ Mike Osman, comedian Jimmy Tarbuck, radio producer Ted Beston, former BBC producer Wilfred De'ath and broadcaster Paul Gambaccini (who spent a year on bail) were all arrested but never charged.[14] Whether these men were guilty or not, the damage was done. The accusations were enough to cast their names and reputations under permanent suspicion.

As the truth about Savile came tumbling forth, more and more people began to ask hard questions about how the eccentric performer could have been allowed to operate so prolifically. He had been given keys to Broadmoor and Stoke Mandeville, after all, that had allowed him access to his most vulnerable victims at all hours of the night and day.[15] At the BBC, he was often allowed to be left alone in his dressing room with children.

Four years after Savile's death, the truth came out – people had been trying to blow the whistle on Jimmy Savile for decades.

In a 2015 interview with Piers Morgan, musician John Lydon (better known as Johnny Rotten of the Sex Pistols) spoke of an interview he recorded in 1978. Morgan played an excerpt of the 1978 interview in which Lydon makes reference to Savile:

> I'd like to kill Jimmy Savile. I think he's a hypocrite. I think he's into all kinds of seediness that we all know about but we're not allowed to talk about. I know some 'rumours'. I'll bet none of this will be allowed out ... Nothing I've said is libel.

In fact, the interview was not aired in 1978 and the 2015 Piers Morgan programme was the first time Lydon's claims were ever heard by the public.[16]

Even worse, a 2014 inquiry found that up to a thousand people, most of them children, had been abused or assaulted by Savile on BBC premises for over 40 years. While it was happening, the inquiry revealed, a huge number of BBC staff knew what was going on and, rather than protecting the children, they stood by and let it happen.

Peter Saunders, Chief Executive of the National Association for People Abused in Childhood, consulted on the inquiry. '[One] thing I have found extraordinary, and very sad,' Saunders said, 'is the number of people I have spoken to connected to the BBC, and that is a lot of people, who said: "Oh yes, we all knew about him."'[17]

The BBC was so eager to protect itself, however, that when reporters for its *Newsnight* programme spoke with the former students of Duncroft Approved School for Girls immediately following Savile's death in November 2011, the company pulled the episode, showing tributes of Savile over the Christmas holiday instead. The *Newsnight* episode exposing Savile, in fact, never aired.[13]

The BBC wasn't the only prestigious British establishment to uphold the image of the iconic Jimmy Savile over his victims. January 2014 saw the publication of fourteen reports detailing decades of abuse at Savile's hands across the NHS. The reports revealed that staff made ten separate complaints against Savile, but that none of these complaints were taken seriously.

The reports indicated that Savile had abused a total of 177 patients aged between five and 75 in 41 different hospitals. When members of staff tried to complain about Savile's abuse, they were 'severely reprimanded' and the complaints were dropped. As one worker was told, 'We have to tolerate him because he makes so much money.'

Despite the ten complaints that were made, senior managers claimed that at 'no stage' were they ever made aware of Savile's 'sexual offending or his unsatisfactory portering'. One excerpt from the report, however, finds that claim difficult to believe:

> *Between 1968 and 1992 Savile sexually abused 60 individuals connected with Stoke Mandeville Hospital. These victims ranged in age from eight to 40 years. The victims were patients, staff, visitors, volunteers and charity fundraisers. The sexual abuse ranged from inappropriate touching to rape.*[18]

It seems almost impossible that Savile could have gotten away with such a serious level of abuse for as a long as he did, but the fact was that he was often dealing with children (and adults) who started out star struck and ended up intimidated.

Take Kevin Cook, who was only nine years old when he went on Savile's *Jim'll Fix It* show, where he'd been told he would be getting a prized Jim'll Fix It badge. At first, Cook said it was 'a fantastic day – we thought we'd died and gone to heaven'. He was dazzled when he saw the *Starsky and Hutch* actors, and was thrilled to be part of the show.

Then Savile took the young Scout into his dressing room where he molested the boy and forced the child to touch him intimately. The fantastic day turned into a day Cook would never forget, for all the wrong reasons:

> *After I'd done up my shorts, Jimmy warned me not to tell. He became really scary and said, 'Don't you dare tell anyone. Don't even tell your mates. We know where you live.' Then he said, 'Nobody would believe you anyway – I'm King Jimmy.'*[19]

For all his many accomplishments and charitable contributions, the name Jimmy Savile is now synonymous with paedophilia. Even though he abused literally hundreds of children, he died without one charge having ever been brought against him. In 2000, Savile boldly told Louis Theroux, 'I could get away with anything'.[5]

In the end, he was right.

Acknowledgements

There are always a number of people I feel compelled to thank for contributing to any book, and this one is no different.

First and foremost is the team at New Holland, including Managing Director Fiona Schultz and publisher Alan Whiticker, editor Diane Wadsworth, designers Thomas Partridge and Andrew Quinlan and printers Toppan Leefung Printing.

Dennis Jarrett and Claire Chambers Calvey were instrumental in their feedback in helping me choose which historic crimes were the most profound, for which they have both earned my eternal gratitude.

A huge thank you goes out to my many friends, acquaintances and former colleagues for their thoughts and opinions on British culture, including Kate Breese, Sue Woodley, Stuart Hart, Heather Gorman, Angela Huddart, Iain Wilkie, Louise Wrankmore, Kirsten Austin, Mairi Claire Dunlin, Jon Muller, Collette Twyford, Joanne Metcalf, Jacqueline Hamood and Tamsin Venter. If I have missed anyone, I do apologise. Please know that I am deeply grateful in my heart.

Many thanks also go to Alex Nasla, Anna McCormack, Nancy Sutcliffe, Terry Fulton, Claire Chambers Calvey, Heather Gorman and Robin Batten for their salient thoughts on Rupert Murdoch. I especially want to thank Scott Douglas for his insight into the daily workings of a Scottish primary school classroom in the 1990s and Tanya Keshavjee for her vital translation of a key Spanish source.

Of course, I could not have written this book without the help of my steadfast editorial assistants Jacob and Nathan, who are becoming masters at the art of making toasted cheese sandwiches, and Isaac and Jonty, who never failed to pretend to be interested in which serial killer I was writing about this week.

Also I have to say a heartfelt thank you to my dear husband Terry Fulton, who was able to explain to me over and over again why the guy sitting opposite me on the train was probably not plotting to follow me home and murder me. After writing this book, everyone looks dodgy.

Endnotes

Chapter One: 1888 - Jack the Ripper

1. Maxim Jakubowski and Nathan Braund (ed) *The Mammoth Book of Jack the Ripper*, Robinson Publishing, London, 1999, p. 17.
2. Jakubowski and Braund p. 17.
3. Peter Thurgood, *Abberline: The Man Who Hunted Jack the Ripper*, The History Press, Gloucestershire, 2013, ebook edition.
4. Steward P Evans and Keith Skinner, *The Ultimate Jack the Ripper Sourcebook: An Illustrated Encyclopedia*, Constable and Robinson, London, 2000, p. 4-7.
5. Dr Rees Llewellyn, Autopsy Report for Mary Ann Nichols, 1888.
6. Dr George Phillips, Autopsy Report for Annie Chapman, 1888.
7. Dr George Phillips, Autopsy Report for Elizabeth Stride, 1888.
8. Jakubowski and Braund p. 39.
9. Dr Gordon Brown, Autopsy Report for Catherine Eddowes, 1888.
10. Dr Thomas Bond, Autopsy Report for Mary Jane Kelly, 1888.
11. Jakubowski and Braund p. 54.
12. Dr Thomas Bond, Report to Inspector Frederick Abberline, 1888.

Chapter 2: 1910 - Dr Crippen

1. John Elmsley, *Molecules of Murder*, The Royal Society of Chemistry, Cambridge, 2008, p. 34.
2. Geoffrey Howse, *Murder and Mayhem in North London*, Wharncliffe, South Yorkshire, 2010, p. 41-42.
3. Howse p. 43.
4. Filson Young (ed), *Notable British Trials*, William Hodge and Company

Limited, London, 1920.

5. Nicholas Connell, *Walter Drew: The Man Who Caught Crippen*, Sutton Publishing Limited, United Kingdom, 2005, e-book edition.

6. Old Bailey Proceedings Online, 'Trial of Hawley Harvey Crippen', October 1910, retrieved 18 January 2016. <www.oldbaileyonline.org>

7. Howse p. 44.

8. Howse p. 46.

9. Richard Cavendish, 'The Execution of Dr Crippen', HistoryToday.com, Volume 60, Issue 11, November 2010, retrieved 18 January 2016. <http://www. historytoday.com/richard-cavendish/execution-dr-crippen>

10. 'Dr Crippen', British Military and Criminal History 1900 to 1999, retrieved 18 January 2016. <http://www.stephen-stratford.co.uk/dr_crippen.htm>

11. Howse p. 50.

12. Howse p. 51.

13. Howse p. 53.

14. Dr David Foran with Beth Wills, Brianne Kiley, Carrie Jackson and John Trestrail, *The Conviction of Dr Crippen: New Forensic Findings in a Century-Old Murder*, The Journal of Forensic Science, Forbio.msu.edu, August 2010, Wiley Online Library, p. 7. Retrieved 20 January 2016. <http://forbio.msu.edu/Crippen%20paper.pdf>

Chapter 3: 1915 – The Case of the Brides in the Bath

1. 'England Emigration and Immigration', Family Search, retrieved 25 January 2016. <https://familysearch.org/learn/wiki/en/England_Emigration_and_Immigration>

2. David Leafe, 'Solved: How the brides in the bath died at the hands of their ruthless womanizing husband', 22 April 2010, retrieved 25 January 2016. <http://www.dailymail.co.uk/femail/article-1267913/Solved-How-brides-bath-died-hands-ruthless-womaniser.html>

3. Eric Watson (ed), *Notable British Trials: The Case of George Joseph Smith*, William Hodge and Company Limited, London, 1922, e-book edition.

4. Meaghan Good, '1915: George Joseph Smith, Brides in the Bath murderer', 13 August 2011, retrieved 25 January 2016. <http://www.executedtoday.com/2011/08/13/1915-george-joseph-smith-brides-in-the-bath-murderer/>

5. Gordon Honeycombe, *Murder of the Black Museum: The Dark Secrets Behind a Hundred Years of the Most Notorious Crimes in England*, John Blake Publishing, London, 2011, e-book edition.

6. Geoffrey Howse, *Murder and Mayhem in North London*, Wharncliffe, South Yorkshire, 2010, e-book edition.

7. Jane Robins, *The Magnificent Spilsbury and the Case of the Brides in the Bath*,

Hatchette, UK, 2010, e-book edition.

8. 'Brides in the Bath Murders', Metropolitan Police, Content.Met.police.uk, retrieved 25 January 2016. <http://content.met.police.uk/Article/Brides-in-the-Bath Murders/1400015481775/1400015481775>

9. Giovanni Di Stefano and Caroline Bayford, 'The Brides in the Bath murders – new evidence suggests George Joseph Smith may have been innocent', OPC Global, 21 December 2013, retrieved 25 January 2016. <http://www.onlinepublishingcompany.info/content/read_more/complexInfobox/site_news/infobox/elements/template/d/active_id/8848>

10. 'Bogus Italian lawyer Giovanni di Stefano found guilty', BBC News, 27 March 2013, retrieved 28 January 2016. <http://www.bbc.com/news/uk-21957686>

Chapter 4: 1953 – 10 Rillington Place

1. Jonathan Oates, *John Christie of Rillington Place: Biography of a Serial Killer*, Wharncliffe True Crime, South Yorkshire, 2012, p. 1-2.

2. 'The Rillington Place Murders', *Murder Casebook: Investigations into the Ultimate Crime*, Volume 1 Part 4, Marshall Cavendish Limited, London, 1990.

3. Oates p. 3

4. Oates p. 5

5. Oates p. 8

6. Oates p. 10

7. Oates p. 12

8. Oates p. 16

9. 'John Christie: Biography', Biography.com, retrieved 30 January 2016. <http://www.biography.com/people/john-christie-17169730#trial-and-aftermath>

10. Burl Barer et al, *Serial Killer Quarterly Vol.1 No.4 "Cruel Britannia"*, Grinning Man Press, 2014, e-book edition.

11. Nigel Wier, *British Serial Killers*, AuthorHouse, Indiana USA, 2011, p. 141.

12. Leonara Rustamova, *Yorkshire's Strangest Tales: Extraordinary But True Stories*, Portico Books, London, 2013, e-book edition.

13. Oates p. 131

14. Kendra Cherry, 'What Is the Average IQ?', Psychology.About.com, 2 January 2016, retrieved 1 February 2016. <http://psychology.about.com/od/intelligence/f/average-iq.htm>

15. Oates p. 174-175

16. Colin Wilson, 'The Two Killers of Rillington Place', JohnEddowes.com, retrieved 1 February 2016.
<http://www.johneddowes.com>

17. Satish Sekar, *The Cardiff Five: Innocent Beyond Any Doubt*, Waterside Press Ltd, Hampshire UK, 2012, p. 162-163.

Chapter 5: 1963 - The Great Train Robbery

1. 'Bruce Richards Reynolds Interview with Julian Broadhead', Nick Reynolds Cons to Icons Exhibition, Clerkenwell Literary Festival, 1999, posted by John McManus 7 March 2013, retrieved 2 February 2016.
<https://www.youtube.com/watch?v=GX_QHfI9644>
2. Sam Delaney, 'The Great Train Robbery: what was Bruce Reynolds really like?' RadioTimes.com, 18 December 2013, retrieved 2 February 2016. <http://www.radiotimes.com/news/2013-12-18/the-great-train-robbery-what-was-bruce-reynolds-really-like>
3. Nick Russell-Pavier and Stewart Richards, *The Great Train Robbery: Crime of the Century: The Definitive Account*, Phoenix, Great Britain, 2013, e-book edition.
4. Maume, Chris, 'Gordon Goody: Criminal who admitted that he had been the mastermind behind the Great Train Robbery', Independent.co.uk, 30 January 2016, retrieved 2 February 2016.
<http://www.independent.co.uk/news/obituaries/gordon-goody-criminal-who-admitted-that-he-had-been-the-mastermind-behind-the-great-train-robbery-a6843246.html>
5. 'Charlie Wilson: The Great Train Robbery', BBC.co.uk, retrieved 2 February 2016. <http://www.bbc.co.uk/programmes/profiles/10Cjx03LCcgjhskBQ9cC9tR/charlie-wilson>
6. 'James "Jimmy" Edward White', ThamesValley.police.uk, retrieved 2 February 2016.
<http://www.thamesvalley.police.uk/aboutus/aboutus-museum/aboutus-museum-gtr/aboutus-museum-gtr-gang/aboutus-museum-gtr-gang-white.htm>
7. 'Ronnie Biggs', Biography.com, retrieved 2 February 2016.
<http://www.biography.com/people/ronnie-biggs-20730907>
8. 'Great Train Robber Tommy Wisbey only regret was "getting caught"', GrimsbyTelegraph.co.uk, 5 August 2015, retrieved 2 February 2016.
<http://www.grimsbytelegraph.co.uk/Great-Train-Robber-Tommy-Wisbey-regret-getting/story-27544563-detail/story.html>
9. Paul Harris, 'Great Train Robber finally admits to coshing engine driver in deathbed confession that solves 49-year-old mystery of who was behind attack during notorious 1963 raid', DailyMail.co.uk, 14 November 2012, retrieved 2 February 2016.
<http://www.dailymail.co.uk/news/article-2232668/Great-Train-Robber-solves-49-year-old-mystery-deathbed-confession-injured-engine-driver-1963-attack.html>
10. 'The Great Train Robbery: 1963', BTP.police.uk, retrieved 2 February 2016.
<http://www.btp.police.uk/about_us/our_history/crime_history/the_great_train_

robbery,_1963.aspx>

11. Tracy McVeigh, 'The quiet Great Train Robber reveals identity of the gang's mystery insider', TheGuardian.com, 28 September 2014, retrieved 2 February 2016.
<http://www.theguardian.com/uk-news/2014/sep/28/great-train-robber-douglas-gordon-goody-reveals-identity-mystery-inside>

12. 'Great Train Robbers' links to Wiltshire and the West', WesternDailyPress.co.uk, 18 December 2013, retrieved 3 February 2016.
<http://www.westerndailypress.co.uk/Ronnie-Biggs-link-Wiltshire-West/story-20336796-detail/story.html>

13. Brett Gibbons, 'The day one of the Great Train Robbers escaped from a Birmingham prison', BirminghamMail.co.uk, 4 March 2013, retrieved 3 February 2016.
<http://www.birminghammail.co.uk/news/local-news/day-great-train-robber-charles-1718100>

14. Matthew Weaver and Jonathan Watts, 'Ronnie Biggs, Great Train Robber, dies aged 84', TheGuardian.com, 18 December 2013, retrieved 3 February 2016.
<http://www.theguardian.com/uk-news/2013/dec/18/ronnie-biggs-great-train-robber-dies-84>

15. 'James "Big Jim" Hussey. Great train robber. Born 1933. Died November 12, 2012. Aged 79.' Express.co.uk, 17 November 2012, retrieved 3 February 2016.
<http://www.express.co.uk/expressyourself/358760/James-Big-Jim-Hussey-Great-train-robber-Born-1933-Died-November-12-2012-Aged-79>

16. 'Brian Arthur Field', ThamesValley.police.uk, retrieved 3 February 2016.
http://www.thamesvalley.police.uk/aboutus/aboutus-museum/aboutus-museum-gtr/aboutus-museum-gtr-gang/aboutus-museum-gtr-gang-fieldb.htm

17. 'Robert Alfred Welch', ThamesValley.police.uk, retrieved 3 February.
<http://www.thamesvalley.police.uk/aboutus/aboutus-museum/aboutus-museum-gtr/aboutus-museum-gtr-gang/aboutus-museum-gtr-gang-wel.htm>

18. 'Train robber John Daly won respect as Launceston dustman', CornishGuardian.co.uk, 1 May 2013, retrieved 3 February 2016.
<http://www.cornishguardian.co.uk/Train-robber-John-Daly-won-respect-Launceston/story-18847198-detail/story.html>

19. Kate Watson-Smyth, '"Weasel" train robber dies, aged 61', Independent.co.uk, 22 August 1997, retrieved 3 February 2016.
<http://www.independent.co.uk/news/weasel-train-robber-dies-aged-61-1246594.html>

20. 'The Great Train Robbers: Who Were They?' BBC.com, 18 December 2013, retrieved 3 February 2016.
<http://www.bbc.com/news/uk-21619150>

21. Steve Boggan, 'Train robber Edwards is found hanged', Independent.co.uk, 30

November 1994, retrieved 3 February 2016.
<http://www.independent.co.uk/news/train-robber-edwards-is-found-hanged-1440017.html>
22. Paul Harris, 'Two fingers to you all: Frail and wheelchair-bound, Ronnie Biggs, 83, makes a feeble gesture of defiance at the funeral of one of his train robber pals', DailyMail.co.uk, 21 March 2013, retrieved 3 February 2016.
23. Duncan Campbell, 'Great Train Robber Bruce Reynolds dies aged 81', TheGuardian.com, 28 February 2013, retrieved 3 February 2016.
<http://www.theguardian.com/uk/2013/feb/28/great-train-robber-bruce-reynolds-dies>

Chapter 6: 1965 – Jack the Stripper

1. 'Jack the Stripper', *Murder Casebook: Investigations into the Ultimate Crime*, Volume 2 Part 33, Marshall Cavendish Limited, London, 1990.
2. Alan Whiticker, *101 Crimes of the Century*, New Holland Publishers, Sydney, 2007, p. 114-116.
3. Tony Moore, *Policing Notting Hill: Fifty Years of Turbulence*, Waterside Press, UK, 2013, p. 108.
4. Moore p. 109
5. Moore p. 112
6. Moore p. 106
7. Moore p. 106-108
8. Moore p. 109-111
9. Moore p. 114
10. Moore p. 115-116
11. Moore p. 116
12. Moore p. 117
13. 'The Nude Murders: Jack the Stripper', MurderMap.co.uk, retrieved 5 February 2016.
<http://www.murdermap.co.uk/pages/cases/case.asp?CID=597117303>
14. Moore p. 119
15. 'The Nude Murders: Report linking the unsolved murder Bridgette O'Hara with those of …' Discovery.NationalArchives.gov.uk, retrieved 5 February 2016.
<http://discovery.nationalarchives.gov.uk/details/r/C10888055>

Chapter 7: 1966 – The Moors Murders

1. Leslie Roberts, 'Remembering the words and pictures that exposed Glasgow's slums in the 1940s', DailyRecord.co.uk, 7 April 2013, retrieved 8 February 2016.
<http://www.dailyrecord.co.uk/news/real-life/words-pictures-exposed-glasgows-slums-1815740#vYtfhBK0ZdOMq5vP.97>

2. 'Ian Brady', Biography.com, retrieved 8 February 2016.
<http://www.biography.com/people/ian-brady-17169718>
3. 'Ian Brady: the illegitimate son of a waitress obsessed with torture', Telegraph.
co.uk, 17 August 2012, retrieved 8 February 2016.
<http://www.telegraph.co.uk/news/uknews/9481752/Ian-Brady-the-illegitimate-
son-of-a-waitress-obsessed-with-torture.html>
4. David Collins, 'Medomsley borstal sex ring: Police set to arrest 18 prison
warders in abuse inquiry', Mirror.co.uk, 14 November 2014, retrieved 8 February
2016.
<http://www.mirror.co.uk/news/uk-news/medomsley-borstal-sex-ring-
police-4576925>
5. 'Profile: Moors Murderer Ian Brady', BBC.com, 13 June 2013, retrieved 8
February 2016.
<http://www.bbc.com/news/uk-18690303>
6. Jean Rafferty, 'My friend Ian Brady', HeraldScotland.com, 8 July 2012, retrieved
8 February 2016.
<http://www.heraldscotland.com/news/13064518.My_friend_Ian_Brady/>
7. Carol Ann Lee, *One of Your Own: The Life and Death of Myra Hindley*,
Mainstream Publishing Company, Edinburgh, 2010, e-book edition.
8. 'Death at 60 for the woman who came to personify evil', Scotsman.com, 18
November 2002, retrieved 8 February 2016.
<http://www.scotsman.com/news/uk/death-at-60-for-the-woman-who-came-to-
personify-evil-1-628780>
9. Duncan Staff, 'Portrait of a Serial Killer', TheGuardian.com, 19 November
2002, retrieved 8 February 2016.
<http://www.theguardian.com/uk/2002/nov/18/ukcrime.childprotection>
10. 'Back in the Day; the first of Britain's Moors Murders', EuroNews.com, 12
July 2013, retrieved 9 February 2016.
<http://www.euronews.com/2013/07/12/back-in-the-day-pauline-reades-murder-
first-victim-of-the-moors-murders/>
11. Jean Ritchie, *Myra Hindley—Inside the Mind of a Murderess*, Angus &
Robertson, Sydney, 1988, p. 46-47.
12. Ritchie p. 56-58
13. Carol Ann Lee with David Smith, *Evil Relations* (formerly published as
Witness): *The Man Who Bore Witness*, Mainstream Publishing, Edinburgh, 2011,
e-book edition.
14. Ritchie p. 78
15. Peter Topping, *Topping: The Autobiography of the Police Chief in the Moors
Murder Case*, Angus & Robertson, London, 1989, p. 120-121.
16. Topping p. 122-124
17. Ritchie p. 91

18. Topping p. 35

19. 'I will never forget that awful tape: Daily Mirror reporter recalls sheer terror of Ian Brady torture recording played at court', Mirror.co.uk, 18 August 2012, retrieved 8 February 2016.
<http://www.mirror.co.uk/news/uk-news/ian-brady-and-myra-hindley-court-1266949>

20. Jackie Anderson, 'Ian Brady: Let him rot', ThinkScotland.org, 1 September 2012, retrieved 9 February 2016.
<http://thinkscotland.org/thinkliving/articles.html?read_full=11608&article=www.thinkscotland.org>

21. Topping p. 268

22. Ritchie p. 274

23. Topping p. 146-147

24. Elizabeth Sanderson, 'Hidden face of a monster to be revealed: Ian Brady will be seen in public for first time in 46 years via TV link after Europe ruling', DailyMail.co.uk, 1 July 2012, retrieved 9 February 2016.
<http://www.dailymail.co.uk/news/article-2167033/Ian-Brady-seen-public-time-46-years-TV-link-Europe-ruling.html>

25. Keiligh Baker, 'Moors murderer Ian Brady writes letter from his hospital bed describing how he thinks he will die soon after breaking hip and arm but wishes he had taken his own life years ago', DailyMail.co.uk, 22 January 2015, retrieved 6 February 2016.
<http://www.dailymail.co.uk/news/article-2920420/Moors-murderer-Ian-Brady-wishes-taken-life-years-ago.html>

26. Nikki Murfitt, 'The secrets of my friend the Moors murderer: For 25 years he has been visiting Britain's most notorious killer, now Ian Brady's only confidant - and heir - reveals all', DailyMail.co.uk, 23 June 2013, retrieved 9 February 2016.
<http://www.dailymail.co.uk/news/article-2346498/Ian-Bradys-confidant--heir--reveals-all.html>

Chapter 8: 1968 - The Case of the Torso on the Train

1. 'Left Luggage Killers', *Murder Casebook: Investigations into the Ultimate Crime*, Volume 8 Part 109, Marshall Cavendish Limited, London, 1991.

2. Juan Ignacio Blanco, 'Suchnam Singh Sandhu', Murderpedia.org, retrieved 11 February 2016.
<http://murderpedia.org/male.S/s/sandhu.htm>

3. 'From the Archives: Poster appeal helps catch Torso on Train killer', BirminghamMail.co.uk, 14 October 2012, retrieved 11 February 2016.
<http://www.birminghammail.co.uk/news/local-news/from-the-archives-poster-appeal-helps-catch-180168>

4. W Owen Cole and Douglas Charing, *Six World Faiths*, Cassell Publisher Limited, London, 1982, p. 322-323.

5. Manjeet Sehgal, 'Honour killing in Hoshiarpur: Couple hacked to death by girl's father, family', IndiaToday.in, 5 January 2015, retrieved 12 February 2016. <http://indiatoday.intoday.in/story/honour-killing-hoshiarpur-punjab-dalit-couple-hacked-to-death-by-girls-father-family/1/411556.html>

6. Navjeevan Gopal, 'Punjab "honour killing": Woman hacked to death', 17 July 2015, retrieved 12 February 2016. <http://indianexpress.com/article/india/india-others/punjab-honour-killing-woman-hacked-to-death/>

7. 'India "honour killings": Paying the price for falling in love', BBC.com, 20 September 2013, retrieved 12 February 2016. <http://www.bbc.com/news/world-asia-india-24170866>

8. John Bingham, 'Honour killing: father convicted of murder of Tulay Goren', Telegraph.co.uk, 17 December 2009, retrieved 12 February 2016. <http://www.telegraph.co.uk/news/uknews/crime/6832862/Honour-killing-father-convicted-of-murder-of-Tulay-Goren.html>

9. Sunny Hundal, 'The left cannot remain silent over "honour killings"', NewStatesman.com, 4 August 2012, retrieved 12 February 2016. <http://www.newstatesman.com/blogs/politics/2012/08/left-cannot-remain-silent-over-honour-killings>

10. Emily Andrews, 'Honour killing theory as mother-of-two is found dumped in the street with her hand severed', DailyMail.co.uk, 18 November 2009, retrieved 12 February 2016. <http://www.dailymail.co.uk/news/article-1228561/Woman-dies-hours-mutilated-street-hand-cut-off.html>

11. Peter Walker, 'Geeta Aulakh killing: a brutal murder ordered by a jealous husband', TheGuardian.com, 4 December 2010, retrieved 12 February 2016. <http://www.theguardian.com/uk/2010/dec/03/geeta-aulakh-murder-background-story>

Chapter 9: 1969 - The Kray Brothers

1. Maureen Paton, 'Nuns on the (BABY) run', DailyMail.co.uk, 7 January 2012, retrieved 17 February 2016. <http://www.dailymail.co.uk/femail/article-2082629/Sisters-St-John-braved-squalor-1960s-East-End-London-deliver-babies.html>

2. Leon Watson, 'We always said Reggie was losing his marbles: Never-before-seen honeymoon pictures of Kray brother and his doomed wife at the Acropolis', DailyMail.co.uk, 22 May 2012, retrieved 17 February 2016. <http://www.dailymail.co.uk/news/article-2147735/Never-seen-honeymoon-

pictures-Reggie-Kray-new-bride-Acropolis-auction.html>

3. John Pearson, *The Profession of Violence: The Rise and Fall of the Kray Twins*, Bloomsbury Reader, London, 2013, e-book edition.

4. Wayne Neil et al, *The Krays: From the Cradle to the Grave*, Media Arts, UK, 2013, e-book edition.

5. John Pearson, *Notorious: The Immortal Legend of the Kray Twins*, Arrow, UK, 2011, e-book edition.

6. Charlie Kray, *Doing the Business: The Final Confession of the Senior Kray Brother*, John Blake Publishing Ltd, London, 2011, e-book edition.

7. Geraldine Bedell, 'Coming out of the dark ages', TheGuardian.com, 24 June 2007, retrieved 18 February 2016.
<http://www.theguardian.com/society/2007/jun/24/communities.gayrights>

8. Rachel Bletchly, 'Covered up for 50 years: How Ronnie Kray and top Tory peer "hunted young men"', Mirror.co.uk, 23 October 2015, retrieved 19 February 2016.
<http://www.mirror.co.uk/news/uk-news/covered-up-50-years-how-6686843>

9. Jacky Hyams, 'How an arts-loving schoolgirl so beautiful she was mistaken for Brigitte Bardot ended her life as the tragic first Mrs Reggie Kray', DailyMail. co.uk, 11 March 2015, retrieved 19 February 2016.
<http://www.dailymail.co.uk/news/article-2989569/How-arts-loving-schoolgirl-beautiful-mistaken-Brigitte-Bardot-ended-life-tragic-Mrs-Reggie-Kray.html>

10. '"Wall of silence" around Krays', News.BBC.co.uk, 18 October 2001, retrieved 19 February 2016.
<http://news.bbc.co.uk/2/hi/uk_news/england/1607666.stm>

11. 'The Krays', Content.Met.Police.uk, retrieved 19 February 2016.
<http://content.met.police.uk/Article/The-Kra ys/1400015485453/1400015485453>

12. Lenny Hamilton with Craig Cabell, *Getting Away with Murder*, John Blake Publishing, London, 2006, e-book edition.

13. Warren Manger, 'Krays gangster admits he dumped a body for the twins but insists they were NOT legends', Mirror.co.uk, 9 September 2015, retrieved 19 February 2016.
<http://www.mirror.co.uk/news/uk-news/krays-gangster-admits-dumped-body-6400288>

Chapter 10: 1969 – A Case of Mistaken Identity

1. 'The McKay Kidnap', *Murder Casebook: Investigations into the Ultimate Crime*, Volume 2 Part 17, Marshall Cavendish Limited, London, 1990.

2. Francis Joseph, 'Englishwoman missing for 39 years', Guardian.co.tt, 4 April 2009, retrieved 15 February 2016.
<http://www.guardian.co.tt/archives/news/crime/2009/04/04/englishwoman-

missing-39-years>

3. Alex Day, 'Writer's appeal over landmark Stocking Pelham murder', HertsandEssexObserver.co.uk, 5 December 2010, retrieved 15 February 2016. <http://www.hertsandessexobserver.co.uk/Writers-appeal-landmark-Stocking-Pelham-murder/story-21863336-detail/story.html>

4. 'Rupert Murdoch', Biography.com, retrieved 15 February 2016. <http://www.biography.com/people/rupert-murdoch-9418489>

5. Michael Newton, *The Encyclopedia of Kidnappings*, Facts on File Inc, New York, 2002, p. 248.

6. Shawn Moynihan, '8 steps to negotiate kidnap and ransom demands', PropertyCasualty360.com, 8 July 2014, retrieved 16 February 2016. <http://www.propertycasualty360.com/2014/07/08/how-to-negotiate-kidnap-ransom-demands-8-steps?t=es-specialty&slreturn=1455584215&page=2>

7. 'Italian mobster "killed rival by feeding him ALIVE to the pigs"', DailyMail. co.uk, 29 November 2013, retrieved 16 February 2016. <http://www.dailymail.co.uk/news/article-2515069/Gangster-kills-rival-feeding-alive-pigs-year-feud-members-Italian-crime-syndicate.html>

Chapter 11: 1974 - The Disappearance of Lord Lucan

1. Laura Thompson, *A Different Class of Murder*, Head of Zeus Ltd, London, 2014, e-book edition.

2. Sally Moore, *Lucan: Not Guilty*, Sidgwick & Jackson Limited, London, 1987, p. 49.

3. Moore p. 55-56

4. Patrick Sawer, 'Friend says Lord Lucan killed himself after murdering the family nanny by mistake', Telegraph.co.uk, 12 December 2015, retrieved 21 February 2016. <http://www.telegraph.co.uk/news/uknews/crime/12047289/Friend-says-Lord-Lucan-killed-himself-after-murdering-the-family-nanny-by-mistake.html>

5. Laura Fitzpatrick, 'A Brief History of Antidepressants', Content.Time.com, 7 January 2010, retrieved 22 February 2016. <http://content.time.com/time/health/article/0,8599,1952143,00.html>

6. Moore p. 87

7. Bill Coles, 'Lord Lucan – And the Damning Evidence That Proves He Was A Killer', HuffingtonPost.co.uk, 11 December 2013, retrieved 23 February 2016. <http://www.huffingtonpost.co.uk/bill-coles/lord-lucan-murder_b_4417579.html>

8. 'Earl's Mother Cites Other Man', Daytona Beach Morning Journal, 18 June 1975, News.Google.com, retrieved 23 February 2016. <https://news.google.com/newspapers?nid=1873&dat=19750618&id=tUUfAAA AIBAJ&sjid=dtEEAAAAIBAJ&pg=2132,406595&hl=en>

9. '"There was so much blood": Lord Lucan's son speaks of the "terrible carnage" in the family home on the night his nanny was bludgeoned to death 38 years ago', DailyMail.co.uk, 8 September 2012, retrieved 23 February 2016.
<http://www.dailymail.co.uk/news/article-2200108/Lord-Lucans-son-reveals-thinks-happened-fateful-night-1974.html>
10. Sam Tonkin et al, '"My mother was killed by a hitman paid for by Lord Lucan" says the son of the dead nanny as the long-lost peer is officially declared dead by court', DailyMail.co.uk, 4 February 2016, retrieved 23 February 2016.
<http://www.dailymail.co.uk/news/article-3431225/My-mother-killed-hitman-paid-Lord-Lucan-says-son-dead-nanny-long-lost-peer-officially-declared-dead-court.html>
11. Moore p. 31-32
12. Moore p. 200
13. 'Records found in Australia add intrigue to great Lord Lucan mystery', SMH.com.au, 26 October 2009, retrieved 23 February 2016.
<http://www.smh.com.au/world/records-found-in-australia-add-intrigue-to-great-lord-lucan-mystery-20091025-hf0f.html>
14. Victoria Richards, 'Lord Lucan: Death certificate granted by High Court judge to missing peer's only son George Bingham', Independent.co.uk, 3 February 2016, retrieved 23 February 2016.
<http://www.independent.co.uk/news/uk/home-news/lord-lucan-death-certificate-granted-by-high-court-judge-to-missing-peers-only-son-george-bingham-a6850731.html>
15. Nick Britten, 'Countess Lucan: I would have helped my husband get away with murder', Telegraph.co.uk, 20 February 2012, retrieved 23 February 2016.
<http://www.telegraph.co.uk/news/newstopics/howaboutthat/9092061/Countess-Lucan-I-would-have-helped-my-husband-get-away-with-murder.html>

Chapter 12: 1975 – The Yorkshire Ripper

1. 'The Yorkshire Ripper', *Murder Casebook: Investigations into the Ultimate Crime*, Volume 1 Part 1, Marshall Cavendish Limited, London, 1989.
2. Chris Clark with Tim Tate, *Yorkshire Ripper: The Secret Murders*, John Blake Publishing, London, 2015, e-book edition.
3. Michael Bilton, *Wicked Beyond Belief: The Hunt for the Yorkshire Ripper*, HarperPress, London, 2003, e-book edition.
4. Simon Edge, 'The Yorkshire Ripper: We were gripped by fear', Express.co.uk, 28 May 2010, retrieved 25 February 2016.
<http://www.express.co.uk/expressyourself/177705/The-Yorkshire-Ripper-We-were-gripped-by-fear>
5. Seumas Miller with Ian Gordon, *Investigative Ethics: Ethics for Police Detectives*

and Criminal Investigators, John Wiley and Sons, UK, 2014, e-book edition.
6. Julie Marshall, 'Dennis Hoban – Old School Copper', YorkshirePost.co.uk, 25 March 2015, retrieved 25 February 2016.
<http://www.yorkshirepost.co.uk/news/analysis/dennis-hoban-old-school-copper-1-7176005>
7. Joan Smith, *Misogynies*, Westbourne Press, London, 2013, e-book edition.

Chapter 13: 1993 – Taken Too Soon

1. Nigel Morris, 'The Big Question: At what age should children be held responsible for their criminal acts?' Independent.co.uk, 5 February 2009, retrieved 29 February 2016.
<http://www.independent.co.uk/news/uk/crime/the-big-question-at-what-age-should-children-be-held-responsible-for-their-criminal-acts-1546284.html>
2. Audrey Gillan, 'Did bad parenting really turn these boys into killers?', TheGuardian.com, 2 November 2000, retrieved 29 February 2016.
<http://www.theguardian.com/uk/2000/nov/01/bulger.familyandrelationships>
3. David Hosier MSc, 'When Ten-Year-Olds Turn Killers – The Case of Jon Venables and Robert Thompson', ChildhoodTraumaRecovery.com, 26 March 2014, retrieved 29 February 2016.
<http://childhoodtraumarecovery.com/2014/03/26/when-ten-year-olds-turn-killers-the-case-of-jon-venables-and-robert-thompson/>
4. Dr Mark Griffiths, 'What drives people to torture animals?' Independent.co.uk, 7 November 2014, retrieved 29 February 2016.
<http://www.independent.co.uk/life-style/health-and-families/features/what-drives-people-to-torture-animals-9844721.html>
5. Jane Cornwell, 'The boys who killed James Bulger', DailyLife.com.au, 9 February 2013, retrieved 29 February 2016.
<http://www.dailylife.com.au/life-and-love/real-life/the-boys-who-killed-james-bulger-20130208-2e2nd.html>
6. Paul Bracchi, The police were sure James Bulger's ten-year-old killers were simply wicked. But should their parents have been in the dock? DailyMail.co.uk, 13 March 2010, retrieved 29 February 2016.
<http://www.dailymail.co.uk/news/article-1257614/The-police-sure-James-Bulgers-year-old-killers-simply-wicked-But-parents-dock.html>
7. Ralph Bulger with Rosie Dunn, *My James*, Sidgwick & Jackson, London, 2013, e-book edition.
8. Jonathan Foster, 'James Bulger suffered multiple fractures: Pathologist reveals two-year-old had 42 injuries including fractured skull', Independent.co.uk, 10 November 1993, retrieved 29 February 2016.
<http://www.independent.co.uk/news/uk/james-bulger-suffered-multiple-

fractures-pathologist-reveals-two-year-old-had-42-injuries-including-1503297.
html>

9. David James Smith, 'Secret life of a child killer', DailyTelegraph.com.au, 15
May 2011, retrieved 29 February 2016.
<http://www.dailytelegraph.com.au/secret-life-of-a-child-killer/story-
fn6b3v4f-1226055888081>

10. David Harrison, 'Agony of following Jamie's final footsteps: No details spared
as toddler's loss relived', TheGuardian.com, 8 November 1993, retrieved 29
February 2016.
<http://www.theguardian.com/uk/1993/nov/07/bulger.davidharrison>

11. Antonella Lazzeri, 'Robert Thompson described every piece of James Bulger's
clothing … I knew then we had them. I had stared evil in the face', TheSun.co.uk,
13 February 2013, retrieved 29 February 2016.
<http://www.thesun.co.uk/sol/homepage/features/4790605/20-years-after-James-
Bulger-ex-cop-describes-catching-Thompson-and-Venables.html>

12. Luke Traynor, '"The coldest child I've ever seen": Lawyer for James Bulger's
killer still sickened by evil crime 20 years on', Mirror.co.uk, 9 February 2013,
retrieved 29 February 2016.
<http://www.mirror.co.uk/news/real-life-stories/james-bulger-murder-20-
years-1594811>

13. 'Understand the Effects of Maltreatment on Brain Development',
ChildWelfare.gov, April 2015, retrieved 1 March 2016.
<https://www.childwelfare.gov/pubPDFs/brain_development.
pdf#page=5&view=Effects%20of%20maltreatment%20on%20brain%20
development>

14. Dr Christopher L Heffner, 'The Psychological Effects of Violent Media on
Children', AllPsych.com, 14 December 2003, retrieved 1 March 2016.
<http://allpsych.com/journal/violentmedia/>

15. David Batty et al, 'James Bulger's killers were old enough to face trial, insists
government', TheGuardian.com, 14 March 2010, retrieved 1 March 2016.
<http://www.theguardian.com/uk/2010/mar/13/bulger-jon-venables-maggie-
atkinson>

Chapter 14: 1994 – The House of Horrors

1. Daniel Boduszek with Philip Hyland, 'Fred West: Bio-Psycho-Social
Investigation of Psychopathic Sexual Serial Killer', *International Journal of
Criminology and Sociological Theory*, Vol 5, No 1, June 2012, p. 864-870.

2. Will Bennett, 'The Early Days: Idyllic village childhood hid a darker side',
Independent.co.uk, 2 January 1995, retrieved 4 March 2016.
<http://www.independent.co.uk/news/uk/the-early-days-idyllic-village-

childhood-hid-a-darker-side-1566339.html>

3. Christopher Berry-Dee with Steve Morris, *Born Killers: Childhood Secrets of the World's Deadliest Serial Killers*, John Blake Publishing, London, 2006, e-book edition.

4. 'Fred West', Biography.com, retrieved 4 March 2016.

<http://www.biography.com/people/fred-west-17169706>

5. 'Rose West: New book claims she took lead role in murders', Mirror.co.uk, 27 January 2012, retrieved 4 March 2016.

<http://www.mirror.co.uk/news/uk-news/rose-west-new-book-claims-140356>

6. Howard Sounes, *Fred & Rose: The Full Story of Fred and Rose West and the Gloucester House of Horrors*, Hachette Digital, London, 1995, e-book edition.

7. 'Five key moments in Britain's sexual revolution', News.BBC.co.uk, 18 January 2010, retrieved 7 March 2016.

<http://news.bbc.co.uk/2/hi/uk_news/magazine/8456543.stm>

8. Fergus Linnane, *Madams: Bands and Brothel-Keepers of London*, The History Press, Gloucestershire, 2009, e-book edition.

9. Nicci Gerrard, 'I can still taste the fear', The Guardian.com, 21 November 1999, retrieved 4 March 2016.

http://www.theguardian.com/theobserver/1999/nov/21/featuresreview.review4

10. Ruth Styles, '"I still feel guilty about what happened to the others": Nanny who was raped by serial killers Fred and Rose West says she wishes she had done more to have them jailed', DailyMail.co.uk, 29 August 2014, retrieved 7 March 2016.

<http://www.dailymail.co.uk/femail/article-2737548/Nanny-raped-serial-killers-Fred-Rose-West-says-wishes-jailed.html>

11. Richard Spillett, 'Nanny who worked for Rose and Fred West reveals how sadistic couple tortured and abused her then threatened to bury her "with hundreds of others" at House of Horrors', DailyMail.co.uk, 5 November 2014, retrieved 4 March 2016.

<http://www.dailymail.co.uk/news/article-2821665/Nanny-worked-Rose-Fred-West-reveals-tortured-abused-her.html>

12. Will Bennett, 'The Bodies: Litany of sadness – The lives of West's twelve female victims', Independent.co.uk, 2 January 1995, retrieved 7 March 2016.

<http://www.independent.co.uk/news/uk/the-bodies-litany-of-sadness-the-lives-of-wests-twelve-female-victims-1566334.html>

13. Will Bennett, 'The horrific secrets of 25 Cromwell Street', Independent.co.uk, 7 October 1995, retrieved 4 March 2016.

<http://www.independent.co.uk/news/the-horrific-secrets-of-25-cromwell-street-1576291.html>

14. Elissa Hunt, 'British mum Rosemary West is a shocking serial killer among our female felons in True Crime Scene', HeraldSun.com.au, 12 May 2013,

retrieved 2 March 2016.
<http://www.heraldsun.com.au/news/law-order/british-mum-rosemary-west-is-a-shocking-serial-killer-among-our-female-felons-in-true-crime-scene/story-fnat7jnn-1226639619598>

Chapter 15: 1996 – The Dunblane Massacre

1. 'Dunblane', VisitScotland.com, retrieved 28 February 2016.
<https://www.visitscotland.com/info/towns-villages/dunblane-p235621>
2. James Cusick, 'He must have chased the pupils all over the place, shooting at them till they fell', Independent.co.uk, 14 March 1996, retrieved 28 February 2016.
<http://www.independent.co.uk/news/he-must-have-chased-the-pupils-all-over-the-place-shooting-at-them-til-l-they-fell-1341854.html>
3. Nick Cohen, 'The life and death of Thomas Watt Hamilton', Independent.co.uk, 17 March 1996, retrieved 28 February 2016.
<http://www.independent.co.uk/news/uk/home-news/the-life-and-death-of-thomas-watt-hamilton-1672323.html>
4. 'Thomas Watt Hamilton', Biography.com, retrieved 28 February 2016.
<http://www.biography.com/people/thomas-watt-hamilton-232311>
5. Peter Aylward with Gerald Wooster, *Understanding Dunblane and Other Massacres*, Karnac Books Ltd, London, 2012, p. 167-168.
6. Alan J Whiticker, '1996: The Dunblane Massacre', *101 Crimes of the Century*, New Holland Publishers, Australia, 2008, p. 247.
7. Chris Atkinson and David Truan, 'Protecting children from sexual abuse: A guide for parents and carers', NSPCC, Middlesbrough.gov.uk, 2008, retrieved 28 February 2016.
<http://www.middlesbrough.gov.uk/CHttpHandler.ashx?id=3619&p=0>
8. Ian Wilson, 'Killer Thomas Hamilton was described five years ago by a policeman as scheming, devious, and deceitful … yet, as Iain Wilson reports, he kept his firearms certificate Refusing a call to disarm', HeraldScotland.com, 7 June 1996, retrieved 28 February 2016.
<http://www.heraldscotland.com/news/12119189.Killer_Thomas_Hamilton_was_described_five_years_ago_by_a_policeman_as_scheming__devious__and_deceitful_____yet__as_Iain_Wilson_reports__he_kept_his_firearms_certificate_Refusing_a_call_to_disarm/>
9. Duncan Campbell, 'Understand Dunblane and Other Massacres by Peter Aylward – review', TheGuardian.com, 18 December 2012, retrieved 28 February 2016.
<http://www.theguardian.com/law/2012/dec/17/dunblane-other-massacre-peter-aylward-review>

10. 'The Dunblane Massacre', BBC.co.uk, retrieved 28 February 2016.
<http://www.bbc.co.uk/dna/place-london/plain/A11103580>
11. 'Teachers relive horror of terrible day', Scotsman.com, 3 October 2005, retrieved 28 February 2016.
<http://www.scotsman.com/news/teachers-relive-horror-of-terrible-day-1-1098906>
12. Erlend Clouston and Sarah Boseley, 'From the archive, 14 March 1996: Sixteen children killed in Dunblane massacre', TheGuardian.com, 14 March 2013, retrieved 28 February 2016.
<http://www.theguardian.com/theguardian/2013/mar/14/dunblane-massacre-scotland-killing>
13. Peter Wilkinson, 'Dunblane: How UK school massacre led to tighter gun control', Edition.CNN.com, 30 January 2013, retrieved 28 February 2016.
<http://edition.cnn.com/2012/12/17/world/europe/dunblane-lessons/>
14. 'Dunblane School Massacre', UnforgottenChildren.com, retrieved 28 February 2016.
<http://unforgottenchildren.com/dunblaneschoolmassacre.html>

Chapter 16: 2002 – The Soham Murders

1. Harriet Arkell, 'Girls are the best of friends', Standard.co.uk, 14 August 2002, retrieved 8 March 2016.
<http://www.standard.co.uk/news/girls-are-the-best-of-friends-6303549.html>
2. Olga Craig, 'Please, please give them back. Our lives are so empty without them', Telegraph.co.uk, 11 August 2002, retrieved 9 March 2016.
<http://www.telegraph.co.uk/news/uknews/1404104/Please-please-give-them-back.-Our-lives-are-so-empty-without-them.html>
3. Sean O'Neill and Sue Clough, 'Jessica and Holly doted on Maxine Carr, says teacher', Telegraph.co.uk, 13 November 2003, retrieved 8 March 2016. <http://www.telegraph.co.uk/news/uknews/1446601/Jessica-and-Holly-doted-on-Maxine-Carr-says-teacher.html>
4. John Troup, 'Parents' heart breaking plea to Holly and Jessica's kidnapper', Sun.co.uk, 12 August 1994, retrieved 9 March 2016.
<http://www.thesun.co.uk/sol/homepage/news/150607/Parents-heartbreaking-plea-to-Holly-and-Jessicas-kidnapper.html>
5. Kamal Ahmed, Mark Townsend and Tony Thompson, 'The fury that drove Huntley to murder', TheGuardian.com, 21 December 2003, retrieved 8 <March 2016. http://www.theguardian.com/uk/2012/jul/22/father-soham-schoolgirl-holly-wells>
6. James McKillop, 'They changed into trousers and then left the house. But why?' HeraldScotland.com, 10 August 2002, retrieved 9 March 2016.

<http://www.heraldscotland.com/news/11954979.They_changed_into_trousers_and_then_left_the_house__But_why__Since_they_disappeared_on_Sunday__the_search_for_Holly_Wells_and_Jessica_Chapman_has_become_the_biggest_hunt_for_missing_persons_in_British_police_history__James_McKillop_looks_back_over_six_da/

7. 'Timeline of events', News.BBC.co.uk, 18 August 2002, retrieved 8 March 2016.
<http://news.bbc.co.uk/2/hi/uk_news/england/2180946.stm>

8. Sue Clough, 'Daughter's phone "said goodbye"', Telegraph.co.uk, 13 November 2003, retrieved 10 March 2016.
<http://www.telegraph.co.uk/news/uknews/1446603/Daughters-phone-said-goodbye.html>

9. Nicci Gerrard, 'Holly, Jessica and the unravelling of a dark and terrible mystery', TheGuardian.com, 7 December 2003, retrieved 8 March 2016. <http://www.theguardian.com/uk/2003/dec/07/ukcrime.soham>

10. 'Ian Huntley: The Soham Murderer', CrimeandInvestigation.co.uk, retrieved 10 March 2016.
<http://www.crimeandinvestigation.co.uk/crime-files/ian-huntley-the-soham-murderer>

11. Olga Craig and Rajeev Syal, 'Two bodies found as police arrest couple', Telegraph.co.uk, 18 August 2002, retrieved 10 March 2016.
<http://www.telegraph.co.uk/news/uknews/1404697/Two-bodies-found-as-police-arrest-couple.html>

12. 'Huntley guilty of Soham murders', News.BBC.co.uk, 17 December 2003, retrieved 8 March 2016.
<http://news.bbc.co.uk/2/hi/uk/3312551.stm>

13. 'Soham girls "likely to have been asphyxiated"', TheGuardian.com, 8 November 2003, retrieved 9 March 2016.
<http://www.theguardian.com/uk/2003/nov/07/soham.ukcrime7>

14. Sean O'Neill, 'Huntley's account of how girls died is dismissed as implausible and unlikely', Telegraph.co.uk, 27 November 2003, retrieved 9 March 2016.
<http://www.telegraph.co.uk/news/uknews/1447865/Huntleys-account-of-how-girls-died-is-dismissed-as-implausible-and-unlikely.html>

15. 'Maxine Carr gives birth to her first child - but baby will never know true identity of its mother', DailyMail.co.uk, 14 January 2014, retrieved 11 March 2016.
<http://www.dailymail.co.uk/news/article-2055570/Soham-liar-Maxine-Carr-gives-birth-baby-know-mother-really-is.html>

Chapter 17: 2002 - The Milly Dowler Case

1. Paul Harris, 'Milly's "horrific final moments in killer's lair after 13-year-old was taken from the street"', DailyMail.co.uk, 12 May 2011, retrieved 12 March 2016. <http://www.dailymail.co.uk/news/article-1385894/Levi-Bellfield-trial-Milly-Dowlers-horrific-final-moments-suspected-killers-lair.html>

2. 'Timeline: Milly Dowler', News.BBC.co.uk, 20 September 2002, retrieved 12 March 2016. <http://news.bbc.co.uk/2/hi/uk_news/england/1947954.stm>

3. John McShane, *Predator: The True Story of Levi Bellfield, the Man Who Murdered Milly Dowler*, John Blake Publishing, London, 2011, e-book edition.

4. Peter Sherlock, 'Milly Dowler murder: Surrey Police say mistakes made', BBC.com, 24 June 2011, retrieved 12 March 2016. <http://www.bbc.com/news/uk-england-surrey-13809720>

5. Paul Harris, '"You should have had me aborted": Milly Dowler's heartbreaking message from beyond the grave as father breaks down in court over porn stash', DailyMail.co.uk, 17 May 2011, retrieved 12 March 2016. <http://www.dailymail.co.uk/news/article-1387644/Milly-Dowlers-message-father-Bob-breaks-court-porn-stash.html>

6. John Twomey, 'I was suspect and had stash of porn, says Milly Dowler's father', Express.co.uk, 17 May 2011, retrieved 12 March 2016. <http://www.express.co.uk/news/uk/247151/I-was-suspect-and-had-stash-of-porn-says-Milly-Dowler-s-father>

7. Stephen Wright, 'Milly: The litany of police mistakes which let her murderer escape justice', DailyMail.co.uk, 26 February 2008, retrieved 12 March 2016. <http://www.dailymail.co.uk/news/article-518673/Milly-The-litany-police-mistakes-let-murderer-escape-justice.html>

8. Stephen Wright, 'Blunders of police who insisted: Milly Dowler's dad did it', DailyMail.co.uk, 24 June 2011, retrieved 12 March 2016. <http://www.dailymail.co.uk/news/article-2007543/Blunders-police-insisted-Milly-Dowlers-dad-did-it.html>

9. John McShane, 'Milly Dowler's murderer Levi Bellfield was a sadistic serial killer and stalker', Express.co.uk, 4 September 2011, retrieved 12 March 2016. <http://www.express.co.uk/expressyourself/269117/Milly-Dowler-s-murderer-Levi-Bellfield-was-a-sadistic-serial-killer-and-stalker>

10. 'Levi Bellfield: Profile of "heinous" serial killer', BBC.com, 10 February 2016, retrieved 11 March 2016. <http://www.bbc.com/news/uk-england-35541060>

11. Sarah White, 'Levi Bellfield's daughter recalls father's brutality', BBC.com, 24 June 2011, retrieved 14 March 2016. <http://www.bbc.com/news/uk-13269066>

12. 'Milly Dowler "cause of death not known"', BBC.com, 13 June 2011, retrieved 12 March 2016.

<http://www.bbc.com/news/uk-england-surrey-13752202>

13. 'Bus stop killer's chain of violence', News.BBC.co.uk, 25 February 2008, retrieved 12 March 2016.

<http://news.bbc.co.uk/2/hi/uk_news/7230063.stm>

14. Paul Harris, 'The terrible price Sally Dowler paid for justice', DailyMail.co.uk, 24 June 2011, retrieved 12 March 2016.

<http://www.dailymail.co.uk/news/article-2007543/Blunders-police-insisted-Milly-Dowlers-dad-did-it.html>

15. Caroline Davies, 'Levi Bellfield gets life without parole', TheGuardian.com, 25 June 2011, retrieved 12 March 2016.

<http://www.theguardian.com/uk/2011/jun/24/levi-bellfield-life-without-parole>

16. Nick Davies and Amelia Hill, 'Missing Milly Dowler's voicemail was hacked by News of the World', TheGuardian.com, 6 July 2011, retrieved 12 March 2016.

<http://www.theguardian.com/uk/2011/jul/04/milly-dowler-voicemail-hacked-news-of-world>

17. Nick Davies, 'Phone-hacking trial failed to clear up mystery of Milly Dowler's voicemail', TheGuardian.com, 26 June 2014, retrieved 12 March 2016.

<http://www.theguardian.com/uk-news/2014/jun/26/phone-hacking-trial-milly-dowler-voicemail>

18. John Shammas, 'Sick Levi Bellfield raped Milly Dowler on driveway of mother's home, her parents reveal in heartbreaking statement', Mirror.co.uk, 10 February 2016, retrieved 11 March 2016.

<http://www.mirror.co.uk/news/uk-news/levi-bellfield-raped-milly-dowler-7342509>

Chapter 18: 2004 – A Hammer and a Frying Pan

1. Jane Mishcon et al, *Independent Inquiry into the Care and Treatment of Peter Bryan, Part One: A report for NHS London*, September 2009, retrieved 14 March 2016.

http://hundredfamilies.org/wp/wp-content/uploads/2013/12/PETER_BRYAN_LON_02.04_1.pdf

2. Marie Louise Elias and Josie Elias, *Barbados*, Marshall Cavendish, New York, 2000, p. 18-19.

3. Peter Stubley, 'Peter Bryan: The Real Hannibal Lecter', CourtNewsUK.co.uk, retrieved 14 March 2016.

<http://www.courtnewsuk.co.uk/c_serial_killers/a_peter_bryan/crime_vaults/>

4. Saumya Arya Haas, 'What is Voodoo? Understanding a Misunderstood Religion', HuffingtonPost.com, 25 May 2011, retrieved 15 March 2016.

<http://www.huffingtonpost.com/saumya-arya-haas/what-is-vodou_b_827947.html>

5. Owen Bowcott and Anisha Ahmed, 'Cannibal killer murdered again after mental care failures', TheGuardian.com, 2 September 2009, retrieved 15 March 2016.
<http://www.theguardian.com/uk/2009/sep/03/cannibal-killer-mental-care-failures>
6. 'Cannibalistic killer not watched properly in Broadmoor, inquest finds', TheGuardian.com, 16 September 2011, retrieved 14 March 2016.
<http://www.theguardian.com/uk/2011/sep/15/cannibalistic-killer-not-watched-hospital>

Chapter 19: 2010 – The Cumbria Shootings

1. Peter Wilkinson, 'Dunblane: How UK school massacre led to tighter gun control', Edition.CNN.com, 30 January 2013, retrieved 17 March 2016.
<http://edition.cnn.com/2012/12/17/world/europe/dunblane-lessons/>
2. Jon Swaine, Paul Stokes and Caroline Gammell, 'Cumbria gunman – profile of Derrick Bird', Telegraph.co.uk, 2 June 2010, retrieved 17 March 2016.
<http://www.telegraph.co.uk/news/uknews/crime/7799167/Cumbria-gunman-profile-of-Derrick-Bird.html>
3. Claire Leigh, *Massacre in Cumbria: The Day Gunman Derrick Bird Brought Terror to the Lake*, John Blake Publishing, London, 2010, e-book edition.
4. Severin Carrell, Rajeev Syal and Peter Walker, 'Derrick Bird profile: What motivated the Cumbria gunman?', TheGuardian.com, 3 June 2010, retrieved 17 March 2016.
<http://www.theguardian.com/uk/2010/jun/02/derrick-bird-profile-cumbria-gunman>
5. Andrew Hough and Nick Collins, 'Cumbria shootings: Derrick Bird's "grudges" against massacre victims', Telegraph.co.uk, 3 June 2010, retrieved 17 March 2016.
http://www.telegraph.co.uk/news/uknews/crime/7801618/Cumbria-shootings-Derrick-Birds-grudges-against-massacre-victims.html
6. Helen Carter, 'Derrick Bird talked of suicide before Cumbria shootings, inquest told', 3 March 2011, retrieved 17 March 2016.
<http://www.theguardian.com/uk/2011/mar/02/derrick-bird-cumbria-shootings-inquest>
7. Martin Evans and John Bingham, 'Cumbria shootings: Derrick Bird's jealousy over money may have motivated killing spree', Telegraph.co.uk, 5 June 2010, retrieved 17 March 2016.
<http://www.telegraph.co.uk/news/uknews/crime/7804560/Cumbria-shootings-Derrick-Birds-jealousy-over-money-may-have-motivated-killing-spree.html>
8. Martin Wainwright, 'Police had "no grounds" to ban killer Derrick Bird from owning guns', TheGuardian.com, 3 November 2010, retrieved 17 March 2016.

<http://www.theguardian.com/uk/2010/nov/02/police-no-grounds-derrick-bird-guns-ban>
9. 'Firearms-Control Legislation and Policy: Great Britain', Library of Congress, LOC.gov, 30 July 2015, retrieved 17 March 2016. https://www.loc.gov/law/help/firearms-control/greatbritain.php

Chapter 20: 2012 - King Jimmy

1. 'Sir Jimmy Savile', TheTelegraph.co.uk, 29 October 2011, retrieved 19 March 2016. <http://www.telegraph.co.uk/news/obituaries/8857428/Sir-Jimmy-Savile.html>
2. 'DJ and TV presenter Jimmy Savile dies, aged 84', BBC.com, 29 October 2011, retrieved 19 March 2016.
<http://www.bbc.com/news/entertainment-arts-1550737>
3. Adam Sweeting, 'Sir Jimmy Savile obituary', TheGuardian.com, 30 October 2011, retrieved 19 March 2016.
<http://www.theguardian.com/music/2011/oct/29/sir-jimmy-savile>
4. Lynn Barber, 'Lynn Barber: I was nervous when I told Jimmy Savile, "People say you like little girls"', 2 October 2012, retrieved 19 March 2016.
<http://www.independent.co.uk/arts-entertainment/tv/features/lynn-barber-i-was-nervous-when-i-told-jimmy-savile-people-say-you-like-little-girls-8193169.html>
5. Louis Theroux, *When Louis Met Jimmy*, BBC2, UK, April 2000.
6. Niamh Horan, 'I don't know why nobody took him on sooner – Barry', Independent.ie, 14 October 2012, retrieved 19 March 2016.
<http://www.independent.ie/irish-news/i-dont-know-why-nobody-took-him-on-sooner-barry-28818829.html>
7. Sam Marsden and Richard Alleyne, 'Jimmy Savile interviewed under caution over indecent assault allegation', TheTelegraph.co.uk, 1 October 2012, retrieved 19 March 2016.
<http://www.telegraph.co.uk/news/uknews/9578870/Jimmy-Savile-interviewed-under-caution-over-indecent-assault-allegation.html>
8. 'Former head of Duncroft admits she was "hoodwinked" by Jimmy Savile', <26 March 2013, retrieved 19 March 2016.
http://www.walesonline.co.uk/news/wales-news/former-head-duncroft-admits-hoodwinked-2015914>
9. Emily Allen, 'Savile pictured at the Jersey House of Horrors: Paedophile DJ is surrounded by children at care home where 192 "suffered abuse"', DailyMail.co.uk, 17 October 2012, retrieved 19 March 2016.
<http://www.dailymail.co.uk/news/article-2218517/Jimmy-Savile-pictured-surrounded-children-Jersey-care-home-192-suffered-abuse.html

10. Ben Quinn, 'Jimmy Savile: transcript reveals "policy" used to halt abuse claims', TheGuardian.com, 16 October 2013, retrieved 19 March 2016.
<http://www.theguardian.com/media/2013/oct/15/jimmy-savile-boasted-police-abuse>

11. 'Jimmy Savile: Sussex police confirm 2008 assault claim', BBC.com, 3 October 2012, retrieved 20 March 2016.
<http://www.bbc.com/news/entertainment-arts-19820017>

12. 'Savile abuse claims: Met Police launch criminal inquiry', BBC.com, 19 October 2012, retrieved 18 March 2016.
<http://www.bbc.com/news/uk-20006049>

13. Josh Halliday, 'Jimmy Savile: timeline of his sexual abuse and its uncovering', TheGuardian.com, 26 June 2014, retrieved 19 March 2016.
<http://www.theguardian.com/media/2014/jun/26/jimmy-savile-sexual-abuse-timeline>

14. Martin Evans, 'Operation Yewtree: The success and failures', Telegraph.co.uk, 5 February 2015, retrieved 18 March 2016.
<http://www.telegraph.co.uk/news/uknews/crime/11393099/Operation-Yewtree-The-successes-and-failures.html>

15. Esther Addley, 'Jimmy Savile's Broadmoor role came with a bedroom and keys', TheGuardian.com, 13 October 2012, retrieved 18 March 2016.
<http://www.theguardian.com/media/2012/oct/12/jimmy-savile-broadmoor-volunteer-role>

16. Piers Morgan, *Piers Morgan Life Stories*, ITV, 26 September 2015.

17. Daniel Boffey, 'Revealed: How Jimmy Savile abused up to 1,000 victims on BBC premises', TheGuardian.com, 19 January 2014, retrieved 18 March 2016.
<http://www.theguardian.com/media/2014/jan/18/jimmy-savile-abused-1000-victims-bbc>

18. Tom McTague, 'Why did NHS stay silent on Saville? 177 victims aged from five to 75 at 41 hospitals after bosses missed TEN chances to stop predatory paedophile … and NO ONE will be held responsible', DailyMail.co.uk, 26 February 2015, retrieved 18 March 2016.
<http://www.dailymail.co.uk/news/article-2970049/Abuse-grand-scale-Jimmy-Savile-raped-sexually-assaulted-victims-aged-5-75-41-NHS-hospitals-including-60-Stoke-Mandeville-24-year-reign-abuse.html>

19. 'Jimmy Savile's youngest victim, 9, speaks out against "King Jimmy"', TheTelegragh.co.uk, 15 October 2012, retrieved 18 March 2016.
<http://www.telegraph.co.uk/news/uknews/9608466/Jimmy-Saviles-youngest-victim-9-speaks-out-against-King-Jimmy.html>

First published in 2016 by New Holland Publishers Pty Ltd
London • Sydney • Auckland

The Chandlery, Unit 704, 50 Westminster Bridge Road, London, SE1 7QY, United Kingdom
1/66 Gibbes Street, Chatswood, NSW, 2067, Australia
5/39 Woodside Avenue, Northcote, Auckland, 0627, New Zealand

www.newhollandpublishers.com

A record of this book is held at the British Library and the National Library of Australia.

ISBN 9781742578804

Managing Director: Fiona Schultz
Publisher: Alan Whitcker
Design: Thomas Partridge
Cover Design: Andrew Davies
Production Director: James Mills-Hicks
Printer: Toppan Leefung Printing Ltd

10 9 8 7 6 5 4 3 2 1

Keep up with New Holland Publishers on Facebook
www.facebook.com/NewHollandPublishers

£14.99